Lilacs and Glady

By

Francer Hope

This book is a work of fiction. Places, events, and situations in this story are purely fictional. Any resemblance to actual persons, living or dead, is coincidental.

ISBN: 1-4107-7394-9 (e-book)
ISBN: 1-4107-7395-7 (Paperback)

Library of Congress Control Number: 2003095118

This book is printed on acid free paper.

Printed in the United States of America
Bloomington, IN

1stBooks - rev. 07/11/03

CHAPTER ONE

Glady listened to her daughter on the phone. She just hoped the little slut wasn't pregnant. She'd been sent off for a decent education and now it would be Glady's luck that she'd go out and get knocked up and have to get married. That would be a fine how-ya-do! What would people think?

Carol was living over in Seneca with some friends she had made in nursing school, working at a big hospital and making good money. Glady noticed Carol certainly had enough money to buy a brand new car and had something new to wear every time she graced them with her presence back here at home. Carol didn't come home that often for someone with a new car either. When Carol had graduated from nursing school Glady had come right out and told her that she should come back home and live there. She had used her low-convincing tone of voice when she had talked to Carol.

"You could live here at home and work in Rockwell, right there at the hospital you were born in. Dr. Tott would just love to have you work there. He delivered you, and you would be here, where you could work with him every day. Wouldn't that be nice? You've been gone from home so long now."

Glady figured out that Carol had been away from home for four years. She left for nursing school at eighteen and lived in the dormitory for three years. Glady made that trip to Halsey so many times to bring Carol home for weekends. She noticed that Carol resisted coming home the last year she'd lived in the dorm though. It seemed like she only wanted to come home when she had a date lined up. Carol turned up her nose at the idea of coming back home to live after graduation. She said she wanted to live in a large city, so she had moved to Seneca when she finished her nursing school a year ago.

Glady continued to talk while wondering how in the hell she could find out if Carol was pregnant without coming right out and asking. It wouldn't pay to be direct; Carol was so much like that damned dad of hers she would clam up immediately. She had that way of blatantly ignoring a person, just like he did. Glady knew she'd better think of something right quick because it would

1

be too embarrassing later if she didn't find out now if Carol had to get married.

Carol had called Glady about a month back and told her she was engaged. That really surprised Glady because she didn't even know Carol was dating anyone seriously. Carol hadn't mentioned a date then but now here she was saying she was getting married the Saturday before Thanksgiving. That sure wasn't much notice and she thought that maybe Carol had to rush things along.

Glady put the engagement announcement in the local paper right after Carol first told her, and people were already asking questions about the wedding. Glady hadn't said too much, thinking she had a lot of time, now she wasn't certain what to do. A late fall wedding all decked out in fall colors would be beautiful and she could certainly do that up right. Carol would be coming back home for the wedding ceremony and reception so Glady knew she would have to play her cards just right if she had to cover up a pregnancy.

Glady reckoned that Carol would need to visit soon and in the meantime come up with a way to find out what she wanted to know. She thought it might be easy to cover-up if Carol was pregnant but wasn't showing yet since the wedding was less than five weeks away. She had volunteered to make the wedding dress and she could make any needed adjustments.

"Well Carol," Glady said using the most worn out-weary tone of voice she could mange. "If that's the case, you're gonna hafta get out here pretty quick so you can try on this wedding dress before I get very far along with it. I've cut it real snug in the waist and I haven't made you any clothes for quite awhile, so you'll hafta try it on a couple of times."

Carol sighed so Glady continued her appeal.

"I'll be goin' blind from all this sewin' I'm going to hafta do. I been cuttin' out your little sisters' dresses and I'll need to get started on your dress before my eyes give out. This delustered satin you picked is pretty, but it reflects in my eyes so bad. You remember how my eyes get all bloodshot when I sew shiny material. You don't want the mother-of-the-bride to have bloodshot eyes, do ya? How soon can ya come out to try it on?"

2

Carol had consented to driving out home and here she was, trying on the wedding dress that Glady had been working on practically since the day the engagement was announced. Glady had really been killing herself with working on the wedding preparations and worrying if the dress would even fit, plus the big question on her mind about Carol's condition.

Carol took off her blouse and wanted to leave on the bra she was wearing. Glady insisted that the fit could not be determined unless it was tried on with the right long line bra. She demanded that Carol take everything off and then turned her head away like she was giving her some privacy. Pretending to be picking up the correct bra, Glady rolled her eyes toward her daughter to sneak a look at Carols' bare breasts. They looked full and round and ripe with pink nipples. Glady wondered if they looked like pregnant breasts or just young. Glady couldn't remember what her breasts had looked like at that age. Course she'd had brats by that age, it probably didn't matter whether she could remember or not.

As Glady slowly fastened the boned, long-line bra she made up her mind that she had to find out what the situation was, and it was now or never. Using her low and pleasant tone of voice Glady began what she had been practicing as she sewed.

"I saw Irene Lutz the other day. You remember her daughter Diane? She was two years behind you in school?"

"Of course." Carol replied grumpily, wondering if her mother has lost her marbles. Carol had hated Diane Lutz. Everyone did. Ole Diane was such an aggressive girl with a very loud voice and a big mouth going all the time that she had no friends at all. Who wouldn't remember her? Carol knew that Glady would know that too.

How could anyone forget anyone from Milton High? Good old MHS, there were only sixty-two kids in the whole high school and it was in the same building as the grade school. Everyone knew everyone from little on up. In fact, probably even the grade school kids hated Diane Lutz. She was always yapping and guffawing, trying to get attention from anywhere she could.

"I remember Diane," Carol said testily wondering what point her mother was about to make.

"Well, she got married last summer you know? Her mother went to the trouble of a big church wedding. There she was at the altar, in a pure white wedding gown, veil and all. When Diane got back from her honeymoon she told her mother she was seven months pregnant! There she was pregnant even before she announced the engagement. Poor Irene, she almost died of embarrassment!"

Carol eyed her mother, catching on immediately. She had been manipulated for years with these tricks of hers and she was in no mood for charades. She retorted snottily.

"No mom, I'm not pregnant! In fact I have already seen a doctor and I will start the pill with my next period. Does that make you happy?"

Glady was around behind her pinning the dress bodice closed so Carol did not see her face darken with fury. Glady knew Carol would glare at her, so she stayed behind her back and said nothing but in the recesses of her mind she was thrilled. She had won! She had paid a very small price to find out exactly what she wanted to know. Now Glady could brag to high heaven and all over town about the big upcoming late fall marriage of her successful daughter to a mysterious man from the big city.

***

The wedding day dawned fair and bright for late November. Glady was pleased that the weather turned out as good as anyone could ask. Carol had come out home the night before and slept there and Glady awakened her with a staged gentleness.

"It's your wedding day Carol. You couldn't ask for more beautiful weather. Look the sun is shinin' and not a cloud in the sky, a perfect day."

The wedding ceremony was set for two o'clock in the afternoon and the morning was uneventful. Glady complained that Carol should not do her own hair since she couldn't seem to get it smooth in the back. Carol didn't seem to appreciate her opinion so Glady did her best to stay out of Carol's way. She didn't want anything to ruin her hard work and efforts of the past few weeks. Glady even rode in to the church in a different car saying she wanted to see if the cake had been delivered on time for the reception.

Glady oversaw Carol in the dressing room at the back of the church, and then she watched as the ushers began seating people. Everything was turning out so well and more people were coming than Glady had hoped. She admired how she'd found just the right colors to go together for the decorations and clothes.

Glady had read about all weddings since the engagement was announced. She knew that the mother-of-the-bride she should be in harmony with the wedding party colors but not compete with them. She chose a lace-covered sage green dress for herself and adorned it with a harvest gold corsage with ribbon that matched the dress. She felt lucky to find a pair of pumps in a darker sage color that went well with her outfit. She picked a white pillbox hat and white gloves for just a hint of the bridal white Carol would be wearing.

As mother of the bride, Glady was escorted and seated in the church pew just before the first song that began the wedding ceremony. The soloist began her notes and Glady looked at the seats off the aisle to her right and her mind began to race. Just look at the mother-of-the-groom! There she sits all trigged up in a jersey print in the wrong colors! Where did she get the idea that a brown and blue were late fall colors? And she is so obviously squeezed into a corset! Look at the way her ass is flaring out on the seat behind her! Why, it makes a shelf big enough for a little dog to ride around on!

The first song was over. The groom and groomsmen lined up near the altar and the wedding attendants started down the aisle. The wedding march began and Glady turned slightly as she rose for the bride. She wanted to enjoy the moment but her mind continued to race. She was glad Carol had begun to lighten her hair and it went perfectly with the deep green and gold of the wedding decorations. Glady watched as Carol held on to her dad's arm. Her waist looked tiny in the bride dress and you couldn't even tell that she had saddlebag thighs.

The procession was at the front of the church and the next song began. Glady fumed some more over the mother-of-the-groom then turned her attention to the front of the church. Her lips practically moved and her mind worked furiously when her eyes came rest on the fool up there getting ready to marry Carol. What in the world did Carol see in him anyway? There he stood in the bright lights, practically bald!

When Glady first heard the groom was going to college and worked at the same hospital as Carol her hopes rose. Any thoughts about having a doctor in the family were soon dashed however when she found out he was an orderly! An orderly, for God's sake, what a big disappointment!

Glady finally met Carol's fiancée on one of her trips out to Milton to try on the dress. She asked Harold about the classes he was taking at college. It seemed to her like he had no idea of a future in mind. She picked up on the fact that he was taking some psychology classes though and when people asked about the man Carol was marrying, Glady let it be known that he was studying to be a psychologist.

Glady bought the costume pearls that Carol was wearing with the wedding dress. When she found out the groom had not bought his bride a gift she gave those to him to give to Carol. He was such a fool; he didn't know he was supposed to get anything, and then he didn't even offer to pay Glady. What nerve!

Glady turned her attention to the best man standing beside the groom. She noticed how silly he looked, a short little guy with big ears sticking out. What in the hell was he up to? Making faces at the groom! Is he trying to ruin the wedding? I hope he doesn't act up during the wedding pictures like that!

I wish those younger girls of mine weren't so bashful, Glady thought further as she looked at the wedding party. Vera and Tammy got the tapers lit, but Tammy's slip was showing and they were both looking at the floor the whole time. Gail and Shirley's dresses were cute as they walked in front of the bride as flower girl and ring bearer. They appeared timid and looked afraid though, like someone was going to bite them.

The ceremony ended and Glady immediately planned her write up for the local paper. She would describe the wedding as a family affair. She would tell how all four of the bride's beautiful little sisters were in the wedding party, dressed up in harvest gold. She would report that several of the brothers of the bride were ushers. She would provide details of how the blond bride walked down the aisle on her father's arm in a beautiful white satin gown hand-made by her mother. The mother-of-the-bride and the mother-of-the-groom were lovely in their fall finery. The couple will live in Seneca after the honeymoon where the bride works as a registered nurse and the groom works at a hospital while attending Seneca State where he is studying psychology.

***

The next seven months moved by quickly. Glady hadn't heard from Carol in so long, she finally called her one Sunday to catch up on things. The news floored her.

"I thought you would wait a year or two with the pill and all," Glady whined. "Get to know each other before you saddled yourself with kids. Why are you going to start a family now? You've got a good job and everything and Harold is still in college."

Carol sounded terse when she replied, "Well the baby isn't due until next April, so that is waiting over a year, isn't it?"

Glady thought that Carol was acting like it was none of her business. It made Glady mad that Carol would talk to her that way but she used her pleading tone of voice. "Well, just the other day I told Edna Morrse that you were gonna wait a couple of years. Now what will she say?"

"I've been off the pill for three months. The doctor gave me a shot of Progesterone and I didn't bleed so that means I am pregnant. Harold heard they are going to stop honoring the college student deferment but he thinks they'll still honor the deferment for fathers. He wanted to get a letter to the draft board as soon as possible. The doctor gave the shot so he could confirm that Harold will be a father in seven months."

Glady's mind screamed but she remained silent knowing better than to say what she was thinking. That dumb-looking bald fool! He thinks he's too good to go into the service! My boys and my brothers all went when they were called. They took it like men! I knew Carol was marrying an idiot but I sure as hell didn't know he was a coward. Carol must of hurried to get pregnant against my advice and now she'll have a kid to tie her down. All because she married a chicken-shit!

Using her careful-martyred tone of voice to end the conversation, Glady said, "Well, I thought you would wait, you told me you were goin' to, but I guess its yer life now."

CHAPTER TWO

Glady always had an active imagination. It began with wishing and wishing always turned to dreaming. Dreaming could turn to fact in Glady's imagination. When she was a young teen-ager she would go to sleep at night wishing that she were a rich popular girl. She would close her eyes and make believe that she had on a nice skirt and new shoes. She always imagined a new soft sweater to top it all off.

Lying there with her eyes closed and all dressed up in her pretty clothes, she would pretend to sit on the floor. The floor would open up under her and she would slide gently down a chute right into the middle of a party. There were always different seasonal decorations in Gladys fantasy parties, and there were always sweets, usually a huge cake with ice cream on beautifully patterned dishes.

Best of all, everyone would be happy to see her. They would all come up to her sooner or later. Boys would like her as a friend and girls would admire her new sweater and wish they had one like it. Glady would be nice to everyone. She would have a boyfriend who had a car to drive around in whenever she wanted. They would go places, and he would have money to buy her nice presents for special occasions.

Glady had imagined this scene so many nights that she almost believed it was real at times lying there in bed. Sometimes she would fall asleep while fantasizing and the scene continued into a dream and she partied all night. Glady developed a talent for escape with these early years of practice. Throughout her adult life, Glady could imagine something and eventually tell a story as though it were true. She would plan a situation very carefully noting details, then step by step, she would rehearse it over and over, getting it just right in her mind.

Glady became very convincing as she repeated a story to herself and sometimes to others as well. In fact, she ended up believing many of her own stories. As time passed, she couldn't really remember what had actually happened and what parts she had made up and carefully rehearsed.

Glady hated being poor more than anything. Not that they'd ever had that much anyway but during her early childhood things were pretty good; her dad had a job and they did all right. However, when she was seven, the Great Depression enshrouded the world and lasted ten long years, practically the whole time she was growing up. Times were hard on everybody, most everyone she knew was poor or poorer, and her family was among the poorest. Clothes wore thin and shoes wore out with no new ones to replace the old ones. Glady lived with her parents, Carl and Opal Flowers, an older sister and two brothers, one older and one younger. She grew up living in a town named Rockwell. They grew what little garden they had room for and ate better in late summers but in the windy, cold winters of the Great Plains they almost starved.

One time Glady's dad was so desperate family that he took a club and told Opal that he was going out to get food, one way or another. He had come home with a box of groceries and Opal worried about what he might have done to get them. He told her he had found a temporary job for a dollar a day and the grocery store had given him credit until he got paid. Life was hard for most of the long ten years of the depression and the Flowers family got used to hand-to-mouth living and going to bed hungry.

Truth be-known the damned Depression was the only reason Glady found herself married to the old son-of-a-bitch. In the summer of 1939 her folks told her that even though the depression was relaxing its grip, they could barely afford to support themselves and her youngest brother who was in his early teens. Glady would be eighteen the next May and her mother told her she would need to leave home by then; she added that sooner would be even better. Glady worried how she could be ready to leave in ten months let alone any sooner. Opal didn't make any suggestions but she hinted that girls Glady's age should be thinking about marriage.

Glady had gone to school through the seventh grade and now spent most of her day doing chores. Opal kept a very clean house and she expected Glady to work hard helping around the house. Glady had never worked outside of her home and she'd never looked for a job. Getting work was hard enough for grown men like Carl, let alone a girl who still lived at home.

9

Later when it looked like Opal was not going to change her mind, Glady began to worry at night. What would become of her? Her older sister was married and lived up in Nebraska. Her brother-in-law was a truck driver and had a regular paycheck, but they were struggling. Not only did they have two little kids, but he also supported his widowed mother and two young sisters. There was no hope Glady could ask them for any help.

Nor could Glady ask her older brother for help. He was in the Army because Opal had given him the same ultimatum the year before last. Glady had no other family who were not similarly burdened, and she hardly knew anyone else, let alone someone who could take her in.

Quite a few girls Glady had known in grade school had gotten married over the past year or so. She had quit school so young she didn't have many close friends. She had kept in touch with a couple of girlfriends and occasionally had a blind date one of them set up. No one interesting though, and none of the guys ever called on her after the first date. Glady wondered how a person could find someone to marry if they were too poor to get out and meet anyone? She needed a miracle.

Glady lay in her bed and thought back to the only miracle she had ever experienced. She was almost eleven years old and she had been walking down the sidewalk going to school. She spied a ball of paper, all crumpled up and tucked in beside a bump in the sidewalk. It was like the wind may have blown it there and it caught in the crack. Thinking it could be a discarded gum wrapper she bent over and picked it up. If the wrapper hadn't been lying there long, nor had gotten wet, she could at least smell its peppermint deliciousness.

Glady never got candy or gum anymore and sometimes she wanted it so bad she would have stolen it. She knew she could never take a risk like that though because her mother would take her hide clear off her for stealing. Glady picked up the ball of paper hoping at least to dream about treats. As she smoothed out the paper she almost swallowed her tongue! She was so shocked to find she had found a twenty-dollar bill.

Her mind shrieked. Quick! Someone will see! Her first action was to swallow then cast her eyes furtively around to see if anyone was watching. It didn't seem like anyone was around at all let alone looking at her. She carefully slid her hand down to her side re-crumpling the bill as she walked slowly forward. She sure didn't want to call attention to herself at this precious moment.

It was hard not to shriek with joy. Glady's deprived young mind began to race over how she would spend the money. Candy! Piles of candy, chocolate, gum drops, and licorice. At the same time she became aware that no kid could take a twenty-dollar bill in to buy candy. The people working there would probably call the police, and then they would report it to her to her mother and that would be worse than going to jail. Glady knew that even if the police let her keep it, her mother would take the whole thing, sure as God made little green apples.

It would be a big risk to get caught storying to her mother. Selfishly spending money on herself would be bad enough, and lying was nearly as bad as stealing according to Opal. Glady stood to get the daylights beat out of her and the best way to prevent that was to not get caught. Once Glady had made the decision to lie and keep the money, she began planning how she could spend it to the best advantage. Her mind stumbled on the part of how she could take that much money into a store in the first place? It wouldn't be too hard after it was broken down into smaller bills and coins, but a twenty-dollar bill would arouse suspicion. She thought and thought.

First she thought of clothes. How could she wear new clothes without her mother noticing? Where would she keep them? Glady kept walking and trying to act as if nothing had happened, as if her heart were fairly bursting with joy. Glady went a few more blocks and a thought popped into her head.

Shoes! I could buy shoes! Shoes could be kept in her locker at school. It wasn't unusual for girls to change shoes when they got to school; they did it all the time when it was muddy.

What a wonderful dream come true that would be. I've been wearing these clodhoppers all year and the popular girls have been wearing new spring shoes and anklets. Once Glady settled on shoes to break down the twenty-dollar bill, she went back to the dreams of candy.

During classes that day, Glady decided she would go to the largest, fanciest department store in Rockwell. For one thing she didn't know anyone who shopped there so it was likely no one

11

would recognize her. Glady wondered if the clerks would ask her name. If they did, she would lie. Pure and simple, lying was the only thing that might work.

If she got caught, her mother would beat her to within an inch of her life for lying. However she went ahead and thought up a name and practiced saying it to herself it all day long. Glady could not keep her mind on anything but the money. Time seemed to be standing still, like the end of the school day would never come.

Finally, the last bell rang and her heart began to race. She had practiced the name over and over, even whispering it aloud when no one else was in the bathroom. As she left the school building she looked around to see if anyone was watching her going downtown instead of toward home. Everyone just seemed to be rushing out of the schoolyard, not paying attention to anyone else so she headed toward downtown and walked purposefully to Wagner's Department Store. She blew out a deep breath and swallowed a dry lump as she pushed open the glass door.

Glady glanced quickly around the store looking for the shoe department. When she spotted the shoe aisle, she went over and picked up a shoe that was on display. Her mind reeled, as she smelled the new leather and her hand caressed the smooth heel. There were more shoes here than Glady had ever knew existed. Dreams for the feet! Low top slippers, sandals, shoes of every color.

Glady had a brief moment of uncertainty when the clerk approached her. She was sure she had never seen the woman in her life, so she bit back her fear. This was no time to be afraid.

"I'm glad yer summer shoes'er in," Glady piped up to the clerk. "M'feet grew and m'old shoes'er getting' too little." Glady thought her voice sounded so grown up.

It wasn't unusual in the depression for relatives who were better off to send cash as birthday and Christmas gifts. When the occasion called for it some would be very generous because it didn't look so much like charity to poorer kin. The finer department stores were accustomed to these poorer relatives shopping above their usual element. Glady thought she had undoubtedly been mistaken for a rich kid when the clerk produced a cold smile.

"Kin I try on a pair?"

"Do you know your size, miss?"

A momentary panic threatened to seize Glady's confidence, but just in time the clerk added:

"You might go ahead and try that one on, it looks about right."

Relieved Glady set to work unlacing the long dirty shoestrings from her old shoes. She pulled up her long dingy stockings and pushed her foot into the beautiful new shoe.

"Yer right! It does fit." Glady exclaimed.

The clerk seeming to hope she would get a sale said:

"Of course you will want some new stockings too, won't you?"

Good idea! Glady thought but she said: "Of course." And thought of lovely anklets in pink, lavender and light blue.

Glady felt wonderful. In the shopping sack she carried was not only a pair of glorious summer shoes in sweet smelling leather; she also had two pairs of anklets. Best of all, she had been brave enough to ask for small change from the twenty-dollar bill!

This was a true miracle or was she dreaming? Cold reality was that she could not get caught; she couldn't risk going back to school after hours with packages. Glady stuffed the anklets and all her change except two quarters into the shoebox and folded down the paper sack it was in. She had to find a hiding place and be quick about it because she had one more stop to make.

Glady thought of several good hiding places, but she needed somewhere big enough for a shoebox. She walked over a small bridge and looked down at a place she had in mind. She saw some little boys playing in the gravel though and she'd heard that teenagers met down there to neck sometimes. At a temporary loss for ideas, she looked ahead and saw a culvert with weeds growing up around the opening. It didn't look like anyone had been down there in a while.

Glady walked a few steps past the culvert. Taking the chance of someone finding her prizes would be better than getting caught with them at home. It was getting late and her little brother's school was up ahead, and she didn't want to go much further with her package.

Glady turned around and walked back to the culvert and a ways past it. She bent over and pretended to be adjusting her stocking while she glanced around. No one seemed to be around so she quickly slid down the short steep embankment.

Glady brushed off three rocks and positioned them together inside the culvert; then she placed the shoebox upon them. She made sure it was well up off the sandy ground then she bent some weeds over the opening. She backed up to make sure nothing showed outside the culvert rim then hurriedly moved back up the ditch keeping her eyes on the ground. She spied a greenish rock and a piece of colored glass and made a point of picking them up and wiping them off. She continued to look at the ground as though searching for something as she put the rock and glass in her pocket. She looked a brief while longer and then climbed back up onto the sidewalk.

Casting her eyes about once more and seeing no one watching her, Glady hurried back toward town. She did not take time to stare at the mouth-watering wares at the candy counter. She quickly bought chocolate drops and some fruit-flavored hard candies. She put her dime change back in her pocket.

It was the first time Glady ever felt like the twelve-block walk home was too short. As her legs skipped along quickly, her mouth languished savoring the chocolates. Each one of them were wallowed by her tongue and allowed to melt into chocolate spit that flowed down her throat.

As Glady neared home she pushed the hard candies into her pocket. In case someone saw the bulge in her pocket, she could pull out the treasures she would show what she had found in the ditch. But that rock and colored glass had secret company down deep in her pocket, sweet delicious, company that would be sneaked out at bedtime.

"Where have you been young lady?" Opal queried, as her daughter quickly scooted into the house. "Your brother has been home for three quarters of an hour. Git out here right quick and help with supper."

Glady dashed into her room for a brief moment to collect her wits and get the dime out of her pocket. Then she hurried into the kitchen saying:

"Dorothy had too many books 'n papers from cleanin' out her desk. I helped her carry'em home." Glady gulped as she put on her apron patting it to make certain the candy didn't bulge too much.

"Well I need help more than Dorothy does young lady. You just be careful who yer running off to help before you git home to help me."

Hoping to distract her mother from further questioning, Glady held up the dime.

"Looky what I found on the way home from'er house."

Delightedly Opal snatched the dime from Gladys' hand.

"Every little bit helps, girly. Maybe it was lucky you helped yer friend today. See it don't happen again." Opal put the dime in her own pocket and never mentioned it again.

The next morning Glady was impatient to get out the door to school. She had tossed and turned all night. She was worried about the rain falling out of the heavy skies, but most of the sleeplessness was from excitement over her new shoes.

Glady pulled her long stockings above her knees and laced her raggedy high top shoes trying to contain her excitement. Her mother paid her no attention when she rushed out the door a few minutes early. Glady hoped by being a little early she would be out before most kids started to school. The blocks passed but about the time she reached the culvert, she turned and saw some boy was about a block behind her. She turned on around and went back toward him like she had forgotten something at home. When the boy had moved on past the culvert and his back kept moving toward school Glady went back and slid down the bank.

The weeds and rocks were just as she left them the previous evening. She grabbed the box, scrambled quickly back up the bank and rushed on toward school. Glady went straight to the bathroom and sat down on the floor. She unlaced her old shoes and pulled them off then peeled off the long stockings she had just put on at home.

It was a breeze putting on the new shoes and anklets. They slipped right on and she didn't have to push her foot down hard at all. Glady took the extra socks and the money out of the shoebox and stuffed the box and sack down into the trash bin. She rolled her old socks into a ball put them into here old shoes. She carried them back to her locker and tossed them in. More kids were now arriving at school and Glady walked slowly back to the bathroom with her face glowing and she gazed nonchalantly into the mirror. Gloriously, an older popular girl came in just behind her and exclaimed.

"Oh what pretty shoes you have! Your ankles are so thin. I've always wished I had nice ankles like those."

Glady could barely contain her delight. She always knew she would be noticed if she had nice things. She just knew it! Every day that spring until the end of the term Glady would rush to school to change into her new shoes. One time she became anxious when a girl kept staring at her. It had rained hard the night before so several girls were changing out of boots but this girl was looking right at Glady. Glady nervously dropped her eyes and happened to glance at the poor girl's feet. She saw old winter shoes and long stockings just like she used to wear and knew exactly what the look on the girls face had been: Envy!

On toward the end of the school year Glady was growing concerned about her precious shoes. She thought and thought and then hit upon an idea and began to plan. Her mother usually tended their winter coats and put them away in the back of a closet. No one paid much attention to the coats again until late in the fall. She would hide her shoes in the pockets of her own coat and sneak them back to school when summer was over.

Glady would be able to wear her new shoes at school again in September until it got too cold. She just hoped her feet wouldn't spread too much this summer, nor grow too long. She would need to check and see if her coat had been put away where no one would notice a bulge in her pockets.

As Glady neared home one afternoon she was lost in thought, thinking about hiding her wonderful treasured shoes, she looked down and admired her feet. Those new shoes had brought her admiring glances from several girls. Glady just knew things were going to change for her now. People would notice her, be nice to her, and speak pleasantly to her. One girl who Glady admired but who had certainly never noticed her before had already said 'hello' to her. Maybe she should risk buying a nice sweater to wear next school term when the weather turned chilly.

Glady had quite a lot of money left, in fact she still had over nine dollars. She kept some in her locker and some in three different books in her desk and she carried some in the toes of her shoes. Trying to find good hiding places at home for the summer would prove trickier, but she was certainly trying to think of some as she walked.

Glady couldn't get caught with money this summer; it would be risky if she got caught spending. She might be able to buy some good things to eat once in a while though, depending on where she hid the money and how easy it was to get to. Glady thought that putting the money in several places would be best, then if anybody found one of her hiding places, they would only find part of her treasured stash. Lost in thought she tried to think of places that would be safe, but where she wouldn't have to admit it was hers if it was found.

Glady's mind suddenly screamed at her.

"Look at your feet! You still have your pretty shoes on! Oh no!" Terror seized Glady. She knew if her mother happened to be looking out the window right now, she would notice her bare legs from clear up the street.

Glady had to get all the way back to school and get her old shoes and stockings. Her mind was racing, how could she get back to school and back home without being too late on either end? Whatever would happen if her mother caught her now? Not only would she give her a licking, she would find about the money and take everything. Glady knew she could say good-bye to her money and half of her hide with it. Glady turned and ran as fast as she could back toward school.

Rushing up the walk to the school Glady was relieved to find the door unlocked. She hurried up the hallway and stripping off her good shoes and anklets as she approached her locker. She grabbed her old shoes and long stocking and quickly flopped down right there and tugged them on, keeping them as straight as she could. She jumped up and almost collided with the janitor.

"Uh, uh, I just forgot my homework," Glady mumbled dry-mouthed and breathless, pushing past the old man.

"Good thing I was late locking the door," the old janitor called out in puzzlement.

Glady rushed toward home. Those blocks had never seemed so long and so much was at stake. She could say she forgot her homework, but what if her mother had seen her pale legs flashing from up the street. Glady had thought of no good answers as she flew into the house and went directly into her room. She didn't want her mother to see that she had no books or papers with her. Just as quickly, she went into the kitchen trying to act normal.

"Doggit, girl!" Opal scolded as Glady panicked and began to concoct a story about borrowing another girl's shoes. "I don't know why you can't get home any sooner. Always daydreaming and moping around anymore. What's ever going to become of you, young lady?" Glady listened to her mother scold her, trying to look appropriately concerned while feeling so relieved that she hadn't been caught.

***

Glady became quite ill in the winter she was in the seventh grade. She came home from school one day with a fever and aches. She was aching all over her body, but especially had pains down her legs. Opal took one look at Glady, felt her forehead and sent her to bed.

Glady didn't feel any better the rest of the week and she developed swollen glands in her throat. Her skin was flushed all over her body except around her mouth where she was very pale. Opal determined that Glady was getting worse and she finally sent for the doctor. The doctor told Opal that he thought Glady might have scarlet fever and told her to stay in bed and away from other people.

Glady was down in bed for seven weeks. When she finally got up she didn't seem to have any strength to get around and her legs still ached. Since she had so far to walk to school, she didn't go back that year. After the illness, Glady declared that her left leg had shortened. She would stretch both legs out to show the difference in length. For the rest of her life Glady complained about pains in her legs off and on, especially in cold weather.

Glady repeated the seventh grade the next year and passed, but she felt out of place with the younger kids in her class. She never quite fit in so she did not go back to school for the eighth grade the following year. Since Opal had only completed the third grade and knew she had always gotten by, she didn't push Glady to return to school. She sure didn't want Glady getting sick again, it had been a lot of extra work taking care of her.

CHAPTER THREE

When it looked like Glady was going to stay well, Opal expected her to do more and more of the household chores. She didn't expect much else of her though and gave Glady an ultimatum when she announced that Glady was grown and must leave home by her next birthday in May.

"Leave by my birthday next year," Glady thought. "Well, I'll be eighteen then anyway. I won't be too sorry to get out from under Mom's thumb. And next year will be 1940! Now that really sounds funny, 1940."

Glady didn't have many close girlfriends and after she quit school she lost track of most of her classmates. As she reached her middle teens, she gradually became somewhat reacquainted with several single girls when they found out she was available to double date with them.

In those days, decent folks required their daughters to double date when they dated a boy who had an automobile. If a couple suddenly found themselves without their usual double for one reason or another, they would hastily think of anyone that might be available to ensure their own date. Once in a while, Glady would get invited to go with whatever boy could be similarly found quickly. The couples would usually go to a picture show, or roller-skating since that was about all there was to do in Rockwell. After skating or the show if they thought they could get away with it, the driver would find a place to park and neck.

One night Glady walked up to the picture show alone to see Boys Town. Her dad had sneaked her a little change that week. She happened to run into some girls she knew at the front door of the theater and they sat together for the show. They went out to the lobby during the intermission and one girl started flirting with a boy she had dated once. He was with several other guys and they eventually came over and asked the girls to sit with them for the second half of the show. That is how Glady met George.

George was a tall handsome guy and Glady didn't remember ever seeing him around before. She was pleasantly surprised when he paired off with her. They hit it off and they teased each other and joked after the show. George asked Glady if she would like to double date with him and another couple the next week. Glady thought about George as she walked home that night, thinking about how lucky she was that he was so handsome and nice.

The next week when George drove down the street to pick up Glady the first time, he was surprised at the run down condition of the neighborhood where she lived. He had been interested in Glady and it hadn't entered his mind that she might be poor. George's parents were merchants who owned a store just on the outskirts of Rockwell. They had made it through the hardest times and were now fairly well off in their business. He didn't consider himself rich or snobbish, he just forgot about the hard times other people were still going through.

George seemed to truly enjoy his first real date with Glady. She talked brightly and laughed at his jokes as they roller-skated the evening away. Glady was quite pleased when he asked her out again for the next week. They double dated to the movies, and then he asked her out again.

Glady fell hard for George. She figured out that his family owned a nice store and were undoubtedly well off, but that really wasn't it. She really liked him. They seemed to fit together and in her mind, she and George were made for each other.

Glady would fantasize that her dreams were going to come true. Instead of being a popular single girl though, she would be a popular married woman. Only rarely did any doubt creep into Glady thoughts, and then it was only wondering how George's family would treat her after they were married.

At this point Glady was thinking frequently about her mother's ultimatum. She hoped that if she was engaged to George, her mother would extend the time a little. She was not optimistic though since Opal frequently complained about being financially strapped. She did her best not to show any concern and kept accepting dates with George to keep things moving along with him.

George had borrowed his father's car and he invited two other couples out for a ride. After a while they parked and the two other couples got out and walked out into a deserted wooded area, leaving George and Glady in the car. Glady was so pleased that she and George could do some necking in private. As George tenderly kissed her, Glady began to feel warm and different than she had ever felt with a boy before.

After several minutes, the kissing increased in intensity and both Glady and George were breathing heavily. George's right hand inched its way up to Glady's left breast. Since George's hand was on top of her blouse, Glady did not protest. She felt strangely titillated and was wondering where George would put his hand next and where she should put her hands.

Suddenly, the car door was yanked opened and George's hand flew back to the steering wheel.

"Caught ya!" one boy joked loudly as he and the girl piled into the front seat with George and Glady. He raucously began laughing and talking about the third couple and where they may be. Shortly, the other couple came out of the treed area, laughing and joking.

"Did you get any grass in your pants Johnny?" the loud boy teased the other.

"No, she was on the bottom!" the other boy retorted.

Glady wondered what exactly the other couples had done out there in the trees and she hoped she and George would be alone again soon. When George didn't ask for another date Glady grew very worried.

Her worry evaporated a week later when George drove up to the house in the early evening and asked Glady to go to the picture show. He seemed a little downhearted when they were waiting for their double to collect his date, but he didn't say much. George drove Glady straight home after the show, even before dropping off the other couple.

Glady's concern grew again because George seemed different than she had seen him previously. He gave Glady a kiss at her front door and quickly mentioned that his family had made plans to visit his uncle in Texas. He said he would be out of town for two to three weeks. Noting the fear in Glady's face, George added that before she knew it he would be over to pick her up some evening when he got back to town.

Glady thought George seemed anxious as he was saying this. He was coming back from Texas, wasn't he? Was it just that he was going to miss her so much, or what? She stumbled into the house and went to bed feeling unusually sad.

While George was gone, Glady only went out once, and that was in the first week. Two girls came by and she went to the show with them. She wouldn't have gone out at all but she really wanted to see Jeepers Creepers, and the movie wouldn't be playing much longer in Rockwell. She felt guilty because she wasn't seeing it with George but she came straight home, and went straight to bed after the show. She dreamed that George had taken her to the movie and had her hand on her breast. Only this time it was up under her shirt, not outside of it.

The first week went by quickly. Glady spent most of the time fantasizing about her future with George. She looked forward to his return and knew in her heart that this absence would strengthen their feelings for each other. He would come back; they would fall deeply in love and would soon marry in a big church wedding. Each night Glady expanded on her daydreams about George, the wedding, his hands, and deep, deep kisses. Glady's passion grew.

Two weeks came and went, and then three weeks. Glady was growing alarmed that something terrible must have happened to George and he couldn't get back to town. After a month went by, Glady worried that she may never see George again and she began to mourn the loss of her true love during the day, but continued to dream passionate dreams of him at night.

Finally, Glady went to the movies again with the same two girls. After the show she looked across the lobby, and there was George! He was in a group talking to some boys, and they all seemed to be looking at some pretty girls. George didn't look toward Glady, but he broke away from his friends and started toward the restrooms. Glady quickly followed in that direction; cutting across his path she forced him into a corner.

Glady had been worried sick and she knew she sounded too shrill and demanding.

"Where have you been?"

George reached out and roughly grabbed Glady's left breast through her blouse.

"Where have you been is the real question!"

Glady was shaken and uncertain about what George meant. She stammered,

"George! Wha-what's goin' on here? Wha-what do you mean?"

"You know darned well what I mean!" George hissed. "Did you think I wouldn't find out? What are you, some kind of tramp?"

Glady was aghast as George continued.

"Those guys I hang out with told me about you. How they picked you up as soon as I was gone. How easy it was to get into your pants. They told me how you put out for both of them."

Glady was appalled and sickened. She became defensive cried out explanations to his outrageous ideas.

"Why George," she said. "I-I haven't been anywhere. I stayed home the whole time you were gone. W-Well, I mean, I did come here to the movies one time, but I-I haven't done anything. I certainly haven't seen any boys."

George relaxed his grip and removed his hand and said no more. He pushed passed her and stormed back to the lobby. Glady rushed out of the theater crying with her heart completely broken in two.

Glady was devastated and she obsessed on what she would say to George if she saw him again, but admitting that it was probably hopeless. Sometimes she couldn't blame him if those boys actually said those things about her. But why hadn't he even given her a chance to explain things? Other times she thought perhaps it was his parents. Maybe they had found out about her, a poor girl. Then again, she thought it didn't have to do with that either; they probably had big college plans for him and didn't want him getting serious about anyone. Or maybe George was using her all along. How far would he have tried to go with her that night in the car? Glady never saw George again, but she never forgot him.

CHAPTER FOUR

Glady moped around the house for days and cried at night. She tried to figure out what would become of her in light of her mother's ultimatum. She concealed her heartbreak because her mother didn't know how serious she had been about George. She was glad she hadn't said anything while they were dating because Opal would be asking questions now about where he had gone. Glady finally put her pained thoughts aside when Opal reminded her,

"It's the end of August. Time for the fair again."

The big annual county fair was the one event that virtually everyone in Rockwell, and probably the whole county, came to town for at least one night. It always started the last Wednesday of August, and went strong until midnight Saturday night. By early Sunday morning, everything was loaded up and by Sunday noon, it was all gone without a trace.

Maybe George will be at the fair," Glady's mind raced hopefully. "He will tell me he's sorry, and that he was wrong. He will tell me how much he's missed me. We will ride up to the top of the Ferris wheel and he will tell me how much he loves me. He will ask me to marry him and everything will be all right."

Glady was able to use this hope to look forward to the fair. She also hoped her dad would have a little extra money for fair week. She wanted to have her picture taken there, go on some carnival rides and buy cotton candy. She loved cotton candy, spun sugar. It started out all fluffy and then melted down in your mouth to crunchy bits that left your tongue pink. Even if she didn't have money she would still go. She didn't need money to visit the exhibits and walk around the carnival with her girlfriends.

Glady wondered what she would wear to the fair the first night. If she ran into George she wanted to look her best. She didn't have any new clothes and she wanted to wear something like slacks. They were all the rage right now. She asked her mother several times for any material that that she may have around. Tired of her badgering, Opal threw four white and green flour sacks onto her lap one morning.

25

"You can have these to ruin," she told Glady.

Glady carefully ripped all of the stitches out of the flour sacks and laid out the cloth lengthwise. She couldn't find the tape measure so she used a ruler to gauge her height from waist to ankle and decided she would have just enough material to get one piece from each sack. She measured crosswise over her thin body, stomach, hips and waist, to confirm that the cloth would be wide enough. She marked the material with a pencil to guide her as she cut. After she had cut the cloth, carefully following the lines, she held the pieces up comparing them to herself.

"Looks like a good fit," Glady judged, as she got out a needle, thimble and white thread. She triple stitched the outside and inside seams and left room to lap a placket on one side. She hemmed up the legs and fashioned a waistband with some pieced scraps and attached it at the top. Then she turned the slacks to the right side, heated the iron and took care to not scorch them as she pressed out the seams.

The first day of the fair came. Glady heated the curling iron and made some tight pageboy curls in the ends of her hair. She put on her new slacks and paraded around the house. She liked the freedom pants offered and she was pleased they were stylish. The pants pulled a little at the crotch, but after checking carefully in the mirror, Glady noted that they didn't look bad at all.

As she pressed a cool white blouse to go with the new slacks Glady secretly wished she could tie it up for the new bare midriff look. She knew Opal would scream at her for even thinking about such a thing though. Glady used an old green scarf and bobby pins to make a band around her pageboy hairdo. She admired how the scarf matched the little green flowers in her new flour sack pants. She told her folks that she would be gone until late because she was meeting some of her friends.

Glady actually had no specific plans to meet anyone, but she didn't want to wait around and go with her folks. They were going later in the afternoon with her little brother; she hoped she would find someone to walk around with before they spotted her alone.

The carnival rides had been taken off the trucks in the night and were being set up. Glady marveled at the huge machines that would come alive tonight with lights and laughs. The Ferris wheel was her favorite, but it scared her when it stopped at the top and rocked back and forth as passengers were being loaded on the ground.

Luckily Glady ran into two girls she knew right away. She was happy to see them and they admired her new slacks. They chatted about what boys might be there, and they all laughed as one girl told the new 'knock knock' jokes she had heard on the radio. They looked the boys over as they went by around the grounds, but they were all rushing about and they didn't look familiar.

"They must be carnival workers," one girl said. "Or farm hands helping with the show animals." The boys did take a moment to eye the girls as they hurried by.

The girls whiled away the afternoon, and the sun started to drop in the sky. Lights began to twinkle faintly all over the fair grounds and the cotton candy, popcorn and candy apple stands lit up. The Ferris wheel gradually became a huge circle of bright lights, and the barkers called people into the shows.

By eight-thirty in the evening the carnival was in a full riotous swing. Laughter, talking and whirling rides surrounded the group of girls that had grown to five. Girls, women, young men, old men, more girls, married people, kids and couples were everywhere on the midway milling about and having fun.

Two girls they saw were wearing stylish, beaded Indian moccasins that Glady had never seen before. Even though the girls looked stuck-up and were showing off, she admired the new look in footwear. One had on tan moccasins with red and orange beads and the other girl wore white ones with green and blue beads. Glady wished she had the white pair, they would fit right in with her new slacks and then she would really be in style.

When Glady and her girlfriends approached one of the carnival booths, they saw three boys throwing balls at some pins stacked in a pyramid. The boys kept throwing the balls with full force, but they didn't seem to be hitting anything.

The carnival booth man collected more money and encouraged the boys to try harder. He spotted the three girls and said,

"Come on boys! Win a cupie doll for one of the little ladies."

The boy throwing a ball at that moment turned and saw the girls watching him. He confidently over-handed the ball, firing straight at the target. He threw with such force that the pyramid of pins blasted all over the booth as the hardball hit the mark. One pin almost hit the surprised loud-mouthed booth man in the head.

All the girls cheered the marksman and clapped gaily. The boy bowed grandly from the waist and collected his prize. He turned and handed the prize to the blondest girl in Glady's group. The girl squealed and took hold of the winners arm and their group became six.

A tall, thin boy with a handsome head of strawberry blond hair seemed to find Glady the most interesting and he asked,

"Have you been on this here Ferris wheel yet?"

"Not yet," she replied somewhat shyly. The boy took her arm and led her to the line for the Ferris wheel.

Gesturing up to the large moving circle of lights he stated grandly,

"I'm the captain of this here ship, and you kin just call me Cap."

"I'm Gladys Ann Flowers," Glady replied, smiling prettily and getting into the spirit, "but everyone calls me Glady."

The boy bowed as he held the bar out for her to get into the Ferris wheel seat. Glady took a large step into the rocking seat and had to catch herself from falling too hard as she sat down. As she hit the back of the seat she felt her new homemade slacks rip up the back from the crotch up almost to the waistband.

"Oh my God," thought Glady, "now what am I going to do?" It felt like a huge, gaping rip. "I wonder how bad it is? I wonder how much of my underpants will show?"

All through the Ferris wheel ride Glady worried about her slacks. She hardly even noticed when the seat was swinging at the top during loading. Cap noticed the sudden change in

Glady's behavior and wondered if she was scared or if something else was wrong.

"Whatsamatter," he teased. "Is the little lady scared of my ship?"

Glady admired the boy's friendly, open style and unfaltering told him exactly what her problem was.

"I ripped my slacks getting into the seat," she confessed looking into Cap's bright eyes. Cap laughed wildly.

"Well, that ain't no step for a stepper," he jauntily replied. "After we get off I'll walk behind you out to the edge of the crowd and you can go home to change clothes."

True to his word, Cap walked behind Glady with his hands on her shoulders to the edge of the crowd and asked,

"Are you coming back tomorrow night?"

"Yes, I am." Glady replied.

"We will meet by the Ferris wheel at sundown then," Cap stated matter-of-factly. It was settled, Glady had a date with the nicely odd boy.

For the next three nights Glady and Cap hung around together in the same group experiencing all the fair and carnival had to offer. Glady had her picture taken in the most popular booth. She put on a Mexican hat that had dangling fuzzy balls all around the brim and a black weskit and smiled for the camera. She ate cotton candy and popcorn and saw the free show.

Cap cupped her chin and stole several brief kisses, especially when they were on their favorite ride, the Ferris wheel. He teased and asked if she'd ripped anything he could help her with. He started calling her Glady Blue Eyes, even though Glady insisted that he must be colorblind because her eyes were hazel green.

Glady liked being with Cap, he was so relaxed and fun loving. He seemed to have plenty of money to spend on her. At the end of Saturday night, Cap said a hearty goodnight at the gate and did not mention seeing her again. Glady was slightly disappointed that he didn't mention going out with her again. She had grown attached to him, but she could never ask him about seeing him again. It was unheard of for a girl to do such a thing; it didn't even enter her mind.

"Cap cut me off kinda short," Glady thought as she walked home. Glady had told Cap that she lived here in Rockwell and she knew that he lived out around Front City, but no specific information had ever been exchanged. "Maybe he has a steady girlfriend out in Front City."

Glady walked into the house with a miserable letdown feeling. She had been looking forward to the fair, on the hope of running into George. She'd had fun in spite of not seeing him, but now it was over. In her dark lonely bed, Glady's thoughts returned to George. She replayed their last encounter in the movie theater hallway and agonized over what he could have meant. Again, she mourned the loss of her only true love.

The next day was Sunday. Opal Flowers got religious every now and then and would insist that Glady go down to the Baptist Church with her. Opal was off religion at the moment so she didn't say anything when Glady got up early and said she wanted to go to the fairground one last time. Glady hadn't slept very well and she wanted to hang on to the distraction the fair had provided as long as possible. There would be some activity and exhibits to see as there were being collected by their owners.

A few people were out and about, but the excitement was gone from the fairgrounds. One of the kiddy rides was slowly rotating, barely moving, being checked before being dismantled. The big rides including the Ferris wheel were packed and locked down, ready to be moved out.

The vegetable exhibits lay spoiling on the display shelves, some of them with prize ribbons. The show animals had been auctioned off last evening leaving some of their young owners in tears. Glady sighed. Nothing much was going to happen here today. She wandered over to the sewing exhibits area to see if they had all been picked up or not.

Glady was intent, looking at a displayed quilt. She marveled at how well this particular quilter had matched the colors. Usually Glady hated quilts because the prints seemed so mismatched, putting colors and patterns together that weren't quite right. Her mother's quilts were especially awful since Opal pieced together any old scraps that she had on hand, and didn't seem to even consider colors and print combinations.

"I wouldn't mind having that quilt on my bed," Glady thought.

Suddenly Glady was roughly shoved from the side. She turned and saw a young man hurrying past her with a large wooden box, seemingly unaware that he had run into anyone.

"Are you hurt?" a man's voice behind her asked.

Rubbing her arm, Glady turned to see a rather striking young man. He was deeply suntanned and muscled but somehow also wiry appearing, standing there without a shirt. He holding a box and he had a straw hat balanced upon it.

"Uh-no, I don't think so," Glady said, noting how well the young man's arms flexed just right. His face however, was somehow unbalanced with deep-set eyes and heavy eyebrows.

"That was my sorry brother. That is, I know that he would be sorry if he would wake up long enough to know he just ran into a very pretty girl."

"Thank you," Glady murmured.

"Come out here and let me get you something to drink. I think I saw some lemonade," the young man expanded. "I'll send brother Tim a bill and he can pay for it."

Sipping the lemonade through a straw while sitting at the quiet fairground picnic table, Glady learned that the young man's name was Donald. He was a farmer who had five brothers, three with entries in the fair. The family had sold some livestock the evening before and Tim, the brother who'd run into her, had won the grand champion prize for his steer.

By the time they had finished their drinks, Glady had a date for Saturday. Donald explained that though farms were very busy places, he could probably sneak away by then. Glady felt embarrassed by the way Donald seductively stared into her eyes. She could not hold his gaze as she told him how to find her house.

That Saturday, Glady wore a full print skirt and a white blouse and wished again for a pair of the new fashionable beaded Indian moccasins. Donald hadn't said where they were going, but her choice of clothes would be suitable for about anything there was to do in Rockwell.

Glady heated the curling iron and tried to make her hair curl around her face. The weather was hot and humid the curls relaxed almost the instant they came out of the curling iron. She swept her hair back and smoothed it under and into a roll.

About seven o'clock a pickup truck pulled up in the driveway and Glady answered the door when Donald knocked. As he opened the pick-up door for her Glady realized that this was really the first time she had been alone with a boy in a car. She wondered if she should be worried, but then pooh-poohed her own thoughts.

"And anyway," she secretly teased herself, "it's not a car, it's a truck!"

Donald drove around town saying he never got away from the farm much, so he liked to drive around and look at everything when he did get here. It was still very light outside and Glady wondered again what Donald's plans were for the evening.

When the sky began to darken, Donald drove out the blacktop highway and turned onto a graveled road and pulled into a lightly wooded lane near a river. He pulled off that road back into the trees where there were no tracks.

"Let's just talk for awhile and watch the stars come out from here," Donald said.

Glady felt comfortable and they sat there talking, mostly about themselves and their families. Donald told Glady that he too, had only gone through the seventh grade. He said his folks encouraged him and his brothers to finish through the eighth grade, but once he could read, write and do sums, what else did he need to farm with his folks? Just when Glady noticed how dark the sky was, Donald slid over past the gearshift, until he was very close to her, and pulled her face over to his for a kiss.

Donald gave her a quick kiss and then a more lingering kiss. When he felt Glady stiffening and pulling away he said to her,

"Now I've never forced any body to do anything they didn't want to do, so don't worry. I won't do anything unless you are agreeable. Is that alright by you?" Glady was taken aback at his frankness.

"Alright" she murmured, not quite sure it really was all right as Donald took her into his arms again.

Donald kept kissing her deeper and deeper. His tongue began to explore her mouth and his hand slowly massaged her back. The heat developed under his hands, Glady had never known such heat. She began to breathe heavier and move rhythmically into Donald's hands. When his hands moved simultaneously from her back slowly around to her breasts, she was waiting for it. She gasped softly as his hands covered her breast.

"Do you want me to stop?" Donald asked. Glady rocked her chin horizontally and continued the kiss. Donald began to undo the buttons and fasteners between his hands and Gladys bare nipples. When the blouse and brassiere were undone Donald's mouth moved toward Glady's breast. His hand began to gently massage her stomach and then slid on down to tug up the hemline of her dress.

Glady held onto Donald's strong shoulders pulling back slightly so her clothes would fall away and his mouth could find what it sought. Glady gasped louder with a thrilling sensation as she watched the lower half of her breast disappear into Donald's wet mouth. Just when Glady thought she would burst with anticipation, Donald stopped and said,

"Let's get out and into the back of the truck."

Glady got a hold of herself and seemed hesitant. Donald reiterated that he would not do anything she didn't want to do. Glady had not wanted to stop, she wanted to get back to those marvelous feelings she was having for the first time. She decided to trust Donald and allowed herself to be assisted out of the cab. Donald pulled a blanket out from behind the seat, folded it in two and spread it out on the bed of the pickup. He lifted Glady up onto the blanket giving her a quick kiss as he sat her down. He climbed up beside her and gently took Glady back into his arms.

Glady felt exhilarated lying there kissing. Her blouse was still open in the front and the hem almost up around her waist. Donald kept massaging her, rubbing her and kissing her. Everything he did made Glady want more. Even though Donald still had all of his clothes on, he lay on top of her and spread her legs so he was between them. Glady rocked her pelvis into his rhythmically feeling his hardness against her and marveling how it felt. Donald slid his hand down between them and pulled her underpants down and then off and Glady felt her nakedness moving against his trousers. When Donald reached down between them a second time, Glady was feeling so good she barely noticed.

Suddenly during a thrusting motion, she felt Donald slide deep inside her. Donald continued rocking and thrusting, moving in and out.

"How did that happen?" Glady's mind raced, "I always thought this was supposed to hurt, but I've never felt so good. So deliciously cool and hot at the same time."

As Donald thrust faster, Glady also moved with him, wanting more.

"More, more, deeper, deeper, faster, faster," her mind wildly called as her pelvis lifted off the truck bed. Then Glady felt a scream well up from her throat. She suppressed it as an intense constriction rose from the center deep in her pelvis and then broke in a flood of waves all over her body from her abdomen to her knees.

"Ahhhh, Ahhhh, Ahhhh, Ahhhh," over and over came her voice in rhythm with the thrusting. Just as Glady became aware of herself, Donald began the same chant and she felt his body contract and hot liquid rush out of him and into her in a forceful rhythm that gradually diminished.

They lay there very briefly, when Donald rolled off her without words. Glady came to her senses and then grew concerned about what he was thinking.

"Well, I can see that you like this every bit as much as I do." Donald finally said as he turned his face back toward Glady. She couldn't see his expression in the dark and didn't know how to respond. She was aware of the fluid leaking out of her and over the front of her thigh.

"I thought you were a virgin when I picked you up, but now I see you are an experienced woman of the world," he whispered. Glady stared at him perplexedly, in the dark.

"And that's good 'cause I won't have any of that just-picked cherry nonsense from you, like I get from so many girls." Glady listened in revulsion.

"But, but," she stammered.

"That's alright little lady, I've always thought girls should enjoy getting it just as much as boys. I don't have any reservations at all. Let me help you get your clothes back on and get you back to town before your dad comes looking for me with the shotgun."

Glady was numb all the way back to town and seemed frozen. When Donald parked in front of her house she slowly got out of the truck. It was very late and she suddenly worried about getting into the house without waking her folks. He seemed to notice and said a quick good-bye. He drove off while she went around back to the outhouse.

Glady cleaned up as best she could. It dawned on her then what some of those punch lines to dirty jokes meant as she tried to get rid of the fishy odor Donald had left with her. She crept quietly into her bedroom and got quickly into bed, her anxiety lessening as the house remained quiet.

Glady was bewildered as she lay there. She had never experienced such marvelous ecstasy in her life. Waves of intense pleasure like she never knew existed in this world. But many other things swirled around her mind too. Did she get pregnant? She knew Donald had not used a rubber. She never thought it could happen so easy or fast, especially the first time. She'd heard that sex was painful and awful to experience, like getting your period. But that! That feeling that she had just had! Did other women feel like that and think it was awful?

Glady worried that maybe only whores felt good about sex that way. Was she meant to be an over-sexed wanton whore? What did Donald mean that she wasn't a virgin? Was she normal? Was something wrong with her down there? Would a decent man have anything to do with her now that she wasn't a virgin? Had she wrecked herself and her whole life so effortlessly? Would Donald come back? If he did, would she dare go out with him? Make love with him again? Would it feel that good again? Would he wear a rubber if she asked him to?

Glady began having sexual fantasies in her dreams that night for the first time. She dreamed that men were lined up in a row, sunburned, wearing farmer straw hats and long underwear with large bulges in the front. She went up and down the line, rubbing herself up against them, asking them if they could tell whether or not she was a virgin. She woke up several times feeling a warm throbbing at the midline where her pubic hair parted. The throbbing radiated out and down the inside of her legs and up into her stomach. Once she woke up and her hands were wet and she wondered if it was sweat or if she had been touching herself down there in her sleep.

Glady got her period the next week. She let out a long sigh, it was the very first time in three years of bleeding every month, that she was relieved and happy to see that awful dark stringy mess in her underpants. She wasn't unhappy that Donald hadn't come by again and probably wasn't coming back. She had no idea how she could look at him let alone talk to him. Secretly, she did crave that glorious sensation he had awakened, and then unleashed.

CHAPTER FIVE

Winter was here. The terrible wind swept down the Great Plains from the north, screaming through the Dakotas and Nebraska and clear to Texas. Time was running out for Glady to leave home, it was only few months until she turned eighteen. When the weather turned cold she no longer had any thoughts about Cap or Donald. She knew she would never see either of them again, and really didn't care, but she couldn't give up thoughts and dreams of her darling, George.

She hoped he would come back some day. George was never far from her thoughts in the daytime and her dreams at night. Her fantasies would take her to a wedding with George and they would be so happy together. George was indeed her only love, her lost true love.

Glady would turn fantasies and dreams into a kind of reality that she could believe in. Lying in her bed that cold winter she pretended that it was George, not Donald, in the back of the pickup last summer. After a while, even when she was wide-awake doing housework, she would sometimes forget that it wasn't really George.

"I wonder why George thought I wasn't a virgin that night?" she would ask her bewildered self. No wonder he doesn't come back, he probably thinks I am a whore. Then she would remember that George had only felt her breast through her blouse. She sorrowfully hoped that George would come back and profess his undying love for her so everything would be wonderful again.

When she could think of an excuse to get out, Glady would walk downtown to the picture show or to the roller rink even if the weather was miserable. Lately, it seemed like her mother expected her to do more and more of the housework, sometimes acting like Glady was the maid instead of her daughter. She admitted to herself that she would be glad to leave her controlling, griping mother if only she had a place to go.

One especially cold night Glady was at the roller rink skating around the big circle with a girlfriend.

"There sure is a big crowd here tonight," her girlfriend yelled over the noise.

Glady nodded and glanced behind her at a blond-haired boy who was skating up behind them. As the boy quickly skated past them, he tapped Glady on the shoulder. He looked tall and skinny from his backside and Glady didn't get a good look at his face.

Glady watched the skinny boy skate fast on the opposite side of the rink, she still really couldn't see his face but she didn't think she knew him. She continued to talk and skate around the big circle. Glady felt the tap on her shoulder again and saw the boy whiz by again. She wondered what was going on with him.

Later, Glady and her girlfriend were changing back into their regular shoes; the boy came and flopped down beside them.

"Did all that tapping on my shoulder wear you out?" Glady inquired, looking at the stranger. She saw now that he was older than she thought he was when he had been skating by. The young man looked rather sheepish and smiled.

"We're going to go get something to drink," Glady's girlfriend informed him. "Do you want to come along with us?"

Glady wouldn't have invited him to go anywhere, but she didn't care that her friend did either. The three started out of the spectator seating rows in search of something to drink. On the way out the door, Glady's friend saw a cute boy she said used to be her neighbor. She invited him along too.

Glady preferred the boy-next-door to the shoulder-tapper, so she tried to make conversation and smiled at her preferred. Unfortunately, boy-next-door seemed far more interested in his old neighbor than in Glady. Glady found herself paired off with the gawky, skinny guy, Hank, the shoulder tapper.

As they sat in the booth and talked, Glady was amazed to find out that Hank Wilkey was over twenty-one years old and that he drove a taxicab for a living. She thought that shoulder tapping was pretty foolish behavior for someone that age with a steady job.

Hank told them all some of the strange experiences he had as a cab driver in a rather cute fashion. By the time the evening ended, Glady had warmed to him slightly.

"I'm off next Friday," Hank said as they were saying their good-byes outside the café. "Can I pick you up in the afternoon?"

Glady had been shut up in the house too much this winter and anything would be better than staying in. She readily consented to the date rather than stay home doing whatever chores her mother came up with.

Glady was especially pleased when Hank came to pick her up and she discovered that he had a car of his own. They went back to the skating rink and Glady skated with Hank around the big circle. When Hank dropped her off, he asked Glady for another date and she accepted again mostly to get out of the house.

During the next date Hank drove Glady out into the country and past his folks house on their farm.

Hank told Glady that his folks were pretty strict Adventist so when he'd left the farm over a year ago and started smoking cigarettes and eating meat they'd pretty much disowned him. He said they didn't like him driving a taxicab either, but that a son who didn't stay on the farm to help the family wasn't much use anyway.

Further, Hank said that disowning him didn't mean much since they'd lost the family homestead farm the year before he'd left home. He said, that like a lot of people in those bad time, they'd had their farm mortgaged to the hilt. When the crops failed, they just couldn't make the payments. The bank took the farm.

"But ain't this a farm?" Glady asked Hank as they drove past the driveway of his folk's house again.

"Well it is, but not like the one we used to have. This one is only about a hundred acres and the folks just grow for themselves and their own livestock. We used to have a big farm and ranch, hundreds of acres, and we ran a lot of cattle. My grandpa was a big man around these parts. A rancher and he ran for county sheriff and won three terms."

Glady listened with fascination; she had never known anyone who owned such a large piece of property, even if it wasn't theirs anymore.

"What does your mother think of all this?" Glady wondered out loud.

"It's my stepmother. She's the one who had to get used to the change," Hank said. "My mother died when I was little." Hank was brusque and didn't seem to want Glady to ask any more questions, so she didn't.

Each time Hank brought Glady home, he would ask about another date and she accepted. She liked having something to look forward to and someone to talk to. She usually chatted on about this and that and he listened a lot. She had noticed a certain moodiness to Hank. Sometimes he would be talkative and almost giddy, and then other times he would hardly say a word. He always seemed to like her company whatever mood he was in though. Glady needed to get out of the house, and the car was nice to have to get around.

Hank and Glady never had any physical contact. They hadn't parked, or even kissed at the door. In a way, Glady was content to let things move slowly, considering what had happened last summer. In another way, she knew her time was running out. Glady gradually got to know Hank better and sometimes fantasized what it would be like to marry a wealthy rancher.

Ranchers probably had hired workers to do most of the heavy work and cooking, didn't they? Never mind that Hank didn't even have a real ranch anymore. Glady embellished her fantasizes with making love to a wealthy rancher, but she couldn't imagine how it might be with Hank the shoulder tapper. She sometimes longed for that exhilarating feeling she had experienced in the back of the truck last summer.

Hank seemed wound up when he drove by for Glady one day. He smelled so good in a new leather jacket that he'd just bought. As they were driving away from Glady's folks house, Hank seemed unable to contain himself and words rolled out of his mouth faster than she'd ever heard him speak.

"I've taken a job as a hired farm hand making twice the money as driving the cab here," Hank told Glady. "It's with a farmer who goes way back with my folks. One of his hired men just up and quit. They really needed someone right now. A-and, his wife needs a helper now too. I told them I knew someone, so they are waiting to see if you're interested."

"I-I don't know. I don't know what to say," Glady said stammered. Hank saw her hesitation and became mildly defensive.

"W-We-Well, I thought you might be interested, I don't mean I spoke for you or anything. You'd make up your own mind and all that." Glady looked at Hank's face and thought he looked kind of pitiful.

"Mostly, I thought we could spend more time together," Hank sped on. "Would you like to get married?"

Glady was dumbfounded. What she had just heard? Her mind engaged and started whirling. What does he mean, marry? Get married? To him? Why, I don't even know him. Do I even like him? I certainly never expected anything like that to come out of his mouth! Is that why he seemed so anxious today? Did he plan this or did it just come out? I'd better say something quick!

Glady was finally able to respond.

"Well Hank, th-that, that's a big question to answer on such short notice."

"I know, I know. I was gonna wait for a good time later tonight to ask you. But I guess I got carried away. I don't mean to rush you. I'm sorry. You don't have to answer."

Glady felt sorry for his obvious awkwardness, but needed time to get her wits together.

"You just took me by surprise, is all. I was just wonderin' what that helper job is, then up pops this other question. I want to talk more about this, but let's go somewhere else."

Glady had borrowed some time, but her thoughts pounded in her head as Hank drove in embarrassed silence.

Her voice screamed in her head calling herself an idiot! Here's a guy that wants to marry me. What am I thinkin'? Don't discourage him; he's not so bad. He's kinda pitiful in the way he looks at me. He always seems to listen and care what I say. He's makin' sense and he's tryin' to help out. What in the world would mom say if she knew I was thinkin' twice about a marriage proposal? Here it is March and I'll be eighteen in May. I know mom meant what she said; she'll turn me out then for sure. Where will I go then if I don't say 'yes' now?

Hank drove into a park and pulled into a space. As he turned off the motor, he slowly turned his head to face Glady. He looked so rattled and ill at ease she felt sorry for him.

"Hank, first let's talk about the helper job. I don't know what kind of helper you mean. What does a helper do?"

"Well, it's just helpin' around the house with the chores. It's a big, big farm with, I think, seven hired men. There's probably a lot of cookin' and cleanin' up mostly, I reckon. You're probably already doin' the same things at home, except you would get paid for it.

"Look, I-I want to explain this to you. I found out about this job and when I went over to see about it, Ed told me his wife would need a helper too. The guy that quit was married and his wife was the helper. Then old Ed, ya know, he asked me, h-he asked when I was gettin' married. He said it worked out good when a husband and wife took on the jobs. I got to thinkin' about you, so I told him I might know someone. I think we get along pretty good, don't you?"

Glady softened when she looked at Hank's sincere face. He was talking in earnest as he described what it would be like out there on the farm. The more he talked, the more Glady realized that it didn't sound like such a bad life. It was true that she was slaving away for her mother who did nothing but gripe at her all day long. She only got a few cents from her dad once in awhile for all that house work.

What if she didn't accept the marriage proposal right now? The farmer might find somebody else. If Glady married Hank, she was part of the bargain for the helper job. If her mother found out she'd turned down a marriage proposal, she may throw her out sooner than later.

Glady convinced herself that it wouldn't be all that bad and consented to go out and meet the Morrses'. Hank drove on out from the park to their big farm. Hank introduced Glady and said they were probably gonna get married soon. Glady did not contradict him.

"I knew you must have some a gal you were sweet on Hank." Ed Morrse grinned when he was introduced to Glady. "A man your age is needin' to get a wife and she's a real pretty one too."

Edna was a great big woman and she huffed and puffed as she showed Glady though the big two story farmhouse. Edna explained that she had one daughter left at home, but that she was in high school and couldn't help much with the house anymore. She said when her two older daughters were still home she didn't need any extra help but both of them had gotten married and left home about the same time. As they went from room to room Edna told Glady what the helper responsibilities were in each room.

All the furniture was so nicely polished and well kept that Glady could hardly believe her eyes. There were two living rooms with stuffed chairs and couches, all with white crocheted doilies pinned to them. There was a piano shined to a glow with framed photographs standing on it. There were nice rugs on the floors and drapes at the windows. Glady had only seen lavish homes like this in the movies. She always thought farmers were mostly country hicks. She had never realized how huge and nice a farmhouse could be.

They entered the big country kitchen and Glady's lower jaw fell down to her chest. Just as quickly, she closed it and swallowed hard. She had never seen so much food before in her life. Loaf after loaf of wheat bread and rolls were cooling on racks, bowls catching the whey under cloth bags where cottage cheese was making, a huge basket of fresh brown and white eggs on the counter, gallons of milk and cream, crocks of butter in the cooler, and a butter churn over by the window. There were three different kinds of pie on the counter, each one with a piece missing and a big chocolate cake and cinnamon rolls. A pantry stacked with row after row of glass jars with every type of fruit and vegetable she could imagine, corn, string beans, peas, okra, apples, peaches and plums. There were bins full of potatoes and carrots. A smoke room was hanging with meat, two pigs and part of a cow.

All the time she was touring the kitchen and food storage areas Glady was thinking to herself,

"My God, I never even imagined such food. All that wonderful food around all the time, no wonder Edna is so big."

Edna continued talking as she moved through the house.

"Course, you'll be helping me most at mealtimes serving the men, and you and I'll eat in the kitchen. You'll have a room upstairs here in the house and when you and Hank are married you'll probably want to live over on the old Broward place in that little house."

Glady suddenly remembered that her own mother didn't even know she was getting married. Here this woman she had just met, was telling her where she'd be eating and living after she was married.

In early April, Hank picked Glady up from her parent's home and they went down to the county court house to be married. After they had come back to town from the Morrses' that day they had gone right over and told her folks the news. Opal Flowers beamed at Hank.

"Oh Hank, I thank you for takin' this daughter of ours off our hands." Hank had smiled proudly, thinking Opal was joking.

Glady's dad ignored Opal's comment and heartily shook Hank's hand. Carl told Hank that Glady was a fine daughter and would make a good wife.

Glady had used her first paycheck to buy her wedding dress. She took Opal along shopping.

"Now Gladys Ann, don't waste your money. Pick out something sensible that you can wear for good after you're married. Don't get something that won't be practical," Opal admonished her daughter when she saw Glady looking over a frilly ivory dress.

"You'd only be able to wear that a few times," Opal went on. "Now looky here at this dress, its pretty and practical. You could wear it for good, practically year around, if you were careful with it."

Glady looked at the black crepe dress. It was pretty with set-in cap sleeves and a nice round neckline. It was mostly black but with tiny purple, white and red flowers woven into the fabric. Glady wanted something more like what she thought a bride would wear but she gave in to Opal, deciding that her mother's idea made sense. She would be out on the farm and this dress would wear well and could be used for good.

"You look so pretty today Glady." Hank beamed at his chosen bride as they were driving to the courthouse. Glady showed him the dime store ring she'd picked out the day she bought the dress. It was a silver colored metal circle with twelve clear glass stones set in a row.

"Maybe someday we can get a real one," Hank said looking at the ring.

Unbidden, a thought came suddenly into Glady's head,

"I'll give it two years," she said to herself. "If I don't like him any better by then, I'll get a divorce!"

CHAPTER SIX

Glady had been married to Hank for over three years. They already had two children and Glady had missed her period this month. She was so upset that she could hardly think straight. For as long as she could remember having them, hers always came on or near the last day of the month.

Glady had worked as the helper to Edna Morsse the first year after marrying Hank. Over that year, she forgot about the years of hunger she had experienced before leaving home. She ate heartily at the beginning of her new job, and was truly full after every meal. She got pregnant in the fall and food didn't mean as much to her all the time. Glady stopped working for Edna in April on her first wedding anniversary when was seven months pregnant. In early July, she gave birth to their first child, a son.

By their third anniversary Hank had changed jobs twice. He was still a hired farm hand but he moved to farms where the paycheck was larger as his family grew. He was now working longer hours and had responsibilities at several different farms to earn his meager paycheck.

The young Wilkey family lived about a mile and a half down the hill from the large farm Hank worked. Their house was a small, white frame house that looked well kept on the outside, but it was drafty and needed work inside. There was a big red barn and pastureland on three sides.

Hank took care of the livestock in the pastures and barn where he lived, and then walked up the hill to work at the big farm all day. He walked home again in the evening where he milked cows and tended the livestock at the small house again.

Glady was required to make Hank large meals at breakfast and supper to meet his nutrition and energy requirements. She found out how much farmers eat when she worked with Edna. She was glad that Hank ate his noon meal up at the big house, because she really didn't like cooking.

Glady had never cooked much at home and Edna had done all the cooking that first year when Glady worked there. Glady was happy to follow after her, keeping the nice house clean and washing up the dishes, pots and pans in exchange for all that food and her paycheck.

She and Hank didn't have the money for nice things like Edna had, and Glady didn't feel any reward doing housework at home. She often didn't get the dishes washed and the kitchen clean until she needed to use them again. With two little ones, there wasn't time to get much of anything done except care for them and fix meals. She was almost certain she was pregnant again and she wasn't sure she could endure.

Glady felt so down and blue. She never had much morning sickness or felt bad physically; she just wondered how could she ever put up with two little kids and a new baby. She got so lonesome out here day in and day out.

Hank had never been much of a talker and he was dog-tired every night when he got home. They would have supper and he would go out to finish up the nightly chores while Glady tended to the kids bedtime needs. By the time Hank got back into the house it was his bedtime. Sometimes he took a little time out to play with the kids but farming was a dawn to dusk, seven-day-a-week job and there wasn't much time for anything but work.

Glady had come to realize over the course of the marriage that she had made a big mistake. She often wished she hadn't rushed into marriage with Hank. She told herself frequently that she should have waited, she probably would have found a job in town and possibly lived on her own for a while. She most likely would have met someone better with good working hours and time off. She might have found someone that liked to talk and go places, or at least lived in town where there were things to do.

Glady felt strange and isolated living here in the country, far away from even a little town. There were neighbors and several houses that you could see within a half mile of the house, but Glady never saw any women out in the yards that she could talk to. She figured that they would be old farmers wives anyway. Nothing went by on the road that wasn't a farm machine or a truck.

In town there were always people walking by and things going on. There was always some place to go, even when you didn't have any money. When she had the helper job Glady had Edna to talk to all the time. Edna's daughter was around quite a bit too, and Glady really enjoyed gabbing to someone young.

47

Glady just never knew a person could get as lonesome as she was these days.

She had long since admitted that this marriage wasn't going to get any better, but Glady didn't remember her wedding day promise to herself even as the wedding anniversaries came and went. She was, pregnant again and little Carol was only eight months old and George not yet three. She hadn't had time to think about leaving Hank with two little kids and here she was strapped again.

***

"Well if it isn't Glady Blue Eyes," Glady heard a voice say. She had seen the mail carrier coming and went across the road to wait to see if there was any mail today. She needed something to take her mind off her problems even for a few minutes, anything for a little human contact. She was flabbergasted as she turned to see Cap there in the mail car.

"Well, I'll be darned!" Glady exclaimed. "Cap! Are you the mail carrier?"

"I sure am! Are you the lady of the house?" He quipped.

There he was, Captain Ferris Wheel himself. Glady ecstatically stepped up to lean on the side of the car. She and Cap quickly caught up on each other's lives since the fair. Cap hadn't married and he was quite surprised to learn that Glady was married with two children already. Cap said he had just started the rural mail delivery route but he had been sorting mail at the post office in Rockwell for over a year.

After a few minutes of easy chatting, Glady remembered that she had left the kids in the house alone, so she hurried back on up to the house, musing over the bits of the nice conversation.

"Gee whiz," Glady thought, rushing back to the house. "He looks just like he did at the fair."

Glady remembered what an easy-going person Cap was and what fun she'd had that time at the carnival and fair. On most nice days she made it a practice be outside when Cap drove up with the mail. She always left the kids in the house where he wouldn't see them. She combed her hair and fixed herself up a little and took a short break from the dirty house and bawling kids.

During her brief conversations with Cap, Glady was able to talk some about the problems of her current situation. He would jauntily tease her and suggest that she leave it all behind and run away with him. Of course, Glady didn't take him seriously, but she wondered how life would be married to the rural mail carrier. He would have time off so they could go places, have fun and be carefree just like they were at the fair.

One day Glady was leaning at the car window and let it slip to Cap that she was pregnant again. The teasing stopped abruptly, and Cap made an excuse to quickly get away and hastily drove on. The next day he didn't stop at all and Glady knew good-and-well that he saw her hurrying out the driveway to meet him.

Glady wished she had bitten her tongue off instead of letting the cat out of the bag. Other times she knew she would be showing soon any way and he would have still run like a rabbit. To hell with him! She sorely missed escaping her private hell though, even if only for a few moments a day.

When George was three and Carol was fifteen months old, Glady delivered her third child in the hospital at Rockwell. Opal went out to the little farmhouse to take care of the two kids and cook Hank's meals while Glady stayed in the hospital.

Two weeks later, Glady was so glad to see those two little faces when she was brought home in the ambulance with her new baby boy. Opal had the house so organized and clean that it was practically glowing. Hank seemed pleased to see Glady and the baby that evening when he came in for the supper. He joked with his young son and tickled little Carol under the chin.

The whole family seemed content and Glady promised herself that she would keep the house clean and nice just like this. She hoped that three kids wouldn't be much worse than two. Everything went smoothly with Opal taking care of the older kids, the house and cooking and Glady just took care of the baby. A week later, Opal went home.

***

The housework and kids were really getting Glady down. She was trying to breast feed the new baby, but he cried all the time and seemed like he was starving. She went in for her six-week checkup and Dr. Tott said the baby was indeed starving. He said to begin bottle-feeding immediately with canned milk and recommended adding dark Karo syrup to prevent problems with constipation.

Dr. Tott carefully explained how Glady was to make sure the formula was prepared properly each time. He instructed her how to sterilize the bottles and nipples, how to heat the bottles and test for the right temperature. It seemed like a lot of extra work to Glady.

The other two kids had been easy, as she'd breast-fed them. Carol was only eight months old when Glady stopped breast-feeding her due to this pregnancy. After that the little thing sat up in her high chair at the table next to her brother. Glady fed her macaroni and tomato juice or left over mashed potatoes. Now at seventeen months, Glady called Carol a little roly-poly and thought she was cute as a bug's ear.

George was cute too, and growing up to be a big boy. Hank had never questioned Glady's choice of names for their first-born son. His grandfather's name had been George, so Hank and his father both were pleased that Glady had chosen that name, thinking she had picked it for that reason. He had been no extra trouble at all.

Glady sat listening to the doctor tell her about bottle feeding, all this extra work just to feed this third baby, Alfred. He was so scrawny and cried all the time.

Glady went home facing the extra work and faithfully sterilized the bottles for the baby. She didn't want to be responsible if he got sick. She could barely accomplish any thing else and began complaining of being tired all the time.

Hank was getting mostly biscuits and gravy for breakfast and supper and the house was a mess. Glady whined constantly about the condition of the paint and the cold drafts. She complained about being isolated and not knowing anyone to talk to. Hank seemed to tune out the whining and complaining and seemed to be just hanging on himself.

***

Another year went by and the young family struggled to make ends meet. Baby Alfred had gained weight and was thriving. He had white hair, dark blue eyes and was tall and thin like his dad. Glady was trying to keep up the house better, and was growing accustomed to managing her sanity with three little ones. She could hardly believe it when she missed her period again.

"My God!" she thought. "What will ever become of me? There is no way that I can do more! What in the hell am I going to do? What is Hank going to say?"

One night during the past month, Glady was going crazy for affection. She and Hank hadn't had sex for two months. She had literally taken matters into her own hands when they settled down for the night. She reached over to him and taken hold of his penis. It had become immediately hardened and they coupled quickly, both having an immediate and intense orgasm. They lightly joked and Glady had fallen asleep satisfied.

A week later, remembering the pleasant moment in time, Glady reached over and again took hold of Hank's penis.

"Are you asleep?" she had asked suggestively.

"Well I would be if you would let go of my peter and leave me alone!" Hank had retorted roughly, and twisted away from her. Glady reacted like she had been slapped in the face and felt suddenly whorish. She had fallen into a deeply troubled sleep.

Now, Glady had missed her period again. Glady wished to God that she'd left him alone that first night. Obviously she got pregnant way too easily. The more she thought about it though, she was certain it was Hank's fault after all. His damned come was probably so concentrated from never having sex that he could make any woman pregnant with just a drop of it.

This time her stomach grew big and fast. Glady knew that Hank guessed by now she was pregnant again, but he didn't mention it. He had been burying himself in work, rarely ever getting back in the house to even see the kids before they went to bed. The floor was piled with clothes; some clean, but mostly dirty. The kids smelled like pee most of the time and they slept in their dirty little shirts and underwear. The floors went unswept for days and were never mopped. The dishes sat in stacks all over the kitchen, caked with dry food, sometimes for days at a time.

Glady spent most of her time laying in bed yelling at the kids and over time sprinkled in more and more cuss words. Her belly grew large and she was tired but she had to get up and down frequently to make the kids mind her. She was getting handy at smacking little asses when the kids acted up. Damned little brats, always running through the house, always needing something. When Alfred was a year and eleven months old, Glady gave birth to twin boys.

The first week Glady was home from the hospital Opal seemed to be keeping up with everything. However when it looked like Glady was becoming more helpless and Opal was doing more for the twins as well, she gave up and went home. After that Glady spent her time in bed, only getting up when the twins needed something. But that alone was a night and day job.

She was awake with one or the other of them around the clock. Mixing the formula, changing diapers, feeding babies, napping a few winks and starting over with it all became Glady's life. The older kids virtually took care of themselves. They fixed bread and butter for breakfast and at noon and sometimes got cold leftovers from supper. Whatever they got Glady made sure they ate it outside away from the house. Hank made his own breakfast and cooked supper most of the time the first months after the twins were born.

One spring day Glady hadn't seen hide nor hair of her kids for a while. She went outside to see what in the hell they were up to, since it had been quiet too long. She heard little voices over in the old chicken house and went to investigate. She opened the door and there they were, all three of them caught red-handed, with an open box of kitchen matches. The odor in the air ensured Glady that they had been playing with lighted matches. Glady was both infuriated and frightened nearly to death in one huge ball of emotion.

"My God!" she screamed. "You all know better! What in the hell are you tryin' to do? Burn down the house or kill yourselves? You know momma couldn't take it if one of you kids got hurt bad or died. I would never get over it."

Glady grabbed the matches away from five-year-old George and smacked his little ass. She knew he was old enough to know better. She snatched his hand and forced a match into in his fingers and struck it while screeching about the dangers of children playing with matches.

Glady firmly held the squirming boy's hand and allowed the match to burn down until the flame neared his fingers. Feeling his fingers getting burned, George jerked his hand back and started to cry and the lighted match fell to the floor. Glady stamped it out and then forced Carol into the same situation while little Alfred looked on crying.

When Carol jerked her hand back and started to cry from the burned fingers, Glady soundly spanked each one of the three, and warned them what would happen if they ever played with matches again. She left them all crying in the yard and went back in the house and slammed the door thinking how bad the little assholes had scared her.

The blisters on George and Carol's fingers hurt for days so they knew better than to ever get caught playing with matches again. This incident was to reinforce a perplexing problem in their young minds created by a pattern in their mother's behavior. They noticed that Glady hurt them more than they had ever been hurt doing the things she told them not to do because they might get hurt.

***

As time went by Glady left her children alone and unsupervised more of the time but she progressively imposed more restrictions on them. She enforced rules about where they could and couldn't play in an ever-shrinking vicinity; citing her extreme fear that they would get run over by a car or otherwise hurt or killed. George and Carol were increasingly responsible for supervising the younger children and ensuring that they would not come to any harm.

Though their house was in the country, a little church was just down the road a ways. Except Sundays, the church was usually dark and quiet, but once in awhile, community meetings were held there. Cars came and went at these times and Glady warned the older kids to keep the younger ones away from the road. She also demanded they stay away from the barn and away from the side of the house facing the church when there were any cars down there. She also warned frequently what would happen in terms of severe punishment if she caught any of them doing anything they weren't supposed to be doing.

Carol was showing little Alfred a strange greenish worm and lifted the edge of a large flat rock that it had run under. The rock slipped from her hands and it fell, trapping her index finger nail bed between it and another rock. Carol and Alfred both knew their mother had a rule to not even go near the rock pile, and here Carol was lifting rocks and standing on them. She knew if she told her mother about the injury, she would get screamed at and slapped for playing on the rocks in the first place.

"Don't tell mom," Carol admonished Alfred. Carol was able to successfully hide the finger from her mother's view, though it pained her for several days and she eventually lost the blackened fingernail.

Alfred never told on Carol. Soon 'don't tell mom' became the secret phrase among the kids when they got hurt doing anything they considered even borderline for getting into trouble with Glady.

Later, when the kids were school age, Carol heard that if a person got hit on the back of the head in a certain way, their eyeball would pop out and hang there by the nerves and blood vessels, all gooey. Horrified, the kids discussed the situation as if it could happen at any moment.

Whatever would they do if they got hit in the head this certain way? They could never tell their mother since she would no doubt punish them severely for doing anything that would make their eyeball pop out. But how in the world could they get to the doctor to get their eye put back in, if they didn't tell her? It was an introduction to the dilemmas in life. They'd bring it up every once in awhile just to see if any one had come up with any good answers.

CHAPTER SEVEN

"Goddamned those little brats!" Glady exclaimed. She found the white paper she had wrapped the rest of the bologna in last night after supper. There was only one thin slice of the minced ham left in the wrapper.

"Little sonsabitches won't get any dinner now," she said. Glady had planned to feed the kids bologna and bread at noon, then make pork chops for supper when Hank came home to eat. She went out in the yard and called the kids.

"Now where in the hell did they get off to?" she muttered when there was no response.

The twins were now almost three and Glady could run them out of the house with the older kids. It was summer and George wasn't in school so she had him to help watch the little brats again. She went outside to see if she could find anyone but she saw some ladies coming out of the church. They were all dressed up like they had been at some kind of important meeting.

Glady wanted to get back in the house before any of the women noticed her, but then she caught sight of a little figure and almost fainted. Playing near the church driveway was one of the twins, naked a jaybird. Glady was in a terrible fix. She was barefooted and her dress was filthy dirty. She didn't have any underclothes on, and her unkempt hair was knotted and stringing down her back. She had no choice though; she had to get down there before her kid got run over by a churchwoman.

Glady dashed down the side of the house, across the corner of the churchyard and to the driveway. She snatched up the little boy and his discarded sun suit and quickly turned away.

"Little rascal got away from me," she chuckled over her shoulder and hurried back up toward her own home. The amazed church ladies raised their eyebrows and watched the dirty, slovenly, young woman's actions.

When Glady got back to the house, she yelled at the kids and called them all into the house. After she had chastised the older ones sternly for not keeping an eye on Dale, she confronted them with an empty bologna wrapper.

"Now I don't want any storyin'," Glady said in her firm-no-nonsense tone of voice. "I want to know which one of you kids took the baloney and ate it up from everybody else. Whoever it was won't get a whippin', they just have to eat bread and butter at noon for dinner."

None of the kids seemed to know anything about the bologna. As far as Glady could tell from looking at the innocent faces, no one seemed to be lying.

"Well, we all will just have to eat butter and bread for dinner then," Glady said, secretly happy that there had been one piece of meat left for her sandwich. "Now get on back out of here 'til I call you in, and watch those twins, goddamn it! One of em is gonna get hurt!" The kids hurried back to play leaving their mother alone and puzzled.

A few days later the scene repeated itself.

"Goddamned little sonsabitches!" Glady stormed. "Somebody's got to be lyin' to me."

"What in the hell is goin' on?" she asked after she'd called the kids into the house again. "Which one of you kids is lyin' to me? Who's sneakin' food and eatin' it up from the others? Now, I won't stand for lyin' or stealin'. I don't care if you are hungry, I won't have any goddamned kid of mine stealin'! I won't stand for it!"

When no one confessed and again Glady could detect no lies, she screamed,

"Get the hell out of my sight you lyin' little assholes, you're all in on it." The kids hurried back into the yard to escape their mother's sharp wicked tongue.

That weekend, when Hank got up in the early morning to go milk, he heard a thumping noise. He thought one of the kids must be up, but when he paused he didn't hear anything more. He came in the kitchen just in time to see a huge rat running across the floor with a walnut in his mouth. He flung his shoe, but missed the rat. He went on out to milk and then came back into the house after the kids were outside.

"Did you ever see that pack rat we have in the house?" he asked Glady.

"What in the hell are you talkin' about?" Glady asked. Hank relayed his story from earlier and began searching along the mopboards for evidence of rat holes.

Sure enough, Hank found a chewed hole tucked away in a corner on the far side of the table. He got a hammer and pulled some boards loose. As the plaster dust settled, there between the studs was the pack rat's lair. In the heap was the missing bologna, several pieces of bread, nuts and other scraps. Glady was amazed as she looked at the mess. She had never seen a pack rat lair before.

Hank cleaned out the pile of rubbish and cut up and flattened a coffee can. He nailed the tin can over the holes to block the rat's path. Glady never told the kids about the pack rat, never told Hank about the accusations, and felt justified. After all, she hadn't whipped any of the kids for stealing.

***

"Git in there and stay quiet! Keep those little kids quiet too." Glady admonished. The older kids were frightened and didn't speak. They didn't know why their mother had interrupted their play in the front room. She was crowding them into the entryway at the unused front door and locking them into the tiny space.

The house was drafty and the woodstove could not keep up with the whole house in winter. The living room was closed off during the coldest part of year and the furniture moved out and grouped around the stove where it was warmer. It was almost Christmas and the weather was so nasty and windy that Glady kept the kids inside the house. When they got too rowdy and on her nerves so bad she could scream, she made them put on their coats and play in the closed off living room.

Glady had spied Mrs. Mumford's car turning into the driveway. Glady had been watchful of goings on at the church ever since the incidents down there last summer. Old lady Mumford had been one set of the raised eyebrows the day that Dale was naked in the churchyard and Glady had run down to get him.

Damned if that ornery little Dale had done it again in the fall, only on a Sunday. He had taken off his clothes up near the church again. He was strutting around crowing, with two chicken feathers stuck in his little butt crack. Glady had screamed when she looked out and saw him naked again.

The second time she had yelled at George to hurry down and get him. Ever since then the old Mumford hag would drive by slowly and gawk at the kids playing out in the yard. Glady knew the kids weren't always clean, but she was doing the best she could with five little kids. Glady had once heard about a woman who'd had her kids taken away from her. She was suspicious that the nosy Mumford bitch was out to take her kids away from her.

Now Glady dreaded seeing the Mumford car pulling in the driveway. She quickly pulled her tangled hair up away from her face. She secured it with a bobby pin and put on a headscarf. She pulled her coat on over her dirty dress and shoved her filth-caked feet into her shoes.

"Hello there!" old lady Mumford called cheerily, as Glady approached the car. "I was just wondering how many children you have and how old they all are."

Glady was livid. She knew for sure now that the old bitch was after her kids and was finding homes for them.

"I have five children, but they are all stayin' with their grandmother in Rockwell," Glady replied curtly, turning abruptly away from the car. Mrs. Mumford seemed taken aback at the response from Glady.

"Well, some of the church ladies were just wondering. I'll let you get back to your housework," the Mumford woman said and backed out of the driveway.

Glady watched the car back out and then stayed at the window watching the road to make sure Mrs. Mumford wasn't tricking her. When she was sure the old battleaxe was gone, Glady came into the living room to let the kids out of the locked entry way.

"Why were we in there Mama?" asked Carol in a hushed voice, glancing at her mother's face. "Why were you afraid Mama?"

"Old lady Mumford is trying to take you kids away from me!" Glady told her frightened child. The dirty, snot-nosed children crowded around their mother and she gathered them all into her arms asking, "What will you do if they come to take you away? Will you run and hide so they can't find you?"

"Yes, Yes," the children chorused, confused by their mothers strange request. Then they went back to playing in the cardboard box in the cold living room.

By that weekend the weather had turned out sunny and the wind wasn't bad, so Glady sent the kids outside to play.

"You've been indoors so long, get out there and get some of the farts blown out of your hair," Glady told the kids. They giggled and gladly bundled up to go out. Glady had about five minutes peace when a car pulled in again.

"Shit!" she thought, "I hope those damned kids aren't in plain sight. I wish Hank was back up here from the pasture." Glady waited to see who it was before dashing out. After just a few seconds she saw the car back out again.

When the car was down the road and out of sight, Glady opened the back door and peeked out. She could see all the kids playing over by the chicken house. When she was sure no strangers had gotten out of the car, she opened the door and went out onto the porch. She was suddenly infuriated when she spied the covered bushel basket sitting on the step.

"Those goddamned nosy old bitches!" she yelled.

The kids watched their mother snatch up a basket and take it onto the porch. They went to investigate and by the time they got there Glady had removed the clean baby blanket covering a bushel basket. She was looking at the contents and cussing.

Little Alfred spied a toy on top of the basket and grabbed it up. It was a rubber Elsie the Borden Cow and he began to squeak it with a delighted look on his tiny face. Glady snatched the toy away from him and smacked his little hands.

"We don't take any goddamned charity!" she yelled at the little towhead. "Get yer mitts out of that basket! And stay out of it, you grabbin' little bastard."

When Hank came back up the house, Glady shrieked at him about the charity basket. Further, she insisted that he go see Mr. Mumford and get him to tell his old bitch wife to send someone back to pick it up off her porch.

Glady repacked the contents of the basket exactly the way she'd found it and watched out the window Monday morning. As soon as she saw a car pull in she rushed the basket outside and put it on the step then ran back inside. The churchwoman got out of her car, hurriedly picked up the basket off the step and turned toward her car.

"Don't you ever expect me to take a handout from anybody!" Glady proudly yelled through the closed door that hid the pitiful housekeeping and filthy young mother.

The weather was bad and the kids were playing in the closed-off front room in their coats again. Glady tried to clean a little bit after Hank left for work, but she was felt too tired and cold. She laid on her bed reading a book and had no choice but to listen to those brats shriek and scream all day long. At noon Glady handed in some bread and butter and warned the kids not to come out 'til supper as she slammed the door again.

When George came home from school she sent him in to play with the younger kids. Glady told him to keep them quieter until their dad got home. It was nearing suppertime and about time for Hank to come in. Glady knew she'd better get up, change diapers, and find something to cook. She opened the door to let the kids come back into the main part of the house.

"You goddamned little sonsabitches!" Glady screamed, looking in at the mess that had been made all over the floor. "What in the hell have you done?" She grabbed Carol by the hair and smacked her face, then grabbed Alfred by the arm and smacked him on the butt.

Scattered all over the floor were the keepsakes that she kept in a trunk in the front room. The trunk was actually an old long painted wooden box with wheels. The kids had emptied it out and were using it for a cart. They had been taking turns pushing each other around the room all afternoon and there were deep grooves in the wooden floor. Among the keepsakes was a dress that had been reduced to rags.

Alfred was closest so Glady smacked him again and then grabbed Carol's hair. Glady knew George had only been in there a short while, so she only screamed at him.

"Why didn't you come out and tell me what these little bastards were up to when you went in there?"

Glady's rage lasted a few minutes and then she sunk down on the floor holding up the shredded dress.

"Do you kids know what you have done?" she wept, gathering up the black shreds with the little purple, red and white flowers woven in, and held them close. "This is the dress mama got married in. Now you've ruined it so bad it can't be fixed."

The children rubbed the stinging places where their mother had slapped them and gathered around shamefaced at ruining their mother's dress and making her cry.

***

"Who peeked at the presents?" Glady shrilly exclaimed.

"Get the hell in here right now!" she screamed into the cold living room. George was home with a runny nose. He had been happily playing with the other kids, just glad to be home with them on a school day. George, Carol and Alfred came in to their mother who was standing in front of the closet door in her bedroom. She was holding some sacks that were gaping open and the contents peeking out.

"Which ones of you sonsabitches had the guts to look at your presents?" Glady asked in a rage. George and Carol looked ashamed and then confessed in weak voices that they had peeked when she was fixing supper yesterday evening. Glady couldn't believe it.

"I can't believe that you would peek at your presents and ruin my Christmas surprise!" she said as she grabbed Carol with one hand and George with the other. Then she let go of Carol and said,

"You stand right there and don't move young lady!"

She slapped George on the back a few times and then spanked his rear. Carol cried as she waited for her turn, but she knew better than to move. When George was bawling, Glady grabbed Carol's hair and meted out a few slaps to her face, then spanked her butt good. When the two older kids were both crying she turned to Alfred who was beginning to cry also.

"What the hell are you crying for? Do you want some too?" When Alfred didn't stop crying, she slapped his face and then slapped it again when he cried louder.

"You can just have these damned presents right now. There will be no Christmas at our house this year." Glady yelled as she threw the sacks at her kids. Carol and George both stepped around the sacks and went crying to their mother.

"We're sorry Mama," they cried. "We will never peek again. Will you please, please put these away 'til Christmas?"

"Oh, stop your bawlin' and snifflin', you brought this on yourselves. I'll do it this time," Glady relented in her haughty-righteous tone of voice. "But if you ever, *ever* peek at any presents again, we will never have another Christmas. Since you were bad this year, Santy Clause will not stop here. This is all the presents you'll get. If you ever do this again he will never come again."

The kids all tried to quit sniffling and went back to the cold front room, feeling grateful that their mother had relented and they would have Christmas.

"Little sonsabitches!" Glady lamented. "Ruining Christmas! They know damned good and well they're not supposed to even be in the closet, let alone peekin' at presents. I shopped 'til my legs were achin' so bad I coulda cried! The cheatin' little bastards! Now they know what they're gettin'. Takin' away the surprise! My whole goddamned Christmas is ruined!"

***

Glady was so proud. Little Carol had been invited over to a special visiting day in George's first grade classroom. During the singing period, Carol had impressed the teacher with her clear strong voice. The teacher had praised Carol and later asked Glady if Carol could sing a song at the PTA program coming up in mid-February. Glady was thrilled and readily accepted. She convinced herself that Carol's voice was far better than average as she sang little songs around the house.

Glady planned for the event and sewed a little red skirt and matching weskit for Carol. She made a white satin blouse with a big collar and long full sleeves. She pulled out the majorette boots that Carol had gotten for Christmas and polished them up 'til they shone. Carol would be singing Zip-a-dee-do-da without musical accompaniment so Glady coached her, having her sing the song over and over.

The evening of the program came and Hank helped Glady clean up and dress the kids as soon as he got done milking. He admired Glady's handiwork as Carol modeled the new red outfit for him. Just as they were getting ready to rush out the door for the presentation, Carol grabbed for a glass of water to wet her throat as she held her coat over her arm. She slopped a big splash of water on the sleeve of the new satin blouse and her dad saw her. Glady looked in the kitchen and saw Hank's expression.

"What's the matter?" she panicked.

"Carol slopped some water." Hank said.

"Did you get any on your outfit Carol?" Glady yelled.

"No!" Carol lied.

It was freezing out and Hank was concerned about her going out with a wet sleeve. He admonished his daughter sternly,

"Carol, I saw what happened. You got your shirt wet." Hank went on out the door to take the twins to the car.

Glady came rushing out into the kitchen and looked at the growing wet water stain on Carol's sleeve.

"What the hell do you mean 'no'? Look at your sleeve. You can't go like that."

Glady grabbed Carol by the shoulder and slapped her hard on the face and reached out to remove the weskit. She slapped her again after the blouse was off.

"That's for lyin' to me!" she said. Carol felt the tears welling up and spilling out onto her stinging cheek. Glady plugged the iron back in and carefully pressed the sleeve dry.

"Quit your bawlin'! Look at your ole' red eyes. How's it gonna look to people watchin' you up there on the stage singin'. All bawlin' and red-eyed. Now hurry up and git this blouse back on and let's go or we'll be late." Carol followed her mother out to the car, trying to dry her eyes but not rub them too hard and make the redness worse.

When her name was announced Carol climbed the steps and walked out onto the stage, Glady's heart swelled with maternal pride as she saw little Carol in that darling red outfit, up there on the stage. Carol paused and began to sing the song she had practiced so many times. A few lines into the song, Carol paused and frowned. She had obviously forgotten the next line. Mrs. Mumford, as past president of the PTA was seated in the front row.

Trying to be helpful, Mrs. Mumford half rose from her seat and leaned forward, up toward the little singer. She spoke through cupped hands and whispered loudly toward the stage,

"Plenty of sunshine."

Suddenly Carol remembered her place in the song and her young voice picked up the words and went forward from the end of Mrs. Mumford's help line,

"Headin' my way. Zip-a-dee-do-da, zip-a-dee-a," she belted out, and then finished the song. Carol received cheers and resounding applause from the audience as she left the stage. Glady was so proud of her four year old daughter, showing up nosy old lady Mumford that way and stealing the show.

"That's my girl! Now we have to plan what you'll sing and wear next year." Glady confided to Carol when she sat back down.

***

George and Carol learned at a young age how to read Glady's rage and wait for her temper to abate. They knew that Glady was only truly vicious when she was extremely angry and that she never stayed mad very long. Once they had this figured out, they steered clear of their angry mother and were able to avoid many entanglements. However, Alfred suffered the wrath of his mother frequently. He was the third child and Glady always secretly thought that he had come along and spoiled the perfect family.

They'd had a son first and were proud because they were sure that a big brother was needed to protect a little sister. Like it was destiny, sure enough two years later Glady gave birth to a little girl. The young couple had felt like they were proceeding along the path they had chosen, and happily picked the name Carol Ann. They agreed that their family was perfect and complete.

Glady didn't have a period after Carol was born and she hadn't even considered that she might conceive again. She always heard that you couldn't get pregnant while you were breast-feeding. When Glady knew for sure she was pregnant for the third time and knew her perfect family would be ruined; she had been devastated.

Later when she was in labor with Alfred, Glady felt like it was the hardest labor of all. The baby's head was what she blamed and said it hurt her worse than the other two labors put together. Alfred was born a 'blue baby' and they had to dip him in cold water and then hot water and he still wouldn't cry. Glady was scared to death while she waited; she just knew that there was something terrible the matter with him. Just when she was about to panic, the newborn let out a wail and started bawling his head off.

"Praise the Lord!" Glady cried and the nurses cheered. Hank had picked out the name Alfred and Glady tried to make the best of it. The biggest problem with Alfred, though she would never admit it, was that he looked just like Hank. He turned out to be such a bawl baby and he wouldn't even breast feed right.

Glady was proud of George because he did every thing easily and right on time. Then Carol did things even a little earlier than George had. George and Carol were both easy to break to the potty chair. Carol was only thirteen months old when she would come to Glady for help her with her panties. When poor Alfred was still pooping his pants at three years old, Glady was irritated and frustrated with him.

"What will I ever do with him? How can I break him?" she wondered.

Little Alfred was very proud of a Rosie O'Grady doll that he had gotten for Christmas one year. Glady told Alfred that he was Rosie's daddy. He carried that doll around everywhere, never forgetting to take her with him when he found another place to play. Alfred would be playing, taking such good care of his dolly, that he would forget and poop his pants again.

Glady would discover the accident and snatch Alfred up by his arm screaming at him as she smacked his little legs until they were red as a beet.

"What will Rosie think of her daddy, shittin' his pants like this!" she would scream. If Glady got any poop on her hands while slapping Alfred's legs, he would really catch it.

There was another thing that Alfred did that her two older ones did not do. He liked to play with himself. Glady hated it and was horrified the first time she caught him sitting on the floor with his little pecker all stiff, and him playing with it. She slapped him and made him go outside threatening him what would happen if she caught him playing with himself again.

After she'd slapped him so hard the first time, Alfred would sneak off and hide. Glady would catch him off in a corner somewhere, deep in concentration with his own personal toy. One time she caught him winding and trying to tie a shoestring around it and she hit the ceiling. Absolutely enraged, she screamed and began slapping his face and back over and over as he cried and tried to pull away from her, infuriating her more.

"You little son-of-a-bitch! I am not goin' to have a kid of mine actin' like that! If I ever catch you playin' with that goddamned thing again I'm gonna get a butcher knife and cut the damned thing off. I ain't kiddin', just you wait and see!"

The family had lived in the same house for three years and one day a car pulled in the driveway, and up beside the house. Glady could see it was a young woman about her own age with little kids in the car. She quickly ran a brush through her bangs, threw a scarf over the rest of her hair and hurried out the door to see who it was.

"Hi, I'm Neva," a friendly young face said from the car. "I know your husband works up close to where mine does and I've seen your kids out in the yard. I have the car for the day and I stopped by to see if you guys wanted to go into Rockwell to the grocery store."

Glady was extremely happy for any diversion and told the woman to stay in her car, that she would hurry and be right back out. George was in second grade and she and Carol quickly bundled up the twins.

"Hurry up Carol, I don't want Neva to come up to the door and see this filthy house!" Glady breathlessly told her

66

daughter as she changed her own dress and put on her coat. "What in the hell would she think, us livin' this way?"

Glady quickly shoved Alfred's arm into his coat, scrambled back out the door and into Neva's car. The women sat in the front, Glady held Neva's baby while all the kids piled in the back, and away they went.

It was a nice sunny day with not much wind and Glady giddily chatted all the way to town with the young woman. The young mothers took the baby and went into the grocery store while Carol stayed in the car with the kids. Then they ran a couple of smaller errands, taking turns staying in the car. On the way back, Neva's oldest child sat between the two women who were still talking freely.

Neva glanced happily over her son's head at Glady to comment on something Glady had just said. When Neva looked back out the windshield, she panicked as she saw she was heading for the ditch. She yanked the steering wheel back too far over-corrected and spun out of control. The round topped car rolled into the ditch and continued to roll two and a half more times, ending up on its top in a pasture.

It all happened so frightfully quick. Little bodies flying and jumbled everywhere, screaming, crying and the two mothers in terror. Neva was able to shove her door open enough to crawl out and pull her child out of the front seat. Glady handed the baby out to Neva and crawled toward the driver's side door.

As Glady pulled herself out and noticed with horror that gasoline was streaming out of the open gas tank. She looked at the backside window and panicked at the little faces of her own children in the back window. Glady didn't wait for the kids to come out the way she had. She stood on shaky legs and kicked at the backside window, screaming for them to cover their faces from the flying glass. She yanked each child out through the broken glass and shoved them toward the middle of the field.

"Are you hurt? Are you all right? Answer me!" she screamed at each one, as she pulled them out of the wrecked car.

One of the twins looked mute and frightened, but the other one seemed alarmingly unresponsive. To Glady's overwhelming relief, he responded to a hard shaking and crawled off toward his brother.

A man drove by on the highway and jumped out to offer help. He gave a cursory look and told the young women that every one seemed okay. Carol complained of pain in the middle of her chest and one of the twins, still seemed sluggish to Glady.

"Get us to Rockwell to the doctor!" Glady yelled dramatically at the man. He dutifully drove them the short distance back to Rockwell and Glady directed him to wait. The doctors determined there were no serious injuries and treated the minor scrapes. The man dropped Neva and her kids off where her husband worked and Glady insisted on being transported to her to her own driveway.

"My God, my God!" Glady said over and over and did not properly thank the man. When she and the kids got in the house the shock began to wear off. Glady hugged all the kids to her and held them there.

"I don't know what Mama would do if any thing ever happened to any of you kids. I just couldn't take it. I just could not take it"

CHAPTER EIGHT

Glady was always constipated as an adult. Her poor bowels were so sluggish and she continually worked on finding a good solution. She blamed giving birth to so many kids as the cause but she ignored the real reasons such as a lack of physical activity and a diet poor in fiber.

Glady took Carter's Little Liver Pills once in awhile and pronounced to the kids that she had 'shit like a goose'. She had been warned to not to use pills regularly though, because she could get dependent on them. Glady discovered over time that whenever purple plums were in season she had the same result as with Carter's pills, so she gorged on the fruit when she could get it.

Most of the time though, she went through torture every few days passing her usual dry, hard, bloody stools. It seemed like it was when her bowels were the most bound up that she had the most trouble with her damned kids and all their fighting and foolishness.

"Goddamn those kids to hell!" Glady thought from her perch. The kids were outside the door fighting with each other right now and here she was sitting on a damned bucket trying to move her bowels.

There was no indoor plumbing in the house and Glady claimed she just couldn't make that constipated mass come out of her on the outdoor toilet seat. Besides a person could freeze out there waiting for bowels like hers.

Determined to avoid the outhouse Glady devised a primitive means inside the house. She put a heavy board across a sturdy bucket and then put newspapers all around. She sat on the board just so, with her rump hanging just over the back rim of the bucket. If she had to pee while she was waiting, it would go into the bucket. When the stool finally came out, it plopped onto the newspapers behind the bucket. All she had to do then was roll up the newspapers and drop it all in the outdoor toilet hole.

Glady didn't know what people would think if they knew about her way of crapping but it had taken a long time to work out this system. 'So, to hell with them' she would tell herself. By God she had no choice; she had to do it this way!

Glady was in pain. She had waited too many days and she was really bound up. She knew she couldn't put it off any longer so she had to bear it and suffer the consequences and hemorrhoids later. It was too late to buy Carter's and she didn't have any money anyway. Glady hated living out here in the country. Why couldn't they be closer to town when she needed something?

Glady muttered again.

"I wish to hell those brats would go fight somewhere further away from the house."

Suddenly the kitchen door was flung open and one of the twins came bawling in, trying to find her to tell on his older brother.

"Get the hell out of here!" Glady shrieked. "You little bastards don't know what its like to not be able to shit when you need to." Kayle quickly closed the door and forgot his immediate gripe.

Glady had seemingly inherited a tendency for constipation from her mother. Opal used to tell her,

"I just hope you suffer like this some day, then you'll see what I'm going through."

Sometimes Glady wondered if it was her mother's curse that made her this way. She thought her mother was wrong to feel this way and was determined that she would never wish this agony onto her own kids. She just wished she didn't have to suffer either.

Other times Glady knew it was from having delivered so many brats. On top of that, the little bastards wouldn't even try to understand what she had to go through for them. Glady strained and her piles grew and bled, finally she passed a huge stool and a second one tumbled out right after.

"What a relief!" Glady said, almost crying for joy. "My God, look at the size of those things, they're as big as grapefruits, as huge as a man's fist, or a soft ball! I don't believe I could ever suffer through anything like that again."

As she heard the bickering continuing in the yard, Glady thought,

"Maybe I can show those thankless brats what their mother goes through because of them. Maybe next time they'll have some idea of my pain and at least stay outside and keep their damned mouths shut."

Glady cleaned herself up and went to the door. In her low-calm-serene tone of voice she called,

"Carol, you and the boys come in here."

As Carol and the little boys warily approached the house, Glady continued,

"You know how Mama suffers with her bowels. I just wanted you to see what I'm going through. Come here. Come on in the kitchen. Look."

She led the kids into the kitchen and around behind an old ice box,

"Look there over there. No, not in the bucket, behind the bucket."

Carol and the boys cautiously peeked over behind the bucket. What they saw there was to remain clear in their minds for the rest of their lives. Newspapers were spread out behind the bucket and lying on the newspapers was the most awful thing they had ever seen.

Two huge, turds, lying side-by-side, all blood-streaked, smelly and brown, big and round, lying behind the bucket with the board on it. Carol looked horrified and seemed to want to turn and run. It was just too awful, so she just stared without saying a word as if those turds might hear her and rise up. The boys seemed to be in total awe, also stood looking at the soiled newspapers and without uttering a word.

"See what Mama goes through just to shit?" Glady inquired, satisfied that the kids all seemed spellbound with horror. "I try to tell you how I suffer! Now you see what I mean. Remember this next time."

As the kids continued to stare, Glady went on.

"My mama used to tell me she hoped that I would suffer like she did. But I hope you kids never suffer have to suffer the way I do with constipation and piles."

In spite of the words, there seemed to be wickedness in Glady's voice. It some how belied what she was saying, and revealed a secret wish: That they would all die in pain, in the prime of their lives, passing awful turds just like these.

CHAPTER NINE

"Now hold still" Aunt Wilma called as she steadied the camera and snapped a picture of the stoic little ragamuffins, George, Carol and Alfred. Wilma was Hank's oldest sister and she lived way out in California. Every couple of years or so, Wilma and her husband would drive back to her home state to see everyone. She always brought small trinkets and gifts from California.

Carol and George had no concept of travel since they had never been further than Rockwell in their young lives. They could barely remember who Wilma was from one visit to the next. They knew that California was far away and if you lived out there, you didn't get to see your folks very often. Each time they saw Aunt Wilma, they wondered why anyone would ever want to live far away.

Glady would say to the older kids from the time when they were young and just starting school,

"Let's go get a new daddy and move far away from here. Let's get a daddy who will talk to us and buy us things and take us places."

The kids would remember Aunt Wilma and not like the idea of moving far away. Even though they were perplexed, they would grin at their mother and each other self-consciously and chorus,

"No, no, we don't want a new daddy. We love daddy." After a few rounds of this Glady would leave it alone for a while and then bring it up another day.

Glady secretly hoped that the kids would turn on their dad someday and say 'yes'. These days she often thought about leaving Hank and his damned farm life. She hated it, and she thought of Hank simply as 'the old son-of-a-bitch'. She regularly called him that to herself, and worse, she screamed it right in his damned red-sunburned farmer face.

With each passing hour, Glady hated the house they lived in. She hated the neighborhood and remained suspicious of nosy Mrs. Mumford and her motives regarding the kids. Glady sure would never let anyone come in to the house. It was a pigpen. Hank spent less and less time there, always finding work to do on the farm.

They did have a car now, and Glady could drive a little better. But with so many kids to get ready, she could never really go anywhere. She was also afraid of having a wreck like Neva had that day. Glady did drive slowly over to the country store that had opened recently. It was only three miles away but she could only go if Hank was working nearby.

One summer day Glady was driving to the store, overjoyed to be out of the house by herself when a woman came out to the road and flagged her down. She introduced herself and asked Glady if she happened to be going to the store. When Glady replied that she was, the woman asked if her daughter Miriam could catch a ride because they needed a few things. Glady was delighted for Miriam's company.

After that time, Glady would automatically stop by to ask Miriam if she needed a ride to the store. Glady couldn't stay gone long but she welcomed the few chats with Miriam while they drove slowly over to the country store.

One real hot day, Glady was in the mood for some fun. She boldly asked Miriam if she would like to go over to the lake the next day. Miriam was ecstatic and quickly agreed. The two made plans and Glady didn't mention it to Hank. She knew he would be working the fields at the big house the next day.

"To hell with him!" Glady muttered. "The old son-of-a-bitch is never around anyway."

The next day Glady swore the kids to secrecy about going out. She cleaned up and packed the excited kids and a picnic lunch into the car. They stopped by Miriam's house and honked. Miriam and two of her chums came out, and off they all went to the lake. When they arrived at the lake it was so hot the teenage kids jumped in almost immediately. Glady was adamant that her children not go near the water though.

"Just what I need," she said to herself. "Get 'way out here and have one of em drown. I couldn't take it! And Hank would find out I had driven 'way out here myself without tellin' him I was goin'!"

Miriam looked at the little kids on the bank watching her friends have fun cooling off. She finally convinced Glady that she would help watch the kids. Glady relented and let the kids wade after making Miriam walk around a small shallow area to show her there were no drop off areas. She sternly warned her own children to not leave that area. She said they would not only be spanked in front of the company, they would catch worse when they got home.

"Mama is deathly afraid of water," Glady preached. "I don't want you to go into water deeper than your knees because I can't swim. If you started to drown, I wouldn't be able to help you, and then what would I do? Mama just couldn't stand it if any thing ever happened to any of you kids."

The kids waded for a while and Glady called them out to eat. She absolutely forbid any of them to go near the water after eating. After the sandwiches were eaten and they were loading the car, Glady surprised everyone by handing out a new kind of orange bubble gum she had found at the store. She reveled in the surprised looks and thanks she got from the teenagers.

They got back home and Miriam and her friends told Glady they would just walk home from there. Before they left they got involved playing a game of tag and chasing the little kids. George was running from Miriam and he jumped over a low dip in the fence. He landed on a broken pop bottle, which gouged into his heel causing him to nearly inhale the orange bubble gum.

Glady saw all the blood and was scared to death. She got the gum out of George's mouth and then put pressure over the cut using his tee shirt. The cut wasn't very deep and she sent the remorseful teenagers on home. She made George hop on one foot into the house and soaked the cut in Lysol and water. After twenty minutes she found a clean rag to tie around it.

Hank came home that evening and Glady wouldn't let up. She yelled at him over George cutting himself. She screamed that she was deathly afraid that something would happen to one of the kids away off out here in the country, with no doctor for miles. She yelled at him some more when the peeling green paint on the ceiling fell into the macaroni she was cooking and that they would all surely be poisoned. Then she went on to complain that the house was freezing in all but a few months of the year.

The kids ate their supper in silence, warily checking the macaroni for green paint flecks, and willingly hurried to bed as soon as they were told.

***

The Wilkeys' had been living in the drafty damned house for four years and Glady was increasingly sick of it. Hank was sick of Glady complaining about the house morning and night and he was worn out from working the big farm with no foreseeable pay raise. He asked around to see what else he could find; Glady had railed at him long enough.

Hank soon found another job, and even though it was another hired farm hand job, the house that went with it was a vast improvement. It was generally in good condition and at the end of a half-mile long driveway through alfalfa fields lined with Catalpa trees. Best of all for Glady, it was less than five miles out of Rockwell and there was a telephone! Best for Hank was that he would mostly only have chores and be farming the land the house sat on. He would need to go to other locations only occasionally for times like harvest and branding.

Some of the rooms in the house needed work and the people moving out of the house needed to leave some furniture for a week or so. Glady, Hank and the five kids lived in half the house until the other rooms were vacated and finished. It was tight initially but they gradually took over the whole house and after the phone was working Glady was satisfied that it had been a good move.

Hank still had daily chores, getting up and milking, taking care of cattle, pigs and horses, sharing the plowing, planting and harvesting of the alfalfa, hay and wheat. However it was less work that he had been doing and he was around more.

The day they moved, Carol was just getting over the hard measles. Glady made sure that Carol had her sunglasses on before Hank carried her out of one darkened room at the old house, placed her in the car and then moved her into a darkened room at the new house.

Glady was pregnant for the fifth time but she didn't think it was twins again. About three months after they settled in, Glady gave birth to her fifth son and they named him Henry. The neighbors thought Hank's given name was Henry, and they thought it was nice to finally have a junior in the family.

Glady was so irritated when the other hired man's wife, who she barely knew and didn't like at all, came up to the door and wanted to see the new baby.

Glady didn't want to let the woman into her dirty house, but she told the woman it was such a nice day she would bring the baby to the porch. The nice woman was beaming at the baby as she handed Glady a little blue wrapped gift, saying in a glowing voice,

"Oh what a darling baby boy! Little Hank Junior."

"He isn't a junior," Glady snidely retorted to her surprised neighbor.

The neighbor woman scurried away when she realized she wasn't going to be invited to hold the baby or get in off the front porch. Glady remained peevish all day that the woman would even suggest such a thing. She hated it when boys were called 'junior' and she was having none of that for her boys.

***

There were no roads close by the house now. Glady could freely let the twins play outside with the other kids without any concern about them getting run over. Even little Henry played out in the fenced part of the yard before and after his nap. Glady liked the house and liked living here. She didn't know anyone with a telephone except her mom and sister but that helped ease her frustration whenever she wanted to talk. Glady could drive pretty well by now. It wasn't far to town and she liked to go when Hank was nearby to watch the kids. Glady's older sister had been living back in Rockwell for a while and Glady could go visit her when she didn't have money to spend.

Having Hank nearby seemed to make a difference in her motivation to keep house because he was in for three meals. This took more organization especially with cooking and dishes so Glady tried to stay on top of the housework. She would let it get piled up and dirty but then clean it all up. She didn't like cooking on the woodstove any better though. The goddamned things were always too hot, or not hot enough and you had to cook in heavy iron skillets and pans or the food would burn up.

Cooking supper one evening a few days after Carol had started first grade, Glady needed to check the biscuits in the oven and she had already started the gravy.

"Come here Carol," she said. "Stir this gravy while I check the biscuits."

Carol took up the spatula and moved it back and forth through the thin mixture. The biscuits were done and Glady carried them into the dining room table, leaving Carol with the gravy. While she was out of the room, Carol looked at the liquid mass, which had suddenly come alive. It started bubbling and splashing out over the side of the heavy iron skillet. Carol scraped the spatula along the bottom and was horrified to see the gravy rise up out of the pan and began to roll out of the skillet and run all over the stove. It made loud hissing noises as it ran steaming down under the hole covers of the stove and into the flames.

Glady rushed back into the kitchen screaming,

"What in the hell are you doing?" She slapped at Carol and shoved her out of the way. "Don't you have the sense to move the pan off the fire when it starts to boil over?" Glady grabbed the heavy skillet and slid it over to a cooler part of the stove and then reached for Carol in one swift move.

She seized Carol by the hair and slapped her face and then doubled her hand into a fist gave her a good hard hit in the middle of her back.

"You're about as worthless as tits on a boar hog. Get the hell in there and set the table, maybe you can get that done." She then began muttering to herself, "Goddamn it, there probably won't be enough damned gravy left for dinner now. Goddamned worthless kids anyway."

Carol tried to stop crying as she set the table, she tried not to rub her eyes and make them red since she didn't want her dad asking her what was the matter. As the family sat down to eat, Carol stared down at her empty plate and muttered that she was tired of bread and gravy. Glady was fixing the twins plates and didn't pay any attention to her. Hank lightly teased Carol saying,

"Big school girl; too good to eat bread and gravy, huh. Well you eat what's on the table, so you'd better take some and eat it."

Carol sullenly took a small biscuit and put a pool of gravy over it. She ate it three bites, chewing and swallowing it as quickly as she could. Then she sat there staring at the empty plate. Hank looked over at her plate and smiled and winked at her saying,

"It wasn't as bad as you thought it would be huh?" Carol burst into tears and ran from the table going all the way outdoors. Hank looked at Glady with a puzzled expression on his face.

"She's growing up, Hank. You just can't tease her like a little girl anymore," Glady admonished.

CHAPTER TEN

Glady made up new rules for her increasing numbers of children as they grew up. She called this 'laying down the law' and the kids knew from experience they must follow the rules or suffer the consequences if they got caught. Glady didn't have certain punishments attached to breaking 'the' rules but experience told them that a physical punishment would be meted out at the moment.

They grew to accept that getting caught would surely and swiftly unleash the wrath of Glady. Glady would use whatever she could lay hands on in her rage. Glady used her own hands if there wasn't anything else handy.

Some of the rules made sense to the kids. One sensible rule was 'never leave the store if you are lost'. Fear being a great motivator, the kids easily saw that if you left the store, you may never be found. It would be easier to comb one store looking for a lost kid than to search the town, looking in all the wrong places.

Other rules dealt with Gladys' perceptions about family traditions. She made many rules that she called traditions. She hoped to ensure that the Wilkey family had traditions to guide future generations. 'Never, never peek at Christmas presents' was a rule the older kids had broken when they were young and had been sorry for doing so ever since.

Glady's reasoning for this rule was that she put a lot of effort into shopping and no cheatin' little bastard was going to ruin 'her' Christmas by already knowing what was hidden under the tree. The kids were regularly reminded not to cheat their mother out of 'her' Christmas. By now they knew very well that if there was no surprise, there would be no Christmas.

"If any one is going to ruin Christmas, by God, it will be me," Glady bragged each and every year to her kids.

Another tradition was that the Wilkey family only opened gifts on Christmas morning. Every Christmas morning the kids knew to stay in bed no matter what. They would whisper among themselves and wait for Glady to call them into the living room. Glady always left the largest gift for each child unwrapped, under the Christmas tree, telling them it was from 'Ole Santy

Claus'. The kids came when Glady called and dashed in to claim their gifts from Santa. The rest of the gifts were wrapped and placed under the tree.

One Christmas, Carol really longed for a doll buggy. Glady used a ruse on Carol, telling her that nice doll buggies were too expensive that year, and that she wasn't about to buy a cheap one. She promised Carol that next year the nice ones would be more affordable. Glady told this story believably well and Carol stopped hoping and looked forward to a nice buggy next Christmas.

It was Christmas Eve and Carol wondered where her daddy and mama were. It was late but she had gone past their room and knew they weren't there. The boys were already in bed asleep. Carol knew she should be in bed too, but she was excited and wished it was time to get up instead of time to go to bed. She knew she wasn't getting a buggy but she wondered what Santy Clause would bring her. Carol sometimes forgot in the excitement of Christmas what Glady had told her about Santy Clause.

Carol padded silently and quietly stood on the threshold between the dining room and the kitchen. The lower cupboard doors were open in the kitchen and she couldn't figure out why. From the doorway, Carol leaned down close to the floor and peeked under the cabinet door. On the floor she saw some tools lying beside shiny buggy wheels! Her head jerked back, and she leaped back into the dining room, barely able to contain her excitement, she mentally shrieked, I'm getting a buggy! Suddenly she froze, petrified.

"Carol, do not come out here!" Glady yelled roughly as she stormed into the dining room. "Did you come out here? Did you peek out here?" Glady demanded staring down at Carol.

"No, mama, I-I was just goin' to come out, bu-but I didn't," Carol stammered, knowing for the preservation of Christmases forever, that she had to lie.

"Did you peek out here Carol?" Glady asked again, using her soft-friendly tone of voice. Just like it would be okay if Carol had peeked.

"No mama, I didn't. I really didn't. I wondered where you and dad were, but I didn't even make it to the door." Carol repeated.

"Well, then git on back in there and git on to bed, right now," Glady said sternly.

CHAPTER ELEVEN

The kids almost always got into trouble whenever they all had to go someplace in the car with their mother. Especially in warmer weather when they had to wait in the hot sultry car while their mother shopped. They would become short tempered and cranky and in their irritable state, they'd gripe and blame one another. On the way back home they experienced a kind of exhilaration and became overly rowdy.

Assuming no one could hear her on the open road, Glady wouldn't wait until they got home to mete out punishment. She would scream and yell as soon as she was out of the city limits. Finding herself on open roadways while the car was homeward bound, she would pound her right fist over the back of the front seat cussing a blue streak. Guilty or innocent, she would pummel whoever and whatever got in the way. According to her reckoning they all deserved a good beating for one thing or another anyway.

Glady took the kids with her a lot when she went into Rockwell. She still worried about the near incident with nosy old lady Mumford and didn't want someone driving in and catching her gone with Hank so far from the house. She felt like she had to take them with her for appearances sake, but she couldn't very well troop so many of them into the stores. She never would get her shopping done and she wouldn't have a moment's peace. They could just stay in the car and wait for her!

Glady used her cajoling-pitiful tone of voice to make the kids to stay in the car. She promised to come back with candy sometimes, but other times she appealed to their sensibilities of how much easier it was to keep track of the little kids right here in the car.

The older kids dreaded to wait in the hot car with crying babies and whining little kids while their mother shopped. Glady always took longer that she said she would. They would wait and wait, and nine times out of ten, she came back to the car to leave her purchases and go into another store.

Glady usually parked within a block of where she needed to shop then move the car if she had to go very far to another store. The kids would see her coming back to the car and get their hopes up that they could finally go home. When Glady announced that she was finally finished shopping, they would feel so relieved, they would let down and misbehave all the way home. Glady would be driving down the road, pounding her fist over the back of the seat, trying to punch anything she could reach, cussing and threatening all kinds of doom as soon as they got home.

Glady had left Carol in charge of the kids in the car. Carol, Alfred and the twins all watched Glady's back disappear into the grocery store, baby Henry was asleep on Carol's lap. It was September, George had started back to school and it was hot and stuffy in the car. Soon the twins started fussing wanting to go home.

Carol began to get frustrated and Alfred began to whine. It was a busy shopping day and cars were coming and going from the grocery store parking lot. A car pulled into the parking lot and Carol didn't pay much attention since her interest in people watching had long-since worn off. All she wanted was to see her mother coming out that door.

"Eeeeoooouuuu, niggies!" Little Kayle exclaimed in his tiny voice, pointing out the window. Carol looked over to see a large black woman getting out of her car with four little children. She was horrified when she saw the woman approaching their car.

"Oh my God," thought Carol. "What should I do? Where's mama?"

The black woman came right up the car window and glared into open window.

"Who said that?" she asked. Carol felt embarrassed and guilty, wishing she could disappear. Dale and Alfred quickly pointed out little Kayle who was hiding his face in his hands while crouching on the floor of the back seat.

"He did!" they both said and pointed to the floorboard. They were hoping to shift her attention and make sure the blame went on the right person.

"If I was as ugly as you, I'd hide my face too," the woman projected into the car window and proudly turned and marched back her own car. She took up the little hands of her own four children and walked with them into the store.

The twins quit fussing and Carol and Alfred sat rigid and wished fervently that their mother would come out before the woman came back out. They sat and sat there, and then thankfully, Glady finally came out the door and returned to the car. She got in the car making excuses about why she took so long. Just as they drove out, Carol saw the woman and her four children coming out the door, all carrying sacks of groceries.

No one ever mentioned the incident with the black woman to their mother. Carol knew she would be blamed since her mother would claim mortal embarrassment over the whole thing and probably say she had gone to school with the woman. The kids did tell George though and they would relive the story and giggle about it in secret over the years. It dawned on Carol one time as the story was retold, that the woman had gone back over to her car and taken all of her little children into the store. Glady had always told them that a person couldn't be expected to manage with kids in a store.

***

A firm tradition that Glady made and held was to tell each child two things before they started the first grade. She was adamant that her kids would learn these facts at home, not from rumors at school. Beginning with George on the night before he started school she announced to him in private,

"Babies grow in a woman's tummy. When it's time for them to be born, the woman opens up kinda like a gate, and the baby comes out there."

When told this fact of life, each child asked the same question,

"How does the baby get in the woman's tummy?"

"It grows from a tiny seed that is planted there," was Glady's typical response. Any further inquiries about the seed were met with, "You have to have a daddy to plant the seed."

Glady also told each child in turn, another fact of life on the evening before their first day of school.

"There ain't no Santy Clause. Mama and daddy buy those presents and put them there under the tree." Glady would factually make this statement with a straight face and then watch the frown develop on the informed child's face. She watched for the obvious puzzlement, and then proceed.

"Mama wanted to tell you these things so you wouldn't hear them at school and worry about it. Don't ever talk about these things with other kids at school, and never tell the younger kids. I will tell them when it's time. I'll give you a whippin' if I hear of ya tellin' anybody."

As the children grew older Glady was faced with new situations. She learned to make up rules as she went along holding onto them steadfastly as family traditions. She determined what age was right for what information and then she would take the next child aside at that age to pass on the information in strictest confidence. The child was always admonished to never discuss the information with any other children.

Carol was told an additional bit of information though, that Glady did not tell the boys. When it was Carol's turn to be taken aside her mother and added a rule. She told Carol to be careful around strange boys and men. When Carol appeared puzzled by this information she asked,

"Why Mama?"

"Some nasty men want to stick their pee pee in little girls pee pees!" Glady confided. Carol was obviously disturbed and horrified by this bit of information. She had always been very modest about her body and any kind of nudity. She had always been careful even when bathing and kept covered when any one but her mother was around. She couldn't imagine a man so nasty. What kind of person would do such a thing?

"Where are these nasty men?" Carol asked her mother.

"Well just be careful everywhere. Don't ever let them get you to go with them. Sometimes they offer you candy or clothes, but don't believe them. There is an old coot in Rockwell that has been bothering girls since I was a little girl."

"What happened?" Carol questioned.

"Oh, he would follow girls home from school and bother them. Sometimes he'd offer 'em candy to go with him. He still lives over there, I'll show him to you sometime when I see him."

About a month later, when they were in Rockwell, Glady pointed out an old bent man walking down the street and said to Carol,

"That's the old man I was telling you about that time, Carol. You know, the one that bothered girls."

***

Carol stared hard when her mother pointed out the nasty man. She wanted to remember what he looked like and from that time on, she lived in mortal fear of seeing him again but watched for him constantly. Sometimes Carol would be sitting in the car with the younger kids waiting for Glady and see the nasty man coming from way up the street. She would feel panicky and roll up the windows no matter how hot is was until he crossed the street or went past the car and was out of sight. She never looked right at his face and was terrified that he might come up to the parked car while her mother was in a store.

When she was nine Carol was in Woolworth's dime store with her mother. She saw the nasty man coming up the aisle right toward her. She was terrified because she realized at that moment that she had strayed from her mother's side and she couldn't see her.

"Oh my God!" Carol thought. "The nasty man is coming right toward me! What will I do if he stops and offers me candy? Where is Mama? I don't see her anywhere!"

The old man moved steadily up the long aisle toward her and Carol remained frozen in place scanning the store for her mother. Just in the nick of time, Carol spotted a tall floor-to-ceiling mirrored column dividing the aisle. It was just ahead of her, between herself and the nasty man.

Carol watched and waited to see which side of the column the old man would pass on. When his left foot stepped to the right of the column she quickly stepped to the opposite side. When they met, the column was right between them. The old man moved on up the aisle.

Carol was so relieved! She felt suddenly exhilarated, like she had just pulled the most triumphant coup of her young life. She had tricked the nasty man and he didn't get even close to her. Carol finally saw her mother a few aisles over near a back wall among the bolts of fabrics and hurried to her side. With a heady feeling of victory, she said to her mother,

"I just saw that man you told me about. But I got away from him."

"What man?" Glady asked gruffly, her mind obviously occupied with sewing.

"That man, that nasty man. You know, the one you warned me about."

"Oh, I saw the old bastard," Glady said absently. "Did he say something to you?"

"No," Carol replied, suddenly deflated.

"Well just stay away from him then," Glady said as she picked up a spool of black thread and some light yellow seam binding.

CHAPTER TWELVE

One evening, within a year and three months after baby Henry was born, Glady informed Hank that she was pregnant. This being the sixth pregnancy Hank was fairly unresponsive. Glady just let Hank think whatever he wanted to and she was determined to make the best of it. The older three kids were in school most of the year and when they were home they pretty much took care of them selves and the little kids anyway.

"So to hell with you, you old son-of-a-bitch," Glady muttered when Hank left to go back outside.

One Saturday afternoon a little later in the year, Glady was teasing the older kids. She was unaware that Hank was in the house and listening from the other room. She said to Carol and George as she pointed to her growing stomach,

"You guys don't want another baby do you? Let's give this baby away to the Henderson's. They don't have any kids and they really want one." It was a game they had played many times before with their mother and they knew the response she expected from them,

"No, No!" they playfully chorused, looking at each other self-consciously. "We want a new baby."

Later that evening Hank entered into a conversation that he would regret the rest of his life. When he and Glady were alone in their bedroom, Hank looked at his wife. She looked tired and haggard. Her teeth were going bad and she had gained weight with each pregnancy. In recent years, she only rarely combed her hair.

Hank knew that Glady wished for a better life, but he felt helpless to do more than he was already doing, working night and day. He knew the kids were a burden and Glady complained all the time about the responsibility for the six she already had.

"Did you want to adopt this baby out?" Hank inquired in a quiet, sincere tone.

Not believing her ears, Glady leaped up from her side of the bed.

"What are you talkin' about, you son-of-a-bitch!" she screamed shrilly.

Hank was perplexed.

"I heard you talking to the kids about giving the baby to the Henderson's' and I thought you might want to talk about it," he said.

"Don't you ever think I'd give any of my kids away! What in the hell do you think I am anyway? One of that goddamned Taylor outfit, having kids and then givin' em away for other people to raise? You son-of-a bitch, don't you ever suggest such a thing again! I never said anything about adoption I was teasing the kids! What were you doin', sneakin' around the corners? Goddamn you to hell!"

Hank was without words and hung his head as Glady raged on and on.

"Course you didn't have a real mother to raise you. That goddamned aunt and stepmother you had were so tight assed! What would you know about a mother playin' and teasin' her kids?

"It's what you want though, ain't it? That would suit you fine! Don't you ever even think about givin' one of my kids away."

Hank knew when to stay quiet.

In July on the day before baby Henry turned two, Glady gave birth to a baby girl and she was overjoyed. Hank and Carol were also quite ecstatic. Carol was eight and she finally had a sister after four baby brothers in a row. The boys seemed happy, hoping for harmony in the house.

Gladly told herself that this was it now, she would have no more babies. She'd finally had another girl and now the family would settle down and adjust. She had long forgotten that she was similarly satisfied years ago when she delivered Carol and thought one boy and one girl made the perfect family.

Within a few hours after the birth of the new baby girl, Dr. Tott came into Glady's hospital room with bad news.

"Glady, we've been through a lot of years and healthy babies together and now I have some bad news. Your little girl is turning blue and it looks like she may have a bad heart."

Terror seized Glady. "No, it can't be!" she said.

"I'm afraid so Glady," Dr. Tott said. "We'll just wait and see."

After Dr. Tott left the room, Glady gazed at her bedside table past the new aqua nightgown and the Heaven Scent perfume she liked to buy herself to take to he hospital. Her mind whirled.

"It will be alright," she thought. "There can't be anything wrong. The birth was so easy, just like when Carol was born. There won't be anything wrong."

But the heart defects were mortal and the baby girl succumbed in her sleep when she was two days old. The impact on the family was devastating. Hank felt like dying when he heard of the baby's heart condition. When he learned about her death, he stumbled to the car and cried all the way home.

As he drove up to the house, Hank dried his tears and tried to contain himself. He would have to break the news to Opal as she was, again, staying here with the kids. What he dreaded most though, was telling Carol and the boys.

"Hank, what's wrong? Is something the matter?" Opal queried when she saw Hank come in and she noticed how pale he was. Hank almost broke down again when he told Opal the baby had died. Opal, ignorant about past conversations between her daughter and son-in-law, looked meaningfully at Hank and said knowingly,

"Some things happen for the best."

Hank turned toward the door and barely made it outside before he broke down again. He composed himself again and went back into the house to face the children. Opal had collected them into the clean, tidy living room. Hank quietly told the children that the baby girl had died from a bad heart.

Carol burst into tears and ran into her room. She was still crying loudly when Hank came into her room and fell down sobbing beside her on the bed.

Carol was devastated with the news of the baby's death, but she became unsettled and afraid to see her father there beside her weeping. She stopped crying herself when she heard him moaning in agony,

"God took my baby girl away because He thought I didn't want her." Hank sobbed. "I'm so sorry. I'm to blame. I'm so sorry Carol, I'm so sorry."

With his daughter patting his back to comfort him, Hank finally cried himself out. But, he never forgave himself and Glady never let him forget.

Glady came home from the hospital the next day because Dr. Tott felt it was best that she not remain in the hospital with the other new mothers and babies. He told her to go home to her children, but to stay in bed and let the kids wait on her for a change. Carol and the boys were glad to see their mother home, even though they were sad about the loss of the baby.

Before leaving the hospital, Glady had named the baby girl for the birth and death certificates. She had named the baby June, but told Carol she had some middle names picked out but decided not to use them. She said she might need them if she had more daughters.

Hank's folks understood the burden funeral expenses would be for the family. The older Wilkeys' came by and took Hank, Glady and the kids over to Seneca and bought them all clothes for the funeral. Heavily, Glady moved through the large Sears & Roebuck store. She picked out two-tone suits for the boys and bought a pale yellow dress for Carol. She bought a new outfit for baby June and a navy blue suit for herself.

Hank kept his eyes on the kids, who had never been to any town bigger than Rockwell. They looked wide-eyed at the huge store and were amazed, as they looked at all the people passing by them. Then best of all, they saw and rode their first escalator as it moved continuously, carrying people from one floor to the other. Hank had to curb George and Alfred from having too much fun racing each other up and down it.

The baby's funeral was the next day in Rockwell. Hank drove the family to the mortuary and they all trooped in wearing their new clothes. They sat in a row in the front seats. Directly in front of them, little baby June was in a clear bassinet, lying on her stomach with her little face turned to one side, her dark hair curling over her infant forehead. She too, was wearing her new clothes, a beautiful little aqua dress and white booties. Glady sat there morose and dry-eyed, the boys were all quietly solemn and Carol couldn't stop crying. Hank sat there with a stoic look barely managing to hide his broken heart.

***

After the death of baby June, Hank became despondent. He'd always had migraines but they seemed to be worse and coming more often. His stomach was hurting constantly and everything seemed to be going wrong. He was bringing home seventy-two dollars every two weeks as a hired hand, but with six kids it didn't go far and he was still paying the hospital bills on top of that. Glady complained constantly about everything.

One day in August, Glady looked out the window to see Hank running in from the field screaming and holding his head. It scared her half to death fearing that he had been hurt in a terrible accident. When he reached the house she realized it was just the pain from another migraine headache. She yelled at him and demanded that he go see a doctor this minute. Hank took four aspirins and drove over to Rockwell to see the doctor.

Dr. Tott had delivered baby June only a few weeks earlier. He knew Hank was suffering even though Hank didn't provide any details. Here was a man with a big family, working hard trying to make a living as a hired hand, getting migraines and stomach pains for all his trouble.

Dr. Tott gave Hank some stronger pain relievers but he told Hank that he could be allergic to some of the crops he worked with, such as hay and alfalfa. He further suggested that Hank might want to look at alternatives to farming to see if his migraines improved. He told Hank that his own son-in-law had just been hired on at Lin-Aero in Seneca. He said that the airplane factories over there were looking for good, hard-working men. He told Hank that the pay and benefits would look pretty good to a man with a big family to support.

On his way back home from the doctor, Hank thought hard about his situation. He pulled off to the side of the road, feeling dizzy from the pain medicine. He thought about what Dr. Tott had said. Maybe it was a good idea for him to look around for a different kind of work. He didn't seem to be getting anywhere working as a farm hand. There was no future and it and didn't look like he could ever afford a place of his own. It seemed like every time he turned around Glady was pregnant. He had tried his best to do without sex, but it was always Glady who talked him into it.

"Oh come on Hank," she would say. "Don't be like that. Its not close to my period, so it's as safe now as it can be."

Glady, like a lot of people in that day thought conception happened right around the menstrual period. This made sense to most farmers, as the estrus and vaginal discharge that other mammals have is at their fertile time. So Hank would give in and next thing you know Glady would tell him she had missed her period again. If she did get her period after they'd had sex that month, Glady would say something like,

"I must have fallen off the house, because I'm bleeding." Hank would feel like they had gotten away with something those months. Glady would have never brought up the subject of contraception to the doctor though. She wouldn't even have considered it. Sex and pregnancy prevention were not a subject most women would bring up to the family doctor, no matter how many babies he had delivered for her.

Hank sat there until his head had cleared somewhat and he had come to a decision; he turned the car toward Seneca. He stopped and asked for directions to Lin-Aero and drove through the gates and into a parking space designated for applicants. Hank went in and completed the required paperwork and was then called into an office.

A short time later Hank was on the way home again with a new job. He was to report in two weeks in early September. Hank found it hard to believe how easy it had been to get a job and even harder to believe was the money he would be making. Even considering driving expenses he had never dreamed he could earn so much.

Hank knew he would have to move his family out of the house they were in very soon. The new hired man would need to live there. Hank wasn't accustomed to paying for housing since he had always lived rent-free as part of his job. He wasn't sure what was available and had no idea how much rent would be. He didn't want to use any more than necessary on housing though, since they had a lot of bills to pay off.

Hank had an uncle across the county who ranched and farmed. Hank remembered his Uncle Bill had an old vacant farmhouse sitting in one of his cattle pastures. The last he knew, no one had lived in it for years. He figured that the house was about sixty miles from Lin-Aero but he might be able to get it cheap. He decided he better go over soon to see his uncle.

By the time Hank got home that day he had a lot to tell Glady. Actually he had more explaining than telling, since she was fit to be tied by the time he drove in.

"Where in the hell have you been all day? You left here in terrible shape and I've been worried sick that something happened to you." Glady yelled out the door. She calmed down in a little bit and Hank relayed the events of his day.

Glady was surprised but pleased that Hank had a new job that would bring in more money. She was dubious when she heard about the house Hank was thinking about moving her into though. She had been by that old house and she said,

"I remember driving by that damned old house. It's out in a field, in the middle of nowhere!"

"Well we can't afford anything else right now," Hank said. "I'm already hired on and that's it. We have to move somewhere right now and we can't afford a lot until we get some of these bills paid."

Then he told Glady that he would be working second shift, and she really hit the ceiling.

Right after milking on Sunday evening, Hank drove down near Larkin to tell his uncle they needed to move. He had already talked to his current boss and told him he would be leaving and he would have his family out by his last day of work. The farmer said he hated to lose a good man, but he could see that Hank had not felt well since the death of the baby.

Hank went ahead and spoke for the old farm house without Glady's input when his Uncle Bill told him the rent would be ten dollars a month. He also said that he would throw in free milk and eggs if someone would come over and pick them up every day. Free food and cheap rent were too much for Hank to pass up so he paid Bill ten dollars for the month of September.

The kids would need to start at a new school, and Hank wanted things to be settled quickly. He and Glady, along with her older brother Paul, packed up all the kids and belongings and moved to the old house in the pasture a few days before his new job started.

Glady took one short look at the house; which started a long war between her and Hank. The house looked like something out of a nightmare and Glady was furious. It was an old two-story weather beaten farmhouse that was all gray because the white paint had long since worn off. The back porch entry was in poor repair and the front porch was literally hanging off the house. The last tenants from long ago had left a lot of trash and junk laying around the yard and the weeds were tall. Most of the windows were smashed leaving broken glass everywhere. The pump at the well was thirty yards from the back porch door.

While it needed paint and fixing outside, the inside looked worse. Hank was desperate to make this work out. He promised Glady that he would start fixing up the inside of the downstairs as soon as they finished moving. He pointed out that he would have plenty of time to work on the house since his job was on second shift and he would have his mornings free weekdays and have every weekend off. He didn't have any milking or farm chores to do so he would have more time than he'd had since they'd been married.

To keep Glady's temper at bay he promised her a new gas cook stove. When she seemed to be weakening, he told her that after some of the bills got paid off, they could afford a brand new refrigerator. Glady finally relented with the peace offering of new appliances. She agreed to make the best of it for now.

On the way through Rockwell with the last load of belongings, Hank and Glady stopped in to buy some paint and supplies. Glady was pleased when she discovered a type of hiding wall paint that would cover up all those cracks in the plaster. She picked a nice soft gray paint for the dining room and a sunny yellow for the living room and a nice light blue color for the boy's room. For the kitchen, she picked wallpaper that was white with little figures of chickens in black and dark red, and gray linoleum that had a dull red and black border. She chose a soft rose color for her and Hank's bedroom walls.

Glady looked around the store at all the ideas for making a house nicer and felt unexpectedly excited. She began to look forward to decorating the house and thought maybe it wouldn't be so bad. However, once they got the supplies back home and Glady saw the house again, she began to doubt that anything would help this damned old house at all. That night they were all so tired the whole family fell asleep on mattresses they had put down on the bare floors. Glady awakened long before dawn listening to rustling and thumps.

When Hank got up the next morning, Glady began harping about all the noises in the house at night. She insisted that Hank begin the work downstairs that very day. When she discovered that the kitchen wallpaper border was the wrong one, she really lost her temper.

"Goddamnit! Sticking me way out here in this goddamned old house. You better come up with something better than this soon, you son-of-a-bitch."

Hank ignored the outburst and continued tearing out the wall between the living room closet and the kitchen pantry. He had bought some Celotex wallboard and planned to carve out a small bedroom for Carol by remodeling the inside walls. They needed a third bedroom on the first floor immediately because the upstairs would not be habitable for sometime. Carol would sleep in the new small room he was building, the boys in the big back bedroom, Hank and Glady in the front bedroom with the baby crib that little Henry still slept in.

Glady saw that all the complaining wasn't phasing Hank, so she got busy to show him that she could work as hard as he could. She worked with the mismatched border first.

"By, God, I'll make it work," she announced.

She turned the embossed border over and saw that the backside of it was white and the impression showed through making a repetitive pattern for her to follow. She used a black Crayola to fill in the circle and then use the red crayon to make two lines between each circle. Over and over, she repeated the pattern and finished all the rolls of border.

Glady's brother, Paul, arrived at mid-morning to help Hank hang the kitchen wallpaper and lay the linoleum. When the crayoned border was pasted and put up between the ceiling and new wallpaper, Glady pronounced that it looked better than the border in the store that was made for the wallpaper. By the time Paul left late that night, the kitchen was done and the new wall construction was finished so Carol had her little bedroom.

Hank spent the next morning painting the high parts of the living room leaving the rest for Glady to paint. He wanted to leave early for his new job that afternoon. He had a long drive and being a cautious man he wanted to leave time to change a flat tire if he had one. He left at one-thirty in the afternoon since he had to clock in at three.

This schedule became Hank's pattern for years. He figured out that it took him exactly an hour to drive to the Lin-Aero parking lot, and he added an extra half hour for any problems that might occur. He punched in for work just before three o'clock week day afternoons, and punched out at eleven-thirty at night, arriving home just after twelve-thirty.

Hank loved his job in the airplane factory. Having a job where they made big airplanes almost made up for being rejected for military duty to fight in World War II. It still bothered him that he'd been turned down because of his migraines and he always wished that he'd lied about them.

Hank had never imagined working life could be so easy. He quickly established a comfortable routine. He slept eight hours from the time he got home to about nine in the morning then he would get up and do some work around the house. He did some chores, kept his car maintained and in good repair, cleaned up, drove to work, punched in, did his job, took regular breaks, punched out, drove home with his clothes still clean, and went to bed. And then he had every weekend off; Hank had never had so much free time in his life.

Hanks migraines disappeared and his stomach only hurt occasionally. He was providing his family with a decent living, making more money than he ever had in his life. He even appreciated the drive to Seneca, enjoying the solitude. Hank soon moved up to a new position making even more money.

He was the overhead crane operator and was required to walk across a narrow beam high up, near the ceiling, and climb down into a hanging bucket seat. He would then move the overhead crane back and forth across the factory carrying airplane parts. Hank had always been around farm machinery so he was a natural for the job and he loved it.

It wasn't long before Hank had paid off some of the bills and he happily went out with Glady one weekend and paid cash for the new refrigerator he'd promised. He bought the biggest General Electric they made and it had a large freezer across the top. Soon after that, Hank traded in their old car for a nice, reliable second-hand car.

While Hank was so content, Glady had never been more miserable in her life. She was out in this godforsaken house in the middle of nowhere. The kids had to get on the bus early because of the long ride to school and then they didn't get home until almost five in the evening. She was stuck at home with the little farts, all the time with no relief. She missed the telephone and she couldn't even go anywhere after Hank left for work in the car. While it was still warm weather, Glady would send George out across the pastures to Bill and Trudie's every week day evening and then worry until she saw him coming back loaded down with milk and eggs.

Glady had money to spend. Hank cashed his check every two weeks and kept out money for his expenses. He turned the rest over to Glady to pay bills and buy food. She was free to spend the rest on anything she wanted, but what good was that if she didn't have a way to get out and spend it.

Hank's first few paychecks were a luxury for the family. When he woke up the day after payday, they would shop for food. Since that was every other Saturday, they would take the kids and make it a family outing.

They especially liked the Safeway Store and it had a nice convenience for shoppers. They had built a special section with half-walls where kids could read comic books while their parents shopped. The older kids would read comics and watch the younger kids while Hank and Glady bought groceries. Hank was very pleasant as he went through the store choosing items for his lunches and helped Glady with the rest of the food shopping. He seemed proud when he could pay cash for two big carts full of groceries for his family, and he always let the kids buy some comics and gum to take home.

Glady could handle the new car fairly well now and shopping for groceries had become less of a novelty for Hank. Glady willingly took on the responsibility for shopping and went by herself as often as she could, taking his list with her. Now that he wasn't watching her like a hawk, she would buy food that she didn't require as much preparation. She didn't have to cook for Hank much any more, so didn't cook at all if she could get out of it. The new refrigerator held plenty of food that didn't need cooking.

Glady rarely took time to fix the kids any breakfast since they had to rush and catch the bus so early. They usually grabbed some bread and butter if they ate anything at all. Glady hated to hurry fixing school lunches just as much. So damned many to fix and they had to be ready for the kids to rush out the door when that damned bus came. The driver would sit out there and honk if they weren't ready. Often she would grab a can of potted meat, wipe some on white bread or left over cold biscuits, wrap it in waxed paper and throw it in a bag with an orange. She began to tell the kids 'to catch as catch can' for supper. Why should she kill herself making breakfast, lunch and dinner for a bunch of brats who didn't appreciate anything?

One Saturday Glady went to town by herself and shopped the downtown stores in peace. She bought a pair of electric hair clippers that had an attachment foot on them. All a person had to do was run it over the head to make a perfect crew cut. With five boys, Glady thought they would be a godsend. She would sit the boys down one at a time and mow off their hair, and then she would finish by clippering the neckline and around the ears.

Glady was always tired out by the time she finished the third head. Usually the older boys were last since they were off playing more often than not and she could snatch the younger ones more easily. As an older boy sat there trying to hold still and not think about those times the clippers had pinched their neck or ears, he would become lost in thought. Just as he began to slouch forward a bit, Glady would scream.

"Get that hump out of your back! You're making me reach too far and it's killin' me."

As time went by Glady became more proficient at crew cuts and she would no longer warn the unsuspecting boy by yelling first. She would simply double up her fist and paste him in the back between the shoulder blades as she screamed the famous line. No matter how hard the boys would try to sit up straight, it just wouldn't last long. The clippers would jam and buzz loudly from being overworked and they'd have to sit there while Glady cussed and got the clippers adjusted and going again. The boy would relax and begin to settle in to get the haircut over with. Suddenly, he would be brought back to the present when a fist would pound the middle of his back as she screamed,

"Get that goddamned hump out of your back!"

Hank was home with the kids on weekday mornings and weekends so Glady could use then. She used that time to full advantage and came up with excuses to get away from home.

"I just love old people," Glady would say. "They need all the help they can get and I'm glad to do what I can for them."

Glady had taken up with some older people down the road by the name of Hooker. On weekends especially, she would make excuses to look after the Hookers'. She would drive them to their cousin's house across the section or run over to the store for them.

The Hooker household consisted of two brothers, both in their eighties, and their younger sister who was seventy-nine and they all lived on the old family homestead. They had farmed when they were younger, but now they leased out most of their land. Even chickens had become too much of a chore, and they hadn't gotten any new chicks for quite awhile.

Mostly, the two youngest Hookers stayed close around the old house, tending their oldest sibling who was in bad shape with his heart. He was a heavy man and he made a lot work for them; they weren't much younger than he was. The Hookers' were glad for any help or attention and Glady would use any excuse to leave home in the car.

Glady took the clippers up to the Hookers sometimes and clipped their hair. Other times she stayed there half the day doing up the Hookers' laundry while hers lay in souring piles at home.

She would go to the store for them and help do some of the heavy cooking for the Hookers' while her children and husband ate bologna at home.

After Hank had worked at Lin-Aero for a while, listening to Glady complain constantly about being left every evening without a car, he jumped at the chance for extra duty. He volunteered to be an area bus driver for Lin-Aero employees. The company provided a big yellow bus that Hank drove to pick up second shift employees. He had a route from Larkin, through several small towns, and on in to Seneca then out to the plant. He drove the reverse route after work. Hank didn't mind that he had to leave earlier and get home later since Glady would now have the car every evening.

Glady still complained about the house and living in the country, but she loved having the car. She never went too far though while Hank was at work. She worried that the car might not start or have a flat tire but she kept the roads hot within a few miles from home.

"You kids get to go to school and see people all day long, and that damned dad of yours goes to work and talks to people. All I have is little kids all day long," Glady would harp. She used this excuse regularly to leave the older kids to watch the younger ones as soon as they got off the school bus and she went off in the car.

She told herself that all she asked was a little time to get out by her self, without screaming and bawling brats everywhere she turned. Her kids were always acting up and she had to beat their little asses to make them stop. There wasn't much at the little country store at Crocker Corners, but it was a break from home. She'd sometimes stop in to talk with the Hookers' and see if they needed anything as she drove by.

Glady would get in her car and drive slowly, enjoying the peace and quiet. She still did her main grocery buying every two weeks on payday in Rockwell, but in between times, she would run out of things that were easy to fix.

Glady had grown to hate cooking more all the time when Hank was farming. She was sick of all of it and wanted foods that the kids could manage easily without a lot of fuss. Usually she would pick up some bologna and Rainbow bread for their supper.

Sometimes she would buy pop, but most of the time she just got two packs of Kool Aid that they could make for themselves. Other meals consisted of buying a couple of cans of tuna fish and the kids would mix it with Miracle Whip and make sandwiches to eat for supper. George liked hot dogs with ketchup so Glady got those fairly often too. She would bring home the wieners and liked to tease the kids and say,

"Be sure and save that water you boil the weenies in, you can have weenie water soup and potato peelings tomorrow night."

Glady loved having Pepsi around the house. If she had any during the day she would shoo the little kids outside while the big kids were at school. She would try to forget them all and made herself a big glass of Pepsi with ice. She had to watch those kids like a hawk the evenings she brought it home from Crocker Corners to make sure they shared so she could have one left over for the next day. Every now and then Glady got away with hiding a package of cookies or a couple of candy bars to enjoy at home when she could get a moment's peace.

The boys were bad about stealing food, even canned food. Glady would find the empty cans and wrappers under their beds sometimes and she would question them about who was sneaking food. Since all the boys slept in the same room, she couldn't tell who it was, but she knew someone was lying to her.

One time Glady had stuffed a package of cookies under the car seat on the way home from the store. One of the little brats found them and thought they had just fallen out of the sack and happily pulled them out from under there so she'd had to share.

"Dammnit!" she would mutter. "They don't need candy and cookies all the time, but I just feel so much better when I have somethin' sweet to look forward to."

When Lin-Aero employees along the rural routes realized that they were spending too much time riding the bus, they began to buy second cars and drive themselves to work. The Larkin route was one of the first ones Lin-Aero discontinued due lack of riders. Hank went back to driving the car to work in the afternoons.

Glady had gotten used to having a car at her disposal and she was infuriated at being left without transportation in the evenings again. There she was, stuck again, and it seemed twice as bad as before. She made sure that she didn't give Hank a moment's peace over it. She railed loud and long about being stuck out there with all these kids, with no telephone or a *car* if anything went wrong.

Hank got the message.

Glady couldn't believe her good fortune. She looked in the driveway at the gleaming chrome teeth that seemed to be grinning at her. Hank had finally given in and one Saturday took a neighbor man over to Seneca and had driven back a 1950 Buick. It wasn't a brand new car, but someone had taken good care of it. It was blue and white with clean upholstered seats. Glady thought it was the most beautiful sight she had ever seen. Best of all it had a radio in it. Hank came in and tossed the keys at a surprised Glady that afternoon.

"Now you go your way and I'll go mine," he said. He turned and left the room, not even waiting to see what she said about having a car of her own.

"You can count on that, you old son-of-a-bitch!" Glady mouthed to herself. She hadn't told Hank yet, but she was almost seven months pregnant again.

Glady read that a woman loses a tooth with each pregnancy. She thought she must lose at least two for each one. Her teeth were all decayed and the back ones had huge craters in them. They were chipped off and turning brown and the two front ones were just black snags barely hanging there. Hank had a good medical and dental insurance and he kept trying to get Glady to get her teeth taken care of.

"We can afford it, get yourself taken care of, you could get false teeth now," he would say to Glady.

"Oh yes!" Glady would retort. "Then my fake gums would show when I talk or laugh? I couldn't stand that!"

Hank was not one to expend energy trying to get Glady to explain what she meant. He would drop the matter and not have any idea what she was talking about. He quit bringing it up after a while.

"Your goddamned dad wants me to get false teeth!" Glady told Carol. "I've seen those people with false teeth who show a lot of their gums when they laugh. I'm just not going to get my teeth pulled out and then find out I look like that! You don't mind that mama's teeth are bad, do you?"

Carol could tell by her mother's tone to respond in a neutral way even though she hated it when she had to tell girls at school that this snaggle-toothed, plump woman was her mother. And when Glady had to see a teacher it was even worse to watch her go over and talk to them. She secretly wished her mother would rush out this minute and get all those snags yanked out.

"No mama," Carol lied.

In March, Glady delivered her eighth child, another baby girl. Glady let Hank pick out the name for the baby and then she was sorry when he chose Alvera. She hated the name and immediately shortened it to Vera. The whole family felt tentative and fearful to be happy over the birth of little Vera because of what had happened with baby June. They all held their emotions in reserve even when Dr. Tott declared Vera a healthy baby at her six weeks checkup. After awhile though, they began to accept the fact that Vera was thriving and healthy and they began to grow quite proud of her.

Glady started to sew more and bought a new electric Singer sewing machine in a beautiful blond cabinet. She liked making things for the baby, since sewing was more a joy than a chore for her baby girl. Vera was tiny and her clothes always turned out cute, even though Glady refused to waste money on a pattern.

CHAPTER THIRTEEN

Glady got to where she hated springtime after she had a car radio to listen to. It certainly wasn't the beautiful lilacs in full bloom that made her hate spring. She loved the yellow roses, irises and lilies that riotously sprung up everywhere. It was wonderful that the spring rain came to replace the snow and freezing winds. Glady liked the bushes and trees leafing out in bright spring green. But why, in this most beautiful of all seasons, did the damned tornadoes have to come and spoil everything?

Glady's hate for tornadoes wiped out anything good or beautiful that spring could offer. She listened carefully to the car radio for everything she could about tornadoes. She heard about brave people who survived the deadly funnels and what actions had saved them. She heard how to identify the most dangerous type of clouds and loudly proclaimed a deathly fear of tornadoes, but she was ready if any hit.

Glady sat in the car and strained her ears night after spring night, listening for the warnings. She would get out a state map and draw an imaginary line on it with her finger, as the weatherman would call out danger areas, using the names of counties or towns as the boundaries.

"A line from fifty miles east of so and so, to a line a hundred miles north west of so and so."

All spring, Glady would sit in her car with her ear glued to the radio and draw the imaginary lines then announce her decision for the time being. The decision was whether to turn off the radio and ready a shelter or to continue to sit in the car to listen, watch and wait.

If she determined the shelter was not yet needed she resumed her position at the radio. If the announcer gave warnings anywhere close to home, Glady would hurriedly implement the emergency procedures for a shelter she had determined would be adequate.

First, Glady and George would move the dining room table to the inner northeast wall between the dining room and the kitchen. Next, she would take the couch cushions and stuff them vertically between the table legs, leaving an opening at one end the have all her kids except George to crawl in under the table with blankets. She and George would then lift a mattress from one of the boy's beds and place it on the top of the table. Last George and Glady would crawl through the opening and get under the table with the others.

Glady would leave a small peek hole facing the dining room window. She would stare out at the sky and about every twenty minutes she would push away the cushion and crawl out to look out windows that faced in other directions. She would strain her eyes at the ominous sky, knowing she couldn't risk going back out to the car to listen to the car radio at this point. A funnel cloud could come down and sweep her up at any moment.

The kids were fearful during the first few tornado watches of every season. They would whisper in the makeshift shelter and play quiet games like 'When I Go Out West' and tell ghost stories in hushed voices.

Glady would complain loudly from the time the tornado warning was announced cussing and berating the man who had left and gone off to work, leaving her to fend for herself and knowing that tornadoes always come at night.

"Tornadoes always come in the evening and at night when that son-of-a-bitch is gone. He's got us stuck way out here in this god-forsaken rat hole, with no cellar," Glady would yell in her loud-martyred-sanctimonious tone of voice. She hoped the kids would all see how brave she was, and what a bastard their dad was.

Glady related some of the survivor stories to her children and told them what they should do during a tornado to be safe. She told them if they were in a building they were to always crouch in a northeast corner of an inside wall. However if they were outside with no hope of getting inside and saw a tornado coming they were to:

"Run to the lilac bush and take hold of a branch way down close to the ground. Hang on as tight as you can and wait 'til the tornado blows out. Lilac bushes never get blown away." Glady preached this as fact over and over.

After a couple of nights spent under the dining room table with so many other warm bodies and a worried, cussing mother, the kids would lose their fear of tornadoes. They began to take longer to get into the shelter, and then they act up when they were once again confined in the miserable humid space. The games had turned boring and 'When I Go Out West' began to take on a more crude tone.

"Oh yes, someone always has to get dirty!" Glady would say, beginning to lose patience. "You ungrateful sonsabitches better quiet down!"

The kids would all be irritable and tired the next day, hoping that any more tornado warnings would be far away like in Texas.

The kids were always glad when the tornado season ended and the warning stopped being announced on the radio. It was different for Glady though, she knew all she had to look forward to was having a bunch of kids home all day long, a hot summer without a breath of air stirring, and those goddamned rattlesnakes.

"I just saw a huge rattlesnake!" Glady announced to the kids at dusk one summer evening as she was looking out the east living room windows.

"It was over there by the tiger lilies, as big as my arm, just laying there. You kids just all stay in the house tonight, don't go outside anymore."

The boys were just finishing a quick supper of hot dogs. They had been looking forward to going back out to play in the cool night air and she had just dashed their hopes.

"Oh Mom," they groaned. "It will go away in awhile, can't we go back out?"

"You know damned good and well I'd be worried sick the whole time you were out there. I haven't seen it move so it is probably still there. One of you would get bit by the damned thing and be poisoned to death. I just couldn't take it if that happened."

The next day Glady lit into Hank.

"Goddamnit Hank, you listen to me. I can't take it way out here any more. A rattlesnake almost bit one of the kids last night. The poor little fellas were afraid to go outside after supper. What if one of them got bit? I couldn't get them to a town quick enough and they'd be poisoned. What in the hell do you expect me to do, rot out here in this godforsaken damned house?"

"You can leave anytime you want to, you have a car now," Hank retorted.

"You son-of-a-bitch, what in the hell would I do with all these damned kids? Can't you just find something closer to town or at least with a telephone?

CHAPTER FOURTEEN

Glady had been raised to keep things clean and tidy under Opal's careful scrutiny but after she started having babies, she rarely cleaned at all. One of her favorite lines was,

"I'd have to stand with a broom and mop in my hands all the time with all you little sonsabitches always messin' up the place."

Hank's folks were quite religious and very clean and orderly in their households. Hank was raised to clean up after himself and grew up doing his share of the housework as well as farm chores. It always bothered him that his home was so filthy, but he continued the practice of cleaning up after himself.

He learned long ago not to try and do much around the house however. When George was a baby he had picked up the broom a couple of times and swept the floor. Glady had shrieked at him loudly and told him to put the damned broom away.

"What in the hell are you doin'? Tryin' to make out like you hafta come home and clean after workin' in the field all day? You goddamned pitiful son-of-a-bitch!" She had further screamed:

"If you're tired of lookin' at a dirty house, you can leave home anytime."

Glady considered the older Wilkeys' pretty high-falutin' since they'd had money and that big ranch before the depression. She always worried that they would show up unannounced and find out what a terrible mess her house was in. The Wilkeys' hadn't eaten meat since Hank's dad had married his stepmother years ago. That always put Glady on the spot too because she didn't quite understand the belief and just assumed they thought they were better than her.

Glady hid the lard and rushed out and spent money on Crisco if the Wilkeys' were coming or dropped in near a mealtime. Her in-laws always reassured her that they would eat what ever was put before them, and not go to any special trouble. Hank had told Glady that his dad would love it if she served meat, and as a guest, he would be required to respectfully eat it.

Glady ignored Hank and admonished her kids to make a good impression on their paternal grandparents. She taught her kids to do things that the Wilkeys' would approve of so they wouldn't look down their noses at them.

Every year at school picture time, Glady would repeat,

"Now your dad's folks like a pleasant look in pictures. Don't go grinning like a fool at the camera."

When the pictures would come back at least one kid would catch hell.

"Dammnit! Lookit this grin. You look like a goddamned ape. I told you to look pleasant and be careful and not grin too big at the camera."

They'd never heard of other kids with rules like this and Glady's kids had never heard their grandparents say anything about pictures. But, Glady would harp so pointedly at them, it must be true. After their turn in front of the camera every school picture day each kid would wonder if they had they given just the right-sized upward bend to their mouths or would they be cussed by their mother when the disappointing pictures came back?

Glady hadn't cleaned the house since the last holiday when her brother and his family came over. It was spit shined and cleaned top to bottom then but that was months ago. Glady looked around at the piled surfaces and filthy floors and knew she would be mortally embarrassed if any one came by. She would have to stall them at the door and, if possible, she wouldn't let them in the house.

Glady was sitting on an old couch in filthy house in a dirty housedress. She had finally gotten those damned kids run out the door and off away from the house to play. She had just put the little kids down for a nap when a car pulled in the driveway.

"Some son-of-a-bitch!" she muttered as she called out the side door for immediate help as said,

"My God! It's Grandpa Wilkey! Get up here right now and help get this house cleaned up."

Hearing the call the kids rushed in the back and side doors. Glady sent George out to stall the visitors as she rushed into the bedroom and put on a brassiere and the cleanest dress she could find. She grabbed everything piled on the dining room table and threw it onto her bed. She snatched the broom and pushed everything moveable from the living and dining rooms into the bedrooms. She grabbed a wet rag and sponged off all the visible dust on the living room furniture and threw a blanket over the couch and chair. She quickly closed every door to hide as much mess as possible while monitoring Carol who had rag washing the little kids faces.

"Come in!" she called cheerily when the Wilkeys' knocked on the door.

Glady was determined to get out of the house more as she gradually accepted the fact that baby Vera was healthy. These days she was actually thrilled that the sour old son-of-a-bitch worked evenings and wasn't around to glare at her when she wanted to go somewhere. She proclaimed.

"I've finally got a car of my own now, so by God, we are gonna go places! I'm not stayin' in this damned hole any more than I haf' to."

First, Glady got the older kids into 4H and they went to meetings once a month. They held the square dance right after the meetings and Glady enjoyed seeing Carol out there dancing. Carol was almost eleven and had what Glady called a 'peaches and cream' complexion. Glady had turned out some cute square dance skirts for Carol and she looked at her out there moving through the steps to the caller's commands.

"Now star right back home and swing your own little pal."

Glady admired her handiwork as Carol's skirt whirled and Jerry, a big dark-haired older boy, swung her around and they led the promenade.

Next Glady started going to church as an excuse to get out of the house on weekends when Hank was home. There was a little country Methodist church over at Crocker Corners and Glady went there on Sundays. On Sunday mornings Glady would decide who would go with her. If she wanted to leave right after Sunday school she took the little kids, if she wanted to make an impression and stay for the church sermon she only took Carol and the older boys. Some Sundays she was lazy and stayed home altogether. The next week she told the church people that some of the kids had been sick and she just couldn't leave them.

In the summer time, Glady usually left the older boys at home and they didn't care one way or the other. When they stayed home they could bang indoors and outdoors freely since Glady wasn't there to scream at them. The flies were everywhere and they swarmed in and out of the filthy old house right along with the boys.

It was the custom for the church members to invite the preacher and his wife over for Sunday dinner since preachers didn't earn much money and this was one way the congregation helped out. Glady wanted to do her share in her newfound social circle at the church. She invited the preacher over in midsummer for her turn at providing Sunday dinner.

Right after she asked him though, Glady immediately began to fret. She worried about what foods to serve, what dishes to serve on and most of all how to get the house clean enough to look like it was always spotless. She even asked her brother Paul to come out the week before and bring something special to clean the floors.

When Paul arrived he stared at the kitchen flooring that he had helped install and wondered what had happened to it. Glady saw him looking at the mess stuck to the floor and complained,

"Those damned kids have had so much gum lately, Paul. I'm just gonna hafta' quit giving it too them if they can't keep it off the floors."

Paul used Tide and boiling water to make a thick, hot, soapy paste. On his hands and knees, he spread the paste out over a large area of dirt and grime. Then he used his pocketknife to carefully scraped it all up. More than once, Paul wished he had brought something stronger to get the resistant spots off.

Meanwhile the flies continued to swarm the place. The Thursday before the preacher was coming to eat, Glady bought an aluminum pump sprayer and a large can of fly spray. She went through the house three times a day pumping the noxious spray in every nook and cranny, determined that her home would be free of flies when the preacher came to dinner on Sunday.

The big day arrived and Glady decided that she, Carol and baby Vera would go to church that day. For appearances they would need to stay for the church sermon but she planned to sneak out a little early and blame the baby's needs. Glady was apprehensive all through Sunday school and the church service that the boys would mess up the house. She was even more worried that they were letting in the flies.

Hank couldn't take the pressure of the preacher coming to eat so he had volunteered to work an overtime Sunday shift at Lin-Aero. Glady raged at him but he left for work early shortly after she got home from church. Glady ran through the house with the fly sprayer as soon as she got home and saw all the new flies. The preacher and his wife weren't due until one-thirty so she sprayed lightly one more time right before they got there and hoped the smell would air out quickly.

The preacher and his trim little wife were sitting at the table admiring the Dogwood pattern china that Glady had gotten for saving coupons at the grocery store. The little kids were at a small table in the kitchen where Glady could keep an eye on them. The four older kids were sitting stiffly at the big table with Glady, the preacher and his wife. The food was served family style in large bowls that were passed from person to person.

Suddenly Glady shrieked with horror. She was staring at the bowl of coleslaw that Carol had just carefully passed to the preacher. Right at the edge of the dish was a dead fly! Glady snatched the bowl from the preacher and jumped up from her chair.

"Well, I'm mortified!" she huffed.

The preacher, on the other hand, took the presence of the fly in stride calmly saying,

"Well Mrs. Wilkey, it's pretty hard to keep those rascal flies out of the house in the summertime."

Glady whisked the dish into her spotless kitchen, haughtily proclaiming,

"They don't come in to *my* house."

CHAPTER FIFTEEN

One afternoon Glady was just settling down to read. Hank had left for work, the older kids were still at school and the little ones were down for their naps. Glady panicked when a car pulled in the driveway. The house was a royal mess.

Every dish and pan in the house was caked with dried or molding food, and dirty dishes covered every surface in the kitchen. The slop bucket under the sink was smelly and full, and the floors were encrusted with filth. The dining room table was piled halfway to the ceiling with clean clothes and ironing, papers, sewing, magazines, schoolbooks and almost everything else imaginable. The living room furniture was laden with dirt and dust, and trash littered the floors; grimy dirty clothes were tromped all over the bedroom floors.

Glady's long dark hair was oily and stringing down her back. She couldn't remember the last time she had washed it. She had on grubby black print housedress on that was so soiled it was slick across her protruding stomach. Her feet were bare and caked with filth.

Glady didn't have anyone to send out to stall whoever it was and wondered who in the hell it could be pulling in at this time of the day. The car door opened and some people she didn't recognize got out.

"It looks like out of state license tags to me." She muttered. "Maybe they're just lost and need directions."

She waited until someone came onto the back porch knocked on the door.

"Who is it?" Glady shouted. It was no use pretending she wasn't home because one of the little kids had probably peeked out the bedroom window when the dog barked. Glady didn't want any one thinking that she would leave little kids home alone.

It turned out to be strangers from California but they had Hank's nephew Raymond with them. He was Hank's youngest sisters boy and he lived out in California now. The couple and Raymond were down and out and hungry so Glady didn't have the heart to turn them away. They had been broke for days and grateful to get out of the car so they didn't seem to notice the filthy house.

Relieved to be at a seemingly friendly place, the woman filled the teakettle with water and put it on to heat. Then she took the empty water bucket outdoors, pumped it full and brought it back in. She worked hard cleaning up the filthy mess while Glady yammered on about being stuck way out here in this old house that was in such bad shape.

By the time the kids got off the school bus, the kitchen was fairly tidy. The dishes, tables and counter tops were clean and the floor was swept. There was a lot of excitement as the kids showed the company things they brought home from school. Glady whipped up a meal and marveled at how easy cooking was in a clean kitchen. Right after supper the woman guest got up from the table and silently began washing dishes again.

The couple stayed for a day and a half with the woman cleaning the kitchen after each meal. They said they needed to move on and knew some people in Rockwell that might loan them enough money to get back to California. Raymond decided to lighten their burden and stay on for a while. He was family and he had other relatives that might put him up for a while until he was back on his feet. While Hank was asleep and the kids were at school, the couple took off never to be seen or heard from again. It ended up that Raymond stayed for more than a year.

Raymond was sixteen when he came to Glady's house that afternoon. Glady knew he'd had a stormy adolescence and had been in some unnamed trouble and was not highly thought of in the Wilkey family. He had seen Hank and his family a few times over the years and he always liked Glady. He liked her better than his blood uncle Hank, for one reason he could never tell what Hank thought of him.

Glady fixed up a little more beginning the day after he arrived. Raymond seemed to notice saying that they apologized for dropping in before she had a chance to get ready for company the day before. Glady had put on a clean dress and pulled her hair back away from her face. Glady's teeth were bad and she was heavier than she used to be but she talked brightly and Raymond appreciated her attentiveness. He told her tales of his travels in an interesting way.

After the couple had gone, Raymond and Glady were home all day with the little kids and they talked and talked. They talked about all kinds of things, day in and day out. Glady had been so lonesome way out here without even a telephone. Raymond told Glady no one had ever talked to him like he was adult and he listened to Glady as she chattered endlessly. He told Glady all about the places he had been and what it was like out in California.

***

"I didn't know you could read music and play the organ," Glady said. She had taken Raymond with her when she drove the Hookers' over to visit their cousin across the section. Raymond asked permission and sat down at the keyboard of the old organ. His feet worked the pedals and the Hookers' looked on and beamed as Raymond played a familiar hymn.

"I've always wisht' I could get an old piano for the kids to learn to play on," Glady said. "Now that I found out you can play, we'll hafta look into gettin' one."

"Oh gosh," said old Mrs. Hooker, "I know someone who would like to get rid of their old piano. Their daughter bought them a new one for their anniversary quite a while back and the old one has been sitting there gathering dust. I bet they'd let you have it pretty cheap if you'd move it out for them."

Glady was delighted and she and Raymond went over the next day to look at the piano. They paid fifteen dollars for it and took some of the older boys over to pick it up the next Saturday morning. With the help of a couple of men who worked the farm and their truck, they all brought the small upright piano home.

Glady encouraged Raymond to practice playing hymns and praised his skill. She insisted that he teach her and the kids to play too. She used a crayon and put the letter on the front of each key and began to peck out a few tunes on the keyboard with one finger.

***

Except for the short monthly meetings and square dancing, 4H was pretty quiet during winter. Glady sometimes only took Carol over since the boys were bashful and refused to learn to square dance. As Glady watched Carol out on the floor square dancing she dreamed that Carol would be popular when she got older. She hoped she would have a lot of dates and when she was old enough, she would marry someone with good prospects.

The caller was at the part about 'turning your own little pal' again. Glady watched Carol sashay around another dark tall boy. Glady thought it would be perfect if Carol would meet someone just like that to marry when the time came. A dark-haired groom in dark clothes, and then a fair blond bride coming down the aisle in white, now that would be perfect. Glady didn't stop to think that it had been just the opposite of her own wedding to Hank, a dark bride in black and a blond groom in a white shirt.

It was at the square dance late in year that Glady heard about the one annual winter event that the 4H hosted. It drew a big crowd and provided money for many of the 4H activities for the rest of the year. It was the annual Groundhog Day Pancake Supper. The cooks would pass off plump pork sausages as 'groundhog' and serve it up with golden, buttered pancakes and maple syrup.

Glady immediately wanted to go to the big event, then when she heard someone mention a talent show, she really began to scheme. She had always admired the country and western music singers, especially the big families. She'd always dreamed that her kids would be a performing family and she had it on her mind a lot since she found out that Raymond could play the piano.

Glady volunteered her act for the Groundhog Day Pancake Supper talent program at the 4H square dance week right after Christmas. She had until early February to get the act together and her dreams began in earnest.

She believed her vision of a family of famous singers could become reality very soon and thought a good name for her brood would be the 'Singing Wilkey Family'.

"By God, I never had anything in life but a buncha damned kids and this gloomy old house. Maybe together they are destined to make me rich!"

Glady made Raymond practice playing the piano as soon as Hank left for work each afternoon. She didn't want him knowing anything about what was going on, to hell with him. As soon as the kids got off the school bus, she wore them out practicing singing 'This Old House'.

For the first few days the kid sang without music while Raymond practiced separately. When Raymond was pretty good with the timing, Glady had them practice together over and over. Raymond and the kids were sick of the song but they followed her command to sing and play it one more time.

"What ever will they wear?" Glady wondered during one practice session. "I can't have them up there looking like hillbillies. They all have to match so they look nice in front of all those people."

Glady sorted and looked through the clothes, clean and dirty, but found nothing was good enough for the debut of the 'Singing Wilkey Family'. She went to town on payday with an unspoken mission: To come up with outfits that would facilitate immediate world recognition for her family of singers. She came back home with yards and yards of red and white satin and reels of white piping.

Glady set about making western-style red satin shirts with a yolk that came to a V in the back and up over the shoulders in white satin. She set about making shirts for the six older kids and one for Raymond.

In Glady's dream it would be perfect. She would be sitting in the audience, holding baby Vera on her lap and looking up on the stage. There she would behold a brilliant family of singers in perfectly made, gleaming red and white satin shirts. She would hear six perfect voices, beautifully blending, and accompanied by a piano being magnificently played.

It was the end of January and Glady still had three shirts to make. She had started with the smaller ones because they would be more tedious on the handwork. But now she was using up the satin material so fast as she cut out the bigger shirts. Glady had no money between now and payday so she had to be careful to make the material hold out until she got all the shirts cut out. She folded the fabric pieces every which way and was using scraps when she could get away with it.

Finally Glady was starting on the last shirt but she could barely see anymore. She got up and went to look in the mirror.

She thought for a second that she was seeing things. There looking back at her was a hazel green iris peering out through a pool of red. Panic seized Glady, and she thought she must be going blind but she could not stop now. She forged ahead and finished the last shirt moments before they all had to get dressed to go sing.

As the Singing Wilkey Family was introduced, Glady's heart swelled with pride. Every thing was going to be just as she had planned and her dreams were moments away from coming true. The rest of the audience had a little different view however. They all noticed that the piping pulled and puckered at the shirt seams, that the dried milk stain on little Henry' shirt showed, that as the song progressed Raymond missed more notes, that Carol was singing too loud, and that the shy little boy voices were mumbling and off key.

The audience took it for what it was worth though and applauded loud and long for the performing children. The applause elevated Glady's dream far beyond the pancake feed and sent it soaring across the skies and onto the stage at the Grand Ole' Opry. Glady was finally on the way to stardom and riches.

CHAPTER SIXTEEN

Day in and day out since his arrival, Glady and Raymond continued to talk. They sat in the house after Hank left for work every day, and then move out to the Buick after the kids got home. The car was the only place for any privacy in the evening, and Glady would tell the kids that she and Raymond were listening to radio programs.

Glady would sometimes buy a package of good cigarettes, not that homemade kind like Hank rolled out of Price Albert. She and Raymond would smoke as they sat and talked on for hours. Glady led Raymond into discussions of personal issues and feelings as time went by. She found out that Raymond was not a virgin. He'd had a girlfriend the year before he left California and they'd had sex a few times in the back seat of a car. When Glady asked Raymond if the girl had climaxed, Raymond seemed perplexed and didn't seem to know what she was talking about.

"Well you know, women come just like men," she explained in a womanly-knowledgeable-matter-of-fact voice.

Shortly after that, Glady picked up a True Story magazine and told Raymond to read a certain paragraph. Later and over the next few days in their long talks, Raymond asked Glady a few questions about a woman's body. Glady knew very little about her own anatomy, but she described in detail what women like during foreplay and how they felt during sexual intercourse and climaxing.

Further, Glady related to Raymond that Hank did not understand anything about a woman's needs and had never made any effort to find out about them. She told Raymond that she would never talk to Hank the way she talked to him. She said Hank would probably think she was a whore. In the days to come she convinced Raymond to read the good parts of other True Story and True Romance stories.

Raymond kept a low profile around Hank. He was always painfully polite and respectful, but mostly tried to stay out of Hank's sight. For one thing, he didn't know where he would go if Hank asked him to leave.

Raymond cleaned up after himself and washed or dried dishes after every meal. He swept the floors and would go outside and work in the yard work he heard Hank getting up in the mornings. Some days when he couldn't find anything to do outside, he would go into the boy's room and quietly close the door and read.

After Hank left for work one day shortly after the big Wilkey family singing debut, Glady stepped into the room and sat on the corner of the bed where Raymond lay reading.

"Whatcha readin'?" she asked nonchalantly, as she leaned back and reached up over her head to stretch, arching her breasts in the air. She looked over at Raymond and was delighted to see him watching her breasts. Slowly, she reached over and touched at his waist just above his belt. Raymond took a hold of her wrist and she put her other arm around his neck.

About an hour later, the baby woke up and cried. Glady jumped up off the bed and left the room to clean herself before the kids came home on the bus. For several days, when Hank left for work, Glady and Raymond put the kids down for a nap and waited until he'd been gone for at least half and hour and then they would rush quickly into the boy's bedroom. Glady always left her slip on, refusing to be naked in bed. She would tell Raymond that she was too modest to take it off.

Even though Glady knew how easily she got pregnant, they never used any protection. She was more concerned near her period and insisted that Raymond withdraw before he came. For days, Glady waited and watched, but her period never came.

"Shit," she thought, "every goddamned time I've ever missed my period, I've been pregnant." When she was fairly certain she was pregnant, her eyes dimmed and her mind darkened as she tried to remember the last time she and Hank had had intercourse.

"Double shit!" she thought. "Triple shit. I can't even remember when I last convinced that son-of-a-bitch to crawl on top of me, but I'm sure it's been way over a month. Glady lay awake that night until Hank came home from work.

"Hank," Glady said softly to him when she saw him lay down. "I know you're tired, but it's been so long. Can you stay awake long enough for me to get satisfied?"

Hank had heard this plea many times before; he went through the programmed motions, as he tugged his organ awake. He rolled over on top of Glady and began to thrust, when she moaned and arched, he came and rolled off her.

CHAPTER SEVENTEEN

"Oh Dr. Tott," Glady chirped. "We are naming the new baby boy after you. We are going to call him Billy Totten. We thought Billy Tott sounded too cut off so we put the e-n on it. Do you like it?"

Dr. Tott was a pleasant man, who was always cheerful,

"Glady we're just going to have to stop meeting this way. How old is your baby girl?"

"Just over a year and an half, and she is our pride and joy," Glady said. "Little Henry started first grade in September I'll just have the two babies there home most of the time. Hank's nephew is still here visiting from California so I have a lot of help around the house."

Raymond was feeling lost lately. Whatever it was that he and Glady'd had, seemed to be gone. She looked puffy and fat to him, and she complained all the time. She really never talked to him anymore. He thought she was lovely when she was pregnant, with her skin glowing after they made love and lay talking together. Now she treated him like he was the nursemaid and the houseboy.

Raymond looked at the infant Billy Totten as he lay in his arms bottle-feeding. The tiny baby was fair-haired with a wide mouth.

"Just like mine," whispered Raymond.

Since he and Hank were blood related Raymond thought sometimes that he was imagining that Billy Totten looked like him and might be his baby. He hadn't ever asked Glady about any part he might have played when she told him she was pregnant. He wanted to be discreet and he kept thinking Glady would say something. Raymond and Glady had continued sexual intercourse until she got too uncomfortable late in the pregnancy.

"Goddamnit Raymond, don't let him eat so fast. The little fart has been bawling all day and he's so hellishly constipated. Fer chrissake, slow down!"

Glady harped shrilly as Raymond continued to feed little Billy Totten. He really didn't know what he was doing wrong to make Glady so mad, but he tried to slow little Billy T down.

Raymond had looked for work off and on since he had lived here. Sometimes it was only halfhearted, but there didn't seem to be any real work anywhere. He had cut several cords of wood for a guy and helped him deliver them, but that was about it. Winter was coming on again and he thought his prospects looked pretty bleak here. He figured it was time to get on back on out to where the weather was warmer this time of year.

Raymond regretted leaving if Billy Totten was his child, but Glady never said any thing about it. He didn't want to bring it up though, and make an assumption that would make her even madder at him.

"You son-of-a bitch, how dare you desert me with this baby! I need you here to help me out. I'm going to tell Hank that that constipated little brat is yours and then see how your family treats you." Glady screamed when Raymond told her he was leaving. "I hope you run into trouble with the law, hitchhikin' back out there to your damned precious California. It would serve you right if you got thrown in jail, you son-of-a-bitch."

Raymond sadly left her one afternoon, walking out of the yard to hitchhike back out to California. It was two months after his seventeenth birthday and Glady had not really told him, whether or not, Billy Totten was his child.

CHAPTER EIGHTEEN

Glady had lived in the ramshackle farmhouse that she hated for almost four years now. They never had fixed the upstairs. These days there was never any extra money to fix the place up. Glady took Hank's paycheck and spent every dime and they lived from one payday to the next. She never gave Hank a moment's peace no matter what he did, or didn't do. She always railed about living way out here, complaining about the filthy house, making excuses about why she couldn't keep it cleaner.

In nice weather Glady sent Vera and Billy Totten outside to play as early as possible so she could stay in bed and read until the 'old bear' Hank got up off the couch. Hank had been sleeping there every night for quite awhile now.

Some days Glady appeared to hustle when Hank got up. She might offer to fix him food and while he ate she would dab at cleaning some dishes while complaining the whole time about the mess.

As soon as Hank's car was out of sight, Glady breathed a sigh of relief, put the little kids to bed for a nap and read for about three hours until the school bus came just after four-thirty. Many days as soon as the kids got off the bus Glady would announce on her way out the door,

"I'm gonna have to run over to Crocker Corners and get somethin' for supper. Take care of the little kids." Once in awhile she would take one of the older kids if she was too dirty and didn't want to get out of the car. She preferred to go alone, and they preferred to stay home. The kids were tired and wanted to play, they knew she would probably stop at the Hookers' to gab and there was nothing for them to do down there.

In June school let out for the summer, making Glady feel ambivalent about having the kids home all day. In one way, she wouldn't have to take care of those little brats all day long by herself, but the big kids would be yelling and fighting all summer long.

One afternoon Glady announced she was sick of all their fighting and she was getting away from them. She craved adult conversation and needed something sweet to eat. Candy or cookies would be good she thought as she planned how to maximize the cash she had in her purse.

"Carol, you make sure to watch the little kids, I'm going to stop down at the Hookers' to see if they need anything," Glady said, then called out to boys as she drove out of the yard,

"I'm sick of you bastards! Fight all you want to and see if you can kill each other off while I'm gone."

"When are you comin' back, Mama?" called Dale as he ran toward the driveway.

"I'll be back when I'm goddamned good and ready. Maybe not at all, you fightin' sonsabitches."

"I'm sick of summer already, those damned kids and their eternal fighting," she muttered as she sailed past the Hooker's driveway.

Like a lot of times when she told the kids she was going to, Glady had no plans to stop at the Hooker's house. She knew from the other day when she stopped in, that their cousin had taken them to Rockwell this week so they probably didn't need anything. Glady was going over to the store alone to get something sweet to eat and a couple of magazines. Then she was going to find someplace where she could eat and read in peace.

She drove the three miles of gravel road reaching Crocker Corners in just a few minutes.

Glady pulled into the parking lot at the store and saw only one other car there, a maroon one that she didn't recognize. She went into the store and said 'hello' to the clerk that worked there in the afternoons. She noticed a sandy-haired, freckled, short, dumpy woman that she didn't remember ever seeing her before and figured she must be the one driving the maroon car.

"Say hello to our new neighbor," the clerk said to Glady. "This is Arlene Johnston. They just moved into the old Crawford place last weekend."

Arlene turned out to be the gabbiest woman she had met in years and Glady liked her immediately. Arlene had her three kids with her. The two boys kept whining to go home and Arlene kept talking to Glady, following her out to the parking lot and up beside the car.

"My husband works second shift at Lin-Aero and we got moved clear out here. We don't know anybody," Arlene said.

"Well my God," said Glady, "so does my old man!"

"Why don't you bring your kids and come on over tomorrow afternoon after the men go to work. I still have a lot of unpacking to do and you can keep me company." Arlene said happily.

Glady liked Arlene and she loved the invitation to her house. She couldn't very well invite Arlene over to her own pigpen.

"Well, you should know that I have eight kids before you ask me over like that!" Glady said tentatively.

"Oh that's fine, they'll keep my three busy so we can talk," Arlene replied nodding toward the whining children waiting for her in the car.

Glady ate a candy bar on the way back and drove home with some wieners for supper. Carol was surprised to see Glady back home so soon.

"Well the Hookers' didn't need anything, so I didn't stay there very long. But I met a new neighbor over at the store so we're gonna go over there and visit tomorrow afternoon. You'll have someone to play with because she has a girl about your age. Let's do up some wash in the morning when it's cool so we'll have something to wear over there."

Glady and Carol ran five tubs of wash in the Maytag wringer washer and hung them out on the clothesline early the next morning. Glady admired the twelve colored shirts that she had made for the boys in the spring. She had bought every color imaginable from forest green to bright watermelon to sky blue to dark lavender and made two shirts apiece for the boys. Puckered nylon, what a blessing that material was, it was easy to sew and came in ten beautiful colors that didn't fade. It was so lightweight that it dried in just a few minutes out on the line.

Glady was anxious for afternoon to get here. She longed to watch that old bear, Hank, leave for work so she could go visit her newfound friend. So began a long relationship between Glady and Arlene. Almost every weekday for the rest of the summer, Glady forgot all about the poor Hookers' and she and the kids went over to Arlene's house. The kids played while the women talked and talked.

Carol usually had to watch the two youngest kids, but Leanne was a fun girl to be with and as chatty as her mother. The two girls would play house and fit the babies into their games. The boys played rowdy games like 'Kick the Can', soccer and softball workup. The evenings passed quickly and everyone had a good time.

Glady didn't let up complaining about the poor condition of the awful old house she lived in including to Arlene. Arlene told Glady she was welcome at her house and never asked to go to Glady's house. Arlene was a very tidy housekeeper with everything clean and neat and Glady loved going over there to get away from her own mess.

The two women kept the kids outside of the house most of the time they were together. At suppertime they would dole food out the door to the kids. Two pounds of baloney, a loaf of bread, a bag of potato chips and a pitcher of Kool Aid with a couple of ice cubes in it.

"Here's your supper, now get out of here and let us talk in peace!" The two mothers would say, handing food out the door to one of the older kids. The kids didn't mind much though, they loved going over to the Johnston's every day and playing until past dark. Their mother didn't even yell at them much over here.

Once in awhile, one of the kids would slip into the house for one thing or another where the two women were involved in a deep discussion. They had long since wolfed down the food put outside for them and the little face would gaze up in wonderment at the table where the women were sitting.

Huge sandwiches piled high with luncheon meats, tomatoes, and mayonnaise on bread cut diagonal, with cheese showing out the sides. The air would be filled with the scent of chocolate from a package of cookies laying there open with some missing. A good kind of cookies, dipped in chocolate with marshmallow in the middle. There would usually be large glasses filled with Pepsi, which was still fizzing around the ice cubes.

"Mama, can I have a bite of your sandwich?" a younger kid might say.

"Goddamned it!" Glady would yell as Arlene looked on laughingly. "You had your supper. It's not my fault you ate it so damned fast that you couldn't taste it. If I gave you a bite, all those other little sonsabitches would be in here whinin' for a bite, and I wouldn't have any food left. Now get out of here, or you won't get any cookies."

After while, if no one else interrupted the mothers, a bag of cheap sandwich cookies would be handed out the door for all eleven kids to divide up among themselves.

"I see by your outfit that you are a cowboy," Arlene sang while leering at the front of George's pants. He had come in the house for a drink of water one particularly hot night. Glady and Arlene had been listening to the radio while they ate their sandwiches in peace. They had just heard a Marty Robbins ballad, and had been humming the tune when George came in. Glady laughed uproariously at Arlene's joke. George just got a drink and started back out the door.

George was getting accustomed to the coarse atmosphere these days when Glady and Arlene were together. In fact, George knew his mother and Arlene were sometimes repeating the punch lines to dirty jokes they must have been telling each other. He knew they were dirty joke punch lines because he sometimes had heard the whole joke at school. The other kids seemed to have no idea what the women were giggling about. They would try to ignore them if they could, but it didn't stop the mothers from teasing them.

"Woo, woo, must be a Jergen's lotion machine," Arlene said and Glady snorted when Alfred came in to get a drink of water and went back out without comment.

Carol spied a couple of books on the table one evening when she had come in for water. She saw cartoon naked women on the front cover of the top book. She figured that Glady and Arlene must be reading dirty jokes and as she was going back out to play, she heard her mother's leering voice.

"I see by your outfits that you are a cow-girl," Glady called after her, pulling out two points on the chest of her own dress. Arlene really cackled at that one.

In the middle of August, Hank told Glady that he had found another house to live in. She had complained for years about the old farmhouse and Hank had finally taken action. He hoped a move would improve Glady's attitude. He had found a house with cold running water that was vacant now and three miles away there was a bigger house owned by the same man. The bigger house was currently occupied but it would be vacant in less than a year and it had hot and cold running water and an indoor toilet. School was starting and Hank didn't want the kids to change schools in the middle of the term so he thought they should move by fall. He reasoned that it would be better to move twice in one year than to listen to Glady complain for even a few more months.

"Goddamnit Hank. What in the hell are you thinkin'? I don't want to move now and then move again in less than a year!" Glady stormed when she realized that she would actually have to leave her friend, Arlene.

"Listen," Hank said. "You've done nothing but complain since the day we moved in here. You're always goin' on about the fire hazard and the rats. What in the hell are you talkin' about now? This house is available, and I've already spoken for it. It's only five miles into Milton where the kids will go to school and fifteen miles to Rockwell. If you don't want to go now, I'll never discuss moving again!"

Glady weighed the loss of the friendship to never moving again. She hadn't given Hank a moment's peace since they had moved here to this godforsaken, shit hole of a house. She knew that stubborn son-of-a-bitch would live up to his word and never listen to her complain again. There were advantages to the house and the area he was talking about moving to, even though it was too far to see much of Arlene.

"Well, I've hated to tell you something too," Arlene said when Glady broke the news. "We're moving too. This country life ain't for me and we are moving in to Seneca as soon as we can find a place there."

Glady was thrilled that she had not pressed the issue with Hank. She and Arlene blubbered together and vowed to stay in touch.

CHAPTER NINETEEN

Hank and Glady moved just before school started. The cold running water in the house made a big difference in terms of convenience. Dirty dishes didn't stack up quite so high since they could be rinsed under running water after meals. Carol was now assigned to do dishes and did them most evenings without too much complaint. The house had small rooms though and the family never did unpack some of their belongings since they were going to be moving to the bigger house soon.

The house was situated right on the blacktop road with a small yard that wasn't fenced. Glady hated the cramped quarters and worried about sending little kids outside to play. She had to watch them like a hawk so they wouldn't go out on the road and get run over. It was a cold windy winter; so nasty out that the little kids really weren't able to be out much anyway.

When spring came, Hank heard that the renters had given notice early at the bigger house and would they be out in mid April. The kid's school wouldn't be affected by the move this time, since the same school bus would pick up the kids, just further out. They were free to move as soon as the house was vacant.

Over a weekend in mid April, the family moved again. The big house was situated off a little traveled gravel road with a long driveway. They still burned wood for heat so Hank and the boys had to go out and get a load to see them through the chill of spring. There was quite a bit of cleanup to do at the house after the last tenants, but the landlord agreed to pay for new wall paint.

Glady was thrilled with the hot and cold running water. She liked the fact that the house had an indoor toilet so she go and then flush and diapers could be rinsed out before being placed in the bucket.

Glady also liked the rock exterior of the house. After enduring the old weather-beaten wood house in the field for four years, this one looked great outside without any maintenance. Glady picked out fashionable colors to paint her walls. The house had a large bedroom downstairs and two bedrooms upstairs.

Carol and Vera would have the smaller bedroom upstairs, and all the boys would be in the large one. Glady and the youngest child would take the downstairs bedroom. Hank informed Glady that he was putting his bunk in the large old pantry area off the back of the kitchen. He reasoned that for years he had been sleeping on the couch and this way he could sleep in a normal bed and still and not wake any one up when he got home in the night.

"You old son-of-a-bitch," thought Glady to herself. "I know what you're thinkin'. But it's too damned late." Glady had not told Hank that she had missed her period for the second month in a row.

***

"I'm just too tired to ice the cake." Glady told Carol. "I baked it while you were at school and I just can't do anymore." Glady had given birth to another baby girl five months earlier. Carol had been thrilled to have another sister and even more thrilled when Glady told her she could pick the new baby's name. Carol had chosen the name Tammy Ray and she adored both of her little sisters. Carol loved dressing Tammy and Vera and playing with them like they were dolls.

Carol had just gotten off the bus and dashed into the mess they called home. Today was little Vera's birthday and she had been asleep when Carol had gone off to school that morning. Carol was anxious to see her and wish her happy birthday. Last time they went to town, Carol had helped Glady pick out little Vera's birthday present. It was a little fuzzy stuffed chick and it was wrapped up waiting for the cake and happy birthday song from her brothers and sisters.

"Use that powdered sugar in the cabinet to make the icing. Be careful though, it's been open for a while and you'll hafta use a spoon to mash out the lumps before you add any milk. And, only use a little bit of milk at a time 'cause that's all the powdered sugar we got. You'll make it too thin if you don't watch out. Oh, and don't forget to put in about a teaspoon of vanilla for flavor." Glady quickly muttered off the orders to Carol then she went into her bedroom and slammed the door.

Anxious to make a nice icing, Carol tried to follow all the instructions she'd been given. She got out the powdered sugar and poured it into a mixing bowl. The powdered sugar was lumpy, but the dry lumps mashed out fairly easily with a fork and spoon. Carol used a teaspoon and carefully measured the vanilla and then she added what she guessed to be a small amount of milk.

"Uh-oh, this is kind of thin," Carol noted immediately as she stirred the mixture. "Maybe it will get thicker if I stir it faster."

As Carol stirred, the mixture stayed the same. She tried a dab of it on the cake and felt sickened when the mixture soaked right into the cake.

"Oh, no!" Carol whispered as she turned the empty box up over the thin mixture and whacked the bottom. Only a few wisps of powdered sugar were left in the box.

"Now what?" she wondered. She was stuck with a bowl of sticky thin sweet stuff that soaked right into the cake.

Carol hopefully opened the cupboard door to see, if maybe, there was another box of powdered sugar that Glady had missed. Carol's face began to flush when she realized there was nothing up there, then she spied the granulated sugar canister on the back counter top.

"Maybe that'll work," she hoped as she grabbed the canister and poured in some sugar. As she stirred it in, it seemed a little thicker so she tried some more.

"I think it's getting better." Carol continued stirring small amounts of granulated sugar into the mix until it began to look dark and grainy. She dabbed a spoonful of the mixture onto the middle of the first layer and spread it out.

"At least it's not soaking in to the cake anymore," Carol thought as she spread the layer. When she picked up the top layer to place on the first layer, a large corner broke off. In mounting anguish Carol tried to use the grainy icing to make the broken corner stick back on, but it kept sliding away from the cake. She hurried and used up the messy icing to cover the top and sides of the cake, then quickly stuck the whole thing in the freezer. She thought a few minutes in there might help set it up and it would harden.

After about ten minutes Carol dared to look at the cake. It looked awful with the broken piece sagging off to one side. She stuck the store bought colored sugar pieces spelling out 'Happy Birthday' on the top of the ugly and they slipped and slid with the unevenness of the cake.

Carol's mind raced as she remembered they had some toothpicks in a drawer somewhere. She hoped she could find those and they might close the big crack and hole on the corner. She looked sadly upon the sorry sight.

Then terror seized her as she heard Glady's bedroom door being pushed open. Suddenly Glady was upon her. She grabbed Carol by the hair, yanking her head back and pulling hard. She used the other hand to slap Carol's face while she held on to her with the other.

"You goddamned worthless slut!" Glady screamed as she continued to slap. "What in the hell have you done to my cake? Can't you do anything right? I told you not to put too much milk in there. Don't you listen to anything? What in the hell kind of sloppin' mess have you made?"

She slapped Carol once more, let go of her hair and shoved her toward the door.

"Get the hell out of my sight you worthless blond haired hussy." Glady screamed as Carol slunk quickly out the door with her head hurting and her face stinging. Most of all she felt humiliated and sorry that she had ruined her little sister's birthday cake.

"Come in and sing for the birthday girl," Glady sang merrily out the door to the kids. Carol had always been amazed at how quickly Glady's temper would blow over and how she would act like nothing bad had ever happened. Glady would always brag to the kids.

"I've got enough wild Indian blood in me that I lose my temper real quick. I get over it right away though. It just blows away like the wind. In a few minutes, I've fergot all about whatever happened."

Glady never broke or threw things in a fit of anger, she would lash out at whoever was in her path, cussing and hitting with whatever she could get her hands on. If there were no fire shovel, broom handle or plastic belt within easy reach, she would use her hands and fists. The problem with using her hands and fists was that she usually hurt herself and then they would get beat twice as hard.

The kids trooped into the house at Glady's bidding for the birthday party. Carol, who had been dreading this part, marveled to see a beautiful two-layer cake covered with smooth, snow-white icing. The candy letters spelled out 'Happy Birthday' in an arc up over the cake. The candles were lit and Glady led them in the 'Happy Birthday' song. As little Vera delightedly opened the package revealing her new fuzzy chick, Carol finally looked questioningly up at Glady.

"Wh-where did you get the new cake?" Carol asked her mother haltingly.

"Oh, I just scraped off that shitty mess you made of everything and made boiled seven-minute icing. Didn't it turn out good?"

No one mentioned that if she had the energy to whip up boiled icing she could have easily made up the powdered sugar icing in the first place.

***

Glady always complained about suffering from the summer heat. The humidity was always high and all the breezes died down soon after the sun came up. At night she would pass by each window searching for a breath of air to lay in. She would stick her pillow up against the open window screen waiting for any air movement and hope the window wouldn't come down on her neck.

In the hottest part of the year, Glady let the kids take their beds outside and set them up. It got them out of the house and it was almost like camping out for the kids. They would just move the beds over to the shade in the daytime and back out under the stars at night.

During those hot humid days and living way out in the country, Glady took to wearing just a white nylon slip around the house. She had two slips and she would wear the oldest one day and night, until it was grimy and stained and save the newer one to wear under her dress when she went any place.

Glady never had worn undergarments around the house, winter or summer, saying that panties binded her legs, and that 'titty-holders' chafed her so bad under the arms. She would wear these undergarments to town but she would take them off as soon as she came in the door at home.

Glady was heavy and her stomach was pendulous from being stretched out so many times in pregnancy. The old slip usually had a pin holding at least one strap, making it hike up short in the front. It stretched down tight over her stomach and ended quite a ways above her knees. Glady sure wasn't hiding much in that garb.

It was the days just before the Wilkey's had a television set, so most times the boys were off outside playing somewhere away from the house by the time Glady got up in the summer. She would be sitting on the couch by the time they came in. When she needed to get up from the couch, she would slide forward and use her hands to push off the seat.

One hot afternoon Carol was sitting in a chair reading a novel she'd checked out from the summer library and Glady was on the couch as usual. Several of the boys came into the house for a drink of water, hot and tired from play. Then they came in and flopped down, some on the couch and some of them were laying on the floor.

"Well if you hot brats are going to flop on the couch I am going somewhere else," Glady said half in jest, but suddenly she screamed her next sentence.

"You goddamned son-of-a-bitch! You filthy dirty little bastard!"

Startled, Carol and some of the boys looked up to see what had set their mother off.

"You goddamned little cocksucker! Don't you ever look at me again when I'm getting' up off this couch! It's so goddamned hot you know I can't stand to wear any clothes. I'm not having any little son-of-a-bitch sneaking a look up my slip that way!"

For years when Glady even thought one of the boys might be looking at her exposed crotch, she would scream the infamous phrase, she had yelled at Alfred that day,

"Don't you dare look at me, you goddamned pussy-gawker."

***

"Gourds, gourds!" a voice called from up the road. The boys ran out to the road as Carol rode up on George's bicycle. She had been riding out on the gravel road and ran across some huge gourds growing wild in the ditch. She stopped and picked a few but she couldn't manage too many and still control the bicycle safely. She wanted some more gourds to try make birdhouses like she saw in a magazine one time. Hoping some of the boys would walk back and help her carry some more gourds home, she had called out to them. Three of the boys came dashing up to Carol, but their faces fell when they only saw the inedible gourds.

"Oh, gourds," they said disappointedly. "We thought you had somethin' good to eat and said 'gorge'."

The boys were hungry most all the time. They really never got full except on Thanksgiving and then for two weeks during the summer when the field corn ripened.

Every year Glady would tell the kids she had asked one farmer or another if she and her kids could get some corn out of their field. Glady had asked the first year but after that she just figured with acres and acres of corn the farmer wouldn't miss any.

As soon as the corn tassels began to turn brown and the milky fluid came out of a punctured kernel, Glady would take the kids to raid the nearby cornfields after Hank left for work. They would pick all the corn they could carry in a few minutes time and then pile back in the car with armloads of ripe field corn.

Back at home, Glady put a washtub of water on the stove and the kids shucked the corn. Glady dropped the ears one at a time into water when it boiled. When the corn was done, Glady and the kids would load it with margarine and salt and eat until they were so full they would almost pop.

Every night for days in a row, there were ears and ears of corn. They were all sick of corn by the time it got too tough to eat, but the next year the boys couldn't wait to be truly full to the brim.

***

"I'm starvin'. I wish we had somethin' good ta eat, but we don't have anything good here at home," Glady said to Carol one a summer morning. "Hey, I know! Let's go up and visit ole Maizey. She'll kill a chicken and fry it up for us."

Glady and Carol got in the car and drove half a mile up the road to Maizey's house, leaving the hungry boys at home to fend for themselves and watch the younger kids. Maizey was a good old gal who liked having Glady and Carol come to visit since she was stuck with her kids and no car. Maizey was married to a hired farm hand and had three little kids herself. Glady felt sorry for her, remembering her younger days.

"Sure, I'll cook up a chicken for you Glady. Roy will be home in the middle of the afternoon starving and he'll eat up anything that's leftover then."

Carol watched Maizey's three little girls while Maizey killed and cleaned the chicken. Glady kept Maizey company talking about this and that watching her work.

Maizey only had two kids when the Wilkeys' had moved in to the rock house down the road, but she'd been early pregnant at the time. Later in the pregnancy, she got so big and then got sick and her blood pressure went up and the doctor made her stay in bed the last month. Carol had gone up there quite a bit to help with the kids and Glady would come up to visit and help Maizey with her bed bath.

"My God!" Glady told Carol one day, "When I give Maizey her bath, she just opens up her legs and lets me wash her down there. I wouldn't let anyone see me like that in a million years. I guess I'm just modest, that's all."

When Maizey delivered twins girls, no one was very surprised except her husband, Roy, who was astounded. But when the little twins were only two months old, Maizey found one of them dead in her bassinet one morning.

"The doctor told Maizey it was a 'crib death'. I couldn't take anything like that." Glady told her kids. "I just couldn't! I would lose my mind. I shudder to think if any of you kids ever died or got hurt bad. I just couldn't take it."

Glady and was waiting for the chicken to get done. It smelled so good. When Maizey finally put the platter on the table, she, Glady, Carol gorged on fried chicken and ate bread and butter with it. After they had eaten their fill and talked themselves out, Glady and Carol went out to the car.

"Well, that was sure good!" Carol said looking over at her mother.

"Well," Glady said snidely, "it would have been a lot better if she hadn't put so much of that damned black pepper on it. My God, I wouldn't have that crap in my house!"

CHAPTER TWENTY

"Chunks!" George called out as soon as he got off the bus, first to call his favorite again. He liked it when he remembered to call out first. The boys had the chore of bringing the wood that was used to heat the house. It had to be brought in from the woodpile and onto the porch. They had to bring in little wood, kindling and chunks every evening from early fall to late spring.

Whoever got stuck carrying little wood and kindling had to make many trips from the woodpile to the porch. George knew that half the time, when you bent over to pick up more wood, some of the load you were already holding fell back onto the woodpile. It was even worse when the wood would fall out of your arms half way up to the porch.

Chunks were easiest because you picked them up one at time and made a quick trip to the porch. Only five quick trips, and then you were done with the chore. George would tell the younger boys they were too weak to carry the big chunks anyway, as he rushed past them. He would hurry to be finished by the time they were just beginning, so he could relax and tease them while they worked.

One time Glady saw George rushing in with one chunk of wood that he quickly placed on the porch.

"What kind of piddlin' load is that?" she asked him.

"Mom, it's a big chunk of wood. You can only carry one chunk at a time," George explained. "That's why I like chunks, there're heavy but you can still get done quicker."

A few days later, George had forgotten to call 'chunks' quickly enough and got stuck carrying little wood. At least he didn't get stuck with kindling. Knowing his mother was in the house, George remembered her comment about the 'piddlin load' and he was determined to carry a big load.

George took his time selecting each piece of small wood so it would lay against the rest of the load in such a way that he wouldn't lose any of it. He had a huge stack of wood in his arms and he was hoping his mother was watching. Staggering under the load, while taking care not to dump the whole thing, George eased up the steps and through the door, onto the porch. Seeing

Glady watching out the kitchen window, he proudly started to deposit the load he had managed.

"What the hell is that?" Glady called out the window. "A goddamned lazy man's load? Carry so much you don't have to make another trip?"

George thought about this and wondered, where that elusive fine line was between a piddlin' load and a lazy man's load.

***

"Well, you'll need to be careful now!" Glady teased Carol. Carol had just come out of the bathroom and reported privately to her mother that she had finally started her periods. Carol had found out by accident almost ten years ago about girls menstruating. Long ago, she had been talking to her mother who was lying on the bed. When Glady had stood up suddenly, to Carol's horror, dark red blood ran down Gladys legs.

"Oh no, blood!" the four year old had screamed, "I'll go get the boys!"

"No, no Carol. It's okay. Come here and I'll tell you somethin' that's a secret between us girls. When girls get older they have to bleed like this every month. Its just part of being a woman. Some day when you are a lot older, you will bleed like this too. It doesn't hurt; we just hafta wear these pads for a few days, and then the bleeding goes away.

"When mama was a girl, we didn't even have these pads, we had rags and we had to wash them out all the time. So I don't mind much now when I get a period. They're called Kotex and we use them when we 'ministrate'."

Carol and Glady had shared the secret. Kotex was a secret word between them. Carol knew the boys didn't know about 'ministrating' and sometimes Glady would ask her quietly to bring her a Kotex.

Carol had known about periods and pads for years by the time they showed a little education film to the girls at school one day when she was twelve. Carol watched the little cartoon in fascination as it showed the little egg coming out of the ovary, down the tube and landing on a reddish lining. Then the little cartoon lining and egg and all flowed on out of the cartoon uterus. Of course she had known about the bleeding for years but it was so interesting to watch the whole cycle on the screen.

"What do you mean, be careful?" Carol asked, puzzled.

"Well, now you can get pregnant!" Glady exclaimed.

"Do you mean I couldn't get pregnant before this happened?" Carol inquired, puzzlement on her face.

"Well no, silly!" Glady admonished. "Don't you know where babies come from?"

Carol was rather embarrassed as she replied,

"You've told me that before."

"Where do they come from?" Glady asked in her know-it-all tone of voice.

"They come out of the woman's stomach and down and out through, ya know, that gate, in her pee pee. I remember!"

Glady snorted.

"Well, how do they get up there?"

"From an egg and seed that gets in there." Carol retorted, remembering the film from school.

"Well, how does the seed get up there in the first place?" Glady pushed.

Carol's mind began to reel as she thought about the implication of what Glady was telling her.

"Oh my God! Oh my God! No-oo!" Carol moaned as she made a connection with that horror story her mother had told her long ago. She asked in a sickened repulsed tone,

"Do you mean you have to go to see a nasty man?"

When George was almost eighteen the Wilkeys' finally moved close to town. The kids didn't have to ride the school bus any more because they were within a few blocks of school. There were no sidewalks out this far, and they lived at the edge of town, not in it. Their short driveway turned off the blacktop road that ran past their house. Across the road to the north of their house, was fenced pastureland that went on for miles.

To get home from school, the kids would go out the side door of the school, cut across the edge of the baseball field and then through the fence onto the blacktop. They would walk down a long hill and back up the other side and into their driveway. All in all it was a little over half mile from the baseball field to the driveway. If you went on past the house to the east, you came to a Y in the road. The south fork took you about a mile over to the highway that went on in to Rockwell, and north ran out past the places they used to live when they had first moved to Milton. You'd have to go almost thirty miles north before you came to the next little town in that direction.

Glady had kept after Hank for several years until he found this house closer to town. When they had moved here to the edge of Milton, Glady was ecstatic to be near civilization. She announced that she could save a lot of money because the school kids could now come home for lunch. They could eat cheap and help her tidy up before going back to school for the afternoon.

For the first few days of the school year Glady bustled around the kitchen fixing lunches. She made macaroni and cheese one day and tuna sandwiches the next. After a few days of this, Glady proclaimed that she was fixing lunch in shifts and had no time for anything else. What with having kids in three different grade levels all getting out for lunch at different times, it was taking up her the whole day. When the kids came home after school, she claimed to be so worn out from fixing lunches; she never made any effort to fix any supper.

After a short two weeks Glady made her final proclamation on the school lunch topic using her authority-accountant tone of voice.

"It's so much cheaper to eat the school lunches in the cafeteria."

The kids didn't mind at all since their home lunches the past few days had bologna and bread that they had fixed for themselves. Of course, when the kids bought school lunches in the cafeteria again, their mother still didn't fix any supper.

Over time in the house close to town Glady spent less and less time at home. She took off and went places whenever she pleased. Carol didn't get to hang out in town after school any more than she had when she had to catch the school bus though. Glady expected her to come home as soon as school let out to stay with the little kids. Glady always said,

"No daughter of mine will walk the streets. Milton is just full of gossipin' old hags. Some of those sluts from the high school stay out half the night and their mothers just let them get away with it."

Glady had been asked to be one of the sponsors for the teenage dance this week. Sometimes the regular sponsors couldn't come down and Glady enjoyed being a substitute. She would sit at the front table with the other adult sponsor and talk and watch the kids dance. The dance was held in the basement of the Community House in Milton. Nothing fancy, just some folding chairs around the wall, a small table for the sponsors and the record player in the corner. The kids would dance to records, drink pop and talk for a couple of hours on the first Saturday night each month.

It was cold and windy and snow was supposed to blow in before morning. Taking off her coat, Glady sat down in the sponsor chair. Like most teenage dances in Milton, more girls showed up than boys. Couples who were going steady were always present since there was no place else to go. The girls would mostly bebop with each other ignoring the few square, younger boys who did show up. Then everyone would all have to sit there and watch the few couples move to the slow song they had requested.

Tonight there were only eight single girls here and two couples. After an hour or so things were starting to drag with such a miserable turnout. Suddenly the door opened and Suzy Harris came dashing in. Her face was flushed and she told everyone that that her mom had agreed to drive some kids over to Rockwell to the movies. She told them all that 'Jailhouse Rock' was on over there!

Suzie told everyone she was afraid that her mom would change her mind unless she could get a carload of kids. She really talked up the fun they could all have going over to see Elvis. Suzie's pleading made Glady upset. The whole dance was about to be ruined! Everyone would either go to the show, or leave from boredom. Glady wanted her social evening out to last longer. Damn that Suzie.

Carol told Suzie she really wanted to go. It was already so boring here at the dance and if a lot of the girls left to go to the show, there wouldn't be anything to do but sit watch the couples dance.

Carol came over to plead with Glady.

"No, Carol! Absolutely not! There's a storm comin' in. Anything could happen out there on that highway. No kid of mine is goin' out in weather like that."

"Please Mom. Please, I really want to see the show. It's Jailhouse Rock!"

"Carol, you are not going. I'm not gonna let you risk your life in this weather for a hip-swiveling fool like that!"

Glady had watched Elvis Presley on television one time to see what was causing all the commotion among the teen-agers.

"Those big city girls, watching his hips gyratin' around. They're all screamin' and excited about what he's suggestin'. They know!"

CHAPTER TWENTY-ONE

Glady ached. How long had it been? How long would it be? She could last about a month without a climax, but then she just had to have another one soon or she would ache. The bastard she was seeing had told her he maybe could get away again soon. She had waited Wednesday nights at the sewing machine for weeks now watching for him. The clock read quarter past eight and it was getting dark. It looked like he wasn't able to get away again. If he wasn't here by eight, the bastard usually didn't show up at all.

They'd had a system all worked out for the past year. Glady would wait by the window at the sewing machine every Wednesday evening, sewing or at least pretending to. If he could get away that week, he would come by on the blacktop road and pump the brake lights twice. That was their signal for her to come out and follow him. He would drive out the desolate stretch to the north until he was sure no one was following except Glady, then he would stop and they would decide where she should leave her car.

Glady finally gave up and put down the dress material she had been pretending to work on. She used her most tired-worn-out tone of voice to announce,

"My back is so damned tired from all this sewin'. I just hafta' go to bed early, I can't do anymore."

Glady figured she would just have to wait another week. Shit, last week had been so long, and next week would seem twice as bad. Just as Glady started to turn away from the window, she saw a car coming slowly down the hill, but she didn't dare hope. Was it his car? It looked like it might be after all. Yes, yes, her hopes began to soar. And there he was, going past the window. There they were, those fifty-eight Ford brake lights, so distinctive, so bright.

"You better pump them twice you bastard!" Glady muttered. "I need it tonight."

"Oh my God!" Glady turned her voice up dramatically.

Rousing from their regular Wednesday night television programs some of the kids wondered if they should be alarmed by

145

their mother's tone. Maybe she had run the sewing machine over her finger or something.

"What is it, mom? What's the matter?"

"Oh, I just remembered that I'm supposed to pick up Doris Strum and take her out to spend the night with her mother. I was supposed to be there at eight o'clock and here it is twenty after." Glady went on to elaborate on the lie. "You know her mother has been sick and she still isn't very good."

Glady quickly dialed a number on the phone while secretly holding the button down. "Yeah, Doris. Yeah sorry, I forgot, I was so busy sewing I didn't watch the time. Yeah, I'm on my way, I'll be there in just a minute." Glady quickly replaced the receiver and hurried out of the house, continuing the charade.

When the commercial was over and the program was back on the kids turned their eyes back to the screen as their mother rushed out the door without a backward glance. They never questioned why Doris Strum hadn't called there if Glady was so late picking her up.

Glady didn't hear from her good friend Arlene for quite sometime after they had parted that summer when Arlene moved to Seneca and Glady to Milton. However, one day Arlene's husband happened to run into Hank at work. He wrung Hank's hand and told him now he'd be off the hook because Arlene had nagged him for a long time now to find out Glady's address or phone number.

Glady and Arlene had sent each other Christmas cards and occasional letters since that time. Arlene happily reported to Glady that she had gotten a beauty operator's license and that she had a job in a salon in Seneca. She also revealed that her boys were in some trouble with the law. Glady told her they should move back out to the country.

One day after that Arlene called Glady with really good news. They had taken Glady's advice and agreed to move away Seneca to see if the boys straightened up before they got in serious trouble. They would be moving to a rented house near Milton!

Glady and Arlene immediately resumed their close relationship. Arlene set up a beauty shop in her home though, so Glady couldn't go over there every day like the old days. They got together often in the evenings and Arlene liked to fix Glady's thick dark hair. She would save leftover permanent solution from several customers to use on Glady's hair. She warned Glady that she could get into trouble for doing this, and asked that she never to tell anyone. Glady liked having secrets with Arlene.

When the two got together they were even more bawdy and raunchy than ever. It wasn't long before Glady confided in Arlene about the affair with Bud. Arlene would tease Glady about the size of Bud and ask if Bud was any 'gooood', drawing it out like that. Every once in awhile, they bought some apple wine and sipped that while they sat and talked and Arlene smoked.

Both Glady and Arlene's kids became disgusted with their mothers' antics and learned to not respond any more to their foolishness. Their mothers' relationship caused the kids to spend a lot of time together as well. Weekend days and most evenings they were at each other's homes and back and forth. Sometimes they didn't even know where their mothers were; they just knew that they'd better not let any of the little kids get hurt.

CHAPTER TWENTY-TWO

Glady hated the old son-of-a-bitch. She had been married to him a long, long time and she still dreamed of leaving him. She didn't know what she could do though; she still had all those kids to think about. There was no other future evident to her except with him. Hank had worked second shift at Lin-Aero for years now, still too good to spend evenings at home. He would never change! No matter how much she yelled and screamed, he just sat there drinking his coffee, smoking a cigarette, not saying a word. Sometimes he wouldn't utter a word for days on end.

Glady knew Hank left for work before he had to everyday, always claiming he wanted to leave time for any trouble. He left at one-thirty and didn't have to punch in until three. She knew he hung around having coffee with his cronies before and after work. Then he'd come home almost twelve hours later, and since they'd moved in this house close to town, he was back to sleeping on the couch. He made the excuse that he didn't want to wake her or the baby. What the hell was she supposed to do? Sleep alone for years on end?

Glady loved living close to town. The kids walked to school and it was easier to get them out the door when they weren't constantly watching for the school bus. When they'd moved here to the outskirts of Milton, they told Glady that they didn't deliver mail that close to town. She immediately got a post office box number and had a built in excuse to go to town every day.

Now every weekday Glady would go into to town just after nine o'clock to get the mail. She would decide daily whether she would take the little girls with her or leave them home with the promise of candy. Hank was either up by then, or sleeping right there on the couch where they could see him. If they provided her with a good excuse to visit someone, Glady would dress them and take them along.

Glady went to the post office and grocery store every day and then she got to where she would go visit an old woman she referred to as 'Granny'. Granny lived in town and couldn't leave her house, so Glady befriended her and used her as a convenient excuse to stay away from home.

Glady would tell everyone that she was going to check on Granny since Granny hadn't been feeling well lately. Sometimes she would claim she had to go into the store to get so-and-so for Granny. Sometimes she would dress the little girls up and take them to town to see Granny.

Granny this and Granny that, no one could figure out how Glady had come to know Granny. They just knew she spent a lot of time doing things for her. Granny was so forgetful that she couldn't remember how she met Glady either. But, she thought Glady was the nicest person to take such an interest in her and spend so much time helping her out, and sometimes bringing those precious little girls in to visit.

The fact is that Granny was Bud's mother and Glady had to work things around so she could meet Granny and befriend her. No one ever questioned her motives so she and Bud had a neutral place to 'happen' to run into each other or leave messages for one other on a shelf up high over the stove.

One morning the Hank was on his third cup of coffee when Glady got back from town. He didn't eat that much any more. He'd always been a tall, thin, rawboned man, but he used to eat big, regular meals when he was farming. Nowadays he wouldn't eat a regular breakfast and packed a lunch for work. Glady thought he must stop off and get a big meal on the way home because he never fixed food when he got home from work. He just came home, unfolded his bedding, flopped down on the couch and slept in his boxers.

Today was no exception; there was no evidence that he had fixed anything to eat. There he was with a cigarette burning in the ashtray, cup of coffee in his hand and he just glared at her when she came in.

Glady thought he was just too good to even speak to her anymore. Using her soft-helpful-caring tone of voice she asked,

"Hank, do you want some breakfast today? I got some stuff at the store I could fix."

"No, I don't want anything," Hank muttered.

"Well I don't know why in the hell you even come home," Glady stormed. "You never eat here and you're gone all week, then all weekend you act like a goddamned old bear. You always sit there with one damned finger over your mouth and you never say anything. You only come in the house to drink coffee and smoke. You're always workin' on that damned car, or what ever else it is you do out there in the yard."

Hank usually just sat there and let the screeching slide over him. Then, when he was finished with his coffee and cigarette, he would just get up and escape into the peace and quiet of the garage. Today he was in no mood though; he stood up and stubbed out his cigarette, then dumped his unfinished coffee down the drain. He was sick and tired of it all and made a move toward the door.

"You goddamned son-of-a-bitch!" Glady screamed. "Don't you ever walk out on me when I'm talkin' to you."

Hank didn't say a word and moved to go around the table, trying to get out past the screeching banshee. Glady would not step aside, but got in his face and screamed louder, her high-pitched voice cracking under the strain.

"What the hell do you need me for you old son-of-a-bitch?"

Hank glared down into her eyes but she wouldn't budge. He took hold of her forearms and started to pull her to one side so he could pass and get out the door. While he was firm, he was not rough. He had never hit Glady in his whole life and had no intention to ever do such a thing.

Glady flung his hands away and screamed into his face,

"You goddamned old son-of-a-bitchin-bastard! I know you're just aching to hit me, so just go ahead and try it." Glady shoved herself up against him, hatefully spitting and screaming through her screeching mouth and rotting teeth.

Hank never knew what possessed him but he reached over and swiped at her. His fingertips caught Glady at about mid jaw bone and connected. Hank was horrified. He hadn't hit her very hard, but there it was. He had hit her. He went slack jawed, and wondered how he'd ever let her get to him like that. He had gone through similar circumstances at least a thousand times; probably more, and he'd never lost it like that.

Glady grabbed up the skillet, slopping grease over the sides.

"You fucking bastard!" she screamed as she raised the skillet. "You get the hell out of here. If you ever touch me again, I'll shoot you, you son-of-a-bitch."

Hank hurriedly left the house wondering how he could have let things get to this point. He came in a little later, bathed and dressed in his jeans and T-shirt and left for work without saying a word.

"That old son-of-a-bitch hit me!" Glady told Carol after school. Glady had already called her mother in Rockwell and told her as soon as Hank left to work. She told her mother and her daughter that she would make him pay for this.

When Glady got up the next morning, Hank was laying on the couch asleep like nothing had happened. Glady felt her jaw, as she opened and closed her mouth. There was no pain there. She went into the bathroom and looked in the medicine cabinet mirror. There were no marks.

"Goddamn him!" Glady thought. She went in to the dining room and looked closely in the mirror over the buffet. She couldn't see any marks in that light either. She opened the buffet drawer and pulled out a mirror she kept in there intending to check a side view.

As Glady pulled out the hand mirror from under some letters, the pink handle clinked against a bottle of blue Shaffer's' ink. An idea began to take shape in Glady's mind. She took the hand mirror and the blue ink back into the bathroom with her. She quietly closed the door and uncapped the ink. She took a piece of toilet paper and put the edge of it into the little well on the side of the bottle.

Glady thought she had better not over do it. She dabbed a small spot of the ink onto her jawbone with the blued toilet paper. She rubbed paper lightly over the spot where Hank's fingers had caught her the day before. Using a circular motion she rubbed an area about three inches long and wrapped the paper under her jaw a little ways down onto her neck.

Glady blended the line just so, and then examined her handiwork, using the hand mirror to get a side view. She liked the size of the work of art, but she thought it looked too light to be noticeable. She dipped the toilet paper again and re-darkened the whole area.

Glady let the ink dry and then took some liquid makeup out of the cabinet. She put some makeup on her face and carefully applied a thin coat over the ink smudge. She looked in the mirror and was satisfied. She had successfully made it look like she had tried valiantly to cover a horrible bruise with makeup. The old son-of-a-bitch would be sorry now.

When he got up later that morning, Glady told Hank that she had not gone to town to get mail. She said she didn't want anyone to see her. He looked at her face and saw the blueness under the makeup and his face filled with shame. Glady told Hank he would just have to pick up the mail on his way to work for a few days. Then, she advised him that her mother wanted to see him today. She told him she would be riding along with him to Rockwell so she could buy groceries over there where no one knew her.

"Now Hank," Opal said. "I know how hard Glady can be to live with, but you can't let this happen again. I've had to talk to my own sons about this kind of thing once in a while. If I won't let the sons hit the daughters-in-law, I surely can't let the sons-in-law hit the daughters either." Hank's eyes looked toward the floor and he told his mother-in-law how sorry he was. He said he didn't know how things got out of hand and that it would never happen again. He said no more, because there was nothing more to say.

Hank was ever so patient with Glady as she shopped for groceries in Rockwell that day. Then he took her home, unloaded and put away the groceries, and left for work. As soon as he left, Glady examined her facial art. She was satisfied that the son-of-a-bitch was acting so sorry. He had hardly said a word all day and slunk away after her mother had talked to him.

Glady left the ink on her face, carefully washing around it. It wore off in a few days and things went back to usual. Hank never noticed that the bruising didn't go into the usual greenish-yellow fading phase. In fact, he didn't even have the nerve to look at Glady again for quite awhile.

CHAPTER TWENTY-THREE

Carol wouldn't have minded seeing the movie twice. Sampson and Delilah was full of rich color and had good kissing scenes in it. Carol liked Victor Mature as Sampson and thought he was good in the part. He was strong, yet sincere and gentle with Delilah, who was played by Hedy LaMarr. She really liked the part where Hedy LaMarr said that the other woman, whose eyes were liquid brown, had cow eyes. Delilah had green eyes and men made her jewels to match them.

Carol also had green eyes. It was the only feature she had got from Glady though. Glady had dark brown hair and olive skin. Carol was blond and fair. Well she was fair when she was younger, but she was ashamed of her face now. Beginning about the time she was fourteen, she started getting flare-ups of acne, and now it was much worse.

Carol anxiously picked at the cysts constantly. She squeezed them as soon as possible hoping that they would heal and go away, but they only increased in number and severity. Glady screamed at her to leave her face alone. She constantly told Carol that she herself had some pimples when she was young, and if Carol would quit picking them, they would just go away.

"You used to have such beautiful skin when you were young. Now you've ruined it."

Carol had gotten a summer job washing dishes in a local café the summer before. She used some of the money to buy special skin care products. She followed the directions carefully and hoped her skin would clear. The new soap and Noxema didn't seem to help at all though. Sometimes Carol could forget her skin was so bad then she would pass by a mirror and see the ravages and feel ashamed all over again.

Carol left the darkened theater and peeked out to see if Glady was out there yet. Carol had relaxed as the movie credits started for the second time knowing that it would play about a half hour before Glady was scheduled to come pick her up.

Glady had let Carol off in downtown Rockwell right after noon and told her she could shop until the movie started. Carol was glad when the movie theater opened at a quarter 'til two since she'd long since spent the little bit of money Glady had given her.

Carol had enjoyed the show the first time through, not even looking at her watch. Glady was supposed to be back at four thirty, so Carol tried to relax and enjoy the first part of the show again. It was almost five thirty now and Glady still wasn't out there. Carol kept going out to the lobby to check every few minutes.

Going out to check frequently not only interrupted the story line, Carol was concerned that the people that worked there would see her coming and going and say something, maybe even ask her to leave.

It was getting late and Carol getting hungry for supper. Finally a little after five thirty Glady pulled up to the curb in front of the theater. Carol wasn't out there at the moment she drove up, but she came out the door a few seconds later when she finally spotted her mother's car and dashed over and got in.

"You scared me to death when I drove up and you weren't here," Glady wailed. "I didn't know what could have happened to you."

Carol pointed out that Glady was over an hour late.

"I rushed here as quick as I could Carol. My watch stopped and I lost track of the time." Glady huffed.

Glady assumed that Hank wouldn't question where she had been all day if Carol was along. She had used the unsuspecting Carol several times to devise a cover to spend the day with Bud on weekends when Hank was home.

Not that the old son-of-a-bitch gave a damn where she was anyway. But he would glare at her if she was gone all day without an excuse, leaving the kids to take care of themselves. She would tell Hank that Carol was invited to a party at some girl's house in town and that she was one of the chaperones. She would tell Hank that she and Carol had to go early to buy a present. How could he question that? Then Glady would tell Carol some other story, about how she was going to a reunion with her old friends or something. She would tell her not to say anything to her dad. Glady would tell Carol confidentially,

"The old bear just doesn't like it when women get together to gab. He never has understood that kind of thing. Just

154

tell him one of your girlfriend had a birthday party. He doesn't care, so he probably won't even ask anyway."

Then Glady took Carol into her confidence one day when she began to worry that she was going to get caught. Glady's car had been seen one to many Wednesday nights where she had left it on the road when she was out with Bud. She had been following him out for a while now and she thought it would look suspicious if someone saw her out in the country alone.

Bud had started bringing his fishing pole when he was meeting Glady. His wife hated fishing and she would never want to come along on the evenings he told her he was planning to fish after work. Before he learned better, Bud had made up the story he was going out to ride around, but then sometimes his wife would want to come along. Those nights he had hell to pay, because sometimes his wife wanted to ride out the blacktop road that happened to go right past the house where Glady waited for him at the window. He hoped he never had to brake for anything there in front of Glady's house because that was their signal.

Those nights his wife was along, he would speed on by the house and hope Glady wouldn't know it was him and follow. Glady always saw the unmistakable taillights and knew damned good and well that Bud was out on their night without her. It would take most of the time they had together the next time out to get Glady calmed down enough for Bud to get what he needed from her.

That was one thing though; Glady seemed to need it as much as he did. His wife always complained about him hurting her during intercourse until he gave up on her ever getting used to it. His wife seemed quite happy about not having sex anymore, but she wouldn't let him go anywhere alone, except fishing. He could get away with that since she hated it out there on the rivers with all the mosquitoes.

Sometimes Glady and Bud really went to the river and fished. After all, he couldn't go back empty-handed every night he claimed to be fishing after work. Once in awhile he was able get away on Saturday to fish. He would have time to meet Glady and still get over to the lake and catch some fish.

Recently, two different people had asked Glady about her '53 Bel Air parked out there on the country road. Before George went into the service, she could always say it must have been him out in her car. But everyone knew he was out on the East Coast in the Army now. Glady determined that it would be best for someone to bring her out and pick her up to keep from arousing suspicion. She picked her moment and one night she lured Carol into a conversation about life. Using her soft-confiding tone of voice, Glady said,

"I know you won't understand what I'm going to tell you, but you will some day. I am your mother, but I have needs just like anyone else. Your dad has never understood this. The old son-of-a-bitch had ignored me for years.

"He won't even talk to me any more, let alone anything else. He just glares at me all the time. Carol, I have told you about sex and you're getting older now, so try to understand. I hafta have a climax at least once a month. You dad knows this, and he doesn't even care.

"He married me because he needed a mother, not a wife. He's never liked having intercourse. I'd have left him long ago, but I had all you kids to think about."

Glady went on to tell Carol stories about Hank and how he acted in bed.

"I know you don't understand this, but when I reach over and take a hold of his privates, he just acts like I'm poison anymore."

Glady told the graphic story of how Hank told her to let go of his peter that night as an example of his behavior. Carol listened but she didn't know how to respond so Glady forged ahead.

"You remember that man that I thought was following me that time? The one that your dad asked the sheriff about. Well, when I found out he was old Granny's son, I wasn't afraid of him. One day when he was following me, I just drove out of town a little ways and pulled over and stopped by the road. I thought, 'by God, I'll just see what the hell he's up to'. I got out of my car and opened my hood.

"When he saw me he pulled over and stopped and asked if he could help. I asked him what the hell kind of help he thought I would need from him. Well anyway, I've been going out with him. We've almost been caught a couple of times and I need someone to take me out to meet him."

Carol still didn't say anything. What could she say; her mother was telling her she was going out with a man to have sex?

"Well goddamnit Carol! Say something. Are you listenin'? You'll understand this someday."

From that night on, Carol was involved. Glady would sit by the window and then call Carol out to the sewing machine if Bud went by and signaled. Glady would pretend she needed to go somewhere and Carol would be enlisted in the charade to cover for Glady. Hank wasn't home week day evenings, so she just had to cover up to the kids who didn't pay much attention to their mother's comings and goings anymore.

Carol would drive Glady out, go back home to watch the kids and then tell them she had go pick her mother again at what ever time Glady had told her to.

Glady told Carol all kinds of things on the way out and on the ride back home. She went on and on to her sixteen-year-old daughter about how most men could only come once or twice a day, but Bud would be ready again in a few minutes. She told how she and Arlene had met Bud and his brother in a motel several times.

She told her how Bud told her that his brother said, that Arlene had no modesty at all. She just stripped off her clothes and paraded around the room naked. Glady told Carol how she was just so modest she never took off her slip.

Glady told Carol that when she was pregnant with Shirley, she told Bud he was the father. She told how Bud had thrown four hundred dollars in her lap and told her to take the money and leave him alone. How she had refused the money even though she had bills to pay and was tempted to keep it.

Glady told Carol how she took baby Shirley out to see her 'daddy' and they how they would all go to a motel room and pretend to be a family. She said they always went to the same motel and told the manager that they liked to get away from their home to the air-conditioned comfort of the motel room.

A year went by and Glady was still telling Carol stories of life between herself and Bud and expected Carol to continue covering for her. Glady now took baby Gail and little Shirley out to see their 'daddy'. They all four went to the motel room now. She told Carol how proud Bud was of the girls and gave her money to buy them clothes.

One spring Glady bought fabric and sewed cute Easter suits for the two little girls and showed Bud the snapshots she took on Easter morning since he couldn't see 'his girls' on Sunday.

Glady never ceased to fill Carol in on details about her and Bud. Then Glady would lie to Hank right in front of Carol. Sometimes it seemed like Glady wasn't making it up at all, it was like she really believed what she was telling Hank.

CHAPTER TWENTY-FOUR

Glady felt gassy today. Why did she always suffer so with her bowels? She walked over to the buffet in the corner of the dining room. Leaning over the buffet seemed to make the perfect alignment for her colon. Her leaning stance would make the gas come down where it needed to be to get out. She would stand there, bent over just so, reading through a catalogue or magazine to distract herself. Then the gas would come.

The gas bubble ripped out of her loud and long.

"It feels so much better on the outside than it does on the inside," Glady remembered her older brother used to say, as she laughed to herself.

Glady didn't give a damn what her nosy little brats thought when she ripped gas while standing at the buffet. The boys would laugh and make fun of her sometimes though. Then one of them would try to get away with ripping one off in socially unacceptable places. Like in the living room while everyone was eating and watching television. If she scolded them about it, they would bring up the buffet.

"Well, you fart in the dining room all the time! You stand there and rip at the buffet."

"I've suffered all my life with my bowels! I have to get in a certain position to pass gas. It won't come out in the bathroom. You sonsabitches know that! If I hadn't had so goddamned many kids, I might not have this problem! And six of you were hardheaded boys! I could always tell when my labor started if I was having another hard headed boy because it hurt me so bad."

The boys would go back to watching television having heard this line too many times before. They knew it wasn't worth the effort to argue with Glady. She could win any shouting match. And for damned sure, they never got in a gas-ripping match with Glady. They knew damned well that she could blow them clear out of the water, to hell and gone. No contest.

The boys lay awake in their beds early one Saturday morning. They had just determined that after years and years of repeating it, their mother could actually yodel the word 'sonsabitches'. They had giggled about it a few weeks earlier and to confirm their collective suspicions, they had begun to listen carefully whenever Glady began to scream. They knew better than to get caught, but any of them who were out of her eyesight would carefully monitor the tone while their brothers got screeched at.

Yes, yes, there it was. The tone began low, rising on the 'a' and to a high crescendo, wavering at the end, making a yodeling sound like no one ever heard before or since.

"Sonsabitches! All I ever got out of life was a buncha goddamned kids and you sonsabitches would laugh and carry on if I was dead in my coffin in the living room." The boys who were not being directly scrutinized at the moment would giggle quietly and wonder if they would.

"Git downstairs and make my breakfast. Mom bought some bacon yesterday and I'm hungry." George said loudly across the room to his younger brother, Kayle. "Hurry up before Alfred gets up and goes down stairs and grabs the skillet to make his own breakfast. And don't you dare make 'choke bacon' either, like you did last time. I almost gagged on it! It was half raw. I want my bacon crisp. And don't burn it either."

The boys were used to cooking for themselves. During the week they fixed cold cereal and by Saturday they wanted something good to eat. Glady had told them years ago, that she would buy the food, but damned if she would stand there and cook it too.

She warned the boys not to eat it up from their dad in case he wanted to fix something for himself. The boys felt like they had been hungry most of their lives. Glady seemed to always be at the store buying food but there was never anything to eat. Even at school, the hot lunch was limited to one plateful.

"Oh shit!" Henry said to his brothers. "She wants to let out the family jellies for me to wear for the band concerts." All the boys howled with laughter at poor Henry.

Some of Glady's most famous traditions had to do with eighth grade graduation. She proclaimed early on that they would all get their first wristwatch for eighth grade graduation. Then without fail, she approached each child in turn, and fully convinced them that she could not afford a wristwatch that year for their graduation. She took the prospective graduate aside and used her sorrowful-confidential tone of voice to tell them the timeworn story. When the day of graduation arrived Glady would present a brand new watch to the amazed graduate.

The other graduation tradition was born out of necessity. When Alfred was in the eighth grade, money had been tighter than usual that spring. Glady was determined to have enough money to surprise him with the traditional wristwatch so she vowed to save money and have Alfred wear the same pants that George had worn three years earlier.

Alfred was much thinner and taller than George had been at that age, but she took up the waist and let out the legs of the pants. Once her two older boys had worn the same pants for graduation, Glady proclaimed that all her boys would wear the same pants for important school occasions and eighth grade graduation.

When the twins were ready to graduate from eighth grade, Glady had to give a little since they were both in the same ceremony. Glady sent Kayle to the podium in another pair of pants, but Dale was wearing the pants of tradition. She made up for it by sewing a tiny piece of the pants inside Kayle's cuff and making sure Kayle wore the traditional pants to the eighth grade party the night before graduation.

The pants hadn't cost much in the first place. Now they were getting so worn and limp that the older boys had dubbed them 'the family jellies'. Henry had worn the family jellies for his graduation from eighth grade and now Glady had deemed that the high school band concerts were important occasions. She wanted Henry to wear the jellies with his snappy, crisp band jacket.

Much to Henry's relief however Glady gave in and bought him a new pair of pants for his band uniform. She had a mounting concern that if he wore them too much they might wear clear out and be ruined beyond fixing before Billy Totten was able to carry on the tradition.

Sure enough, seven years after Henry's graduation, Billy Totten marched down the aisle in the family jellies. Glady proudly whispered loudly to all the people seated near her.

"All six of my boys have worn that exact same pair of pants to graduate eighth grade."

CHAPTER TWENTY-FIVE

"I jist get such a let-down feeling on Christmas morning!" Glady wailed one year as she was decorating the Christmas tree. "I go out and spend money buyin' presents and then work hard wrappin' everything up. Then you kids get up and open everything in five minutes and it's all over! I just wish there was somethin' I could do about it. I can't have my Christmas ruined year after year this way."

Glady gave it a lot of thought the next year. She read magazines and newspapers to get ideas. The night before Christmas came and Glady told the kids her plan to make herself feel better. A new Wilkey tradition was born.

"On Christmas morning from now on, I'll go into the living room and all of you kids will line up in the kitchen according to age. Littlest ones first, and up the line. You will come slowly into the front room single file and look under the tree to find your present from old Santy Claus. That way I can see your faces when you see what you got. Then we will all sit down and each one of you will unwrap your presents one at a time, starting with the littlest with the others looking on. I will get to see what you think of all your gifts, see if you're surprised, and I won't miss anything. I've spent so much time and energy over the years, and I'm tired of having my Christmases ruined. If anyone's going to ruin Christmas, it will be me!

For years the kids dutifully followed the tradition to the letter. As the family grew and the older kids got married and had kids of their own, Glady insisted that they everyone come home for Christmas morning.

She had written down the chronological list of all family members and insisted that the Wilkey tradition could not be broken. When the boys got engaged to be married, Glady would tell the bride-to-be about the traditions of the Wilkey family. More than once over the years the sons came to Christmas at Glady's without their wives. Glady would have a mouthful to say about the daughters-in-law who didn't respect family traditions.

Sure enough, some of the new families were broken before the tradition was ever broken. Sometimes the older kids would complain that they would rather be in their own homes watching football, instead of waiting for a bunch of kids to open presents. The idea that anyone would dare find something else to do on Christmas morning was just beyond Glady's tolerance. After all, they had Christmas Eve and Christmas night to make other plans!

"I don't give a damn! I never had anything but a buncha goddamned kids. Christmas is for kids and I'm gonna enjoy it! At least you get presents! I never got anything for most of my life, growin' up in the depression.

"I want to see everyone's face when they see what I got 'em."

The kids learned the pitfalls of having their mother scrutinize their faces individually as they opened gifts. Glady always got them what she thought they wanted, mostly based on what they looked at in the stores, or what she had overheard them mention in conversations. Too many times, Glady misread the signals and the kids ended up with something they hated. Glady could tell every time when someone was displeased. She would immediately begin to defend her choice of gifts for them.

"Well you loved it when you saw it in the store." Glady told Carol as her face fell before she could control it. Carol knew she had squealed about the fuzzy jumper in the window, but it was because of its awfulness! It looked like it was made out of a hairy blue blanket. She had looked at the price tag as soon as she went into the store and told Glady how much it cost. Glady assumed that Carol loved it and thought the price too high, so she bought it thinking Carol's face would really light up when she opened it Christmas morning. Carol was able to get out of the situation fairly well.

"Oh, I was just surprised that you would spend this much on me this year, Mom, that's all."

When Carol moved out of the state, Glady bawled her eyes out for several years when it came Carol's turn to open her presents and she wasn't even there.

CHAPTER TWENTY-SIX

"Take your brother, he can dance!" Glady said to Carol.

"I don't want to go with my brother!" Carol retorted.

"Well, it's the only way you'll get to go. You don't have any boyfriends, so you won't be able to go if you don't take him."

American Bandstand had paved the way for local television dance programs and Seneca was no exception. Every afternoon in the half hour time slot just before American Bandstand, Hi Fi Hop would air. Local kids would come into the studio, listen to a deejay and dance to popular hit records and have the chance to be on television. Groups could make reservations if they could meet the minimum number of couples. A group of kids from Milton had made arrangements with the show and had a date set. They were anxious to get enough kids to meet the minimum and Carol really wanted to go.

All the regulars from the community house teen-age dance were making plans to go over if they could find a date. The steady couples were signed up and a few more impromptu dates were quickly arranged from the group of girls and the few square boys who showed up for the local dance.

Most of the girls who danced with each other scrambled to find someone to take. The biggest problem was that if a boy knew how to dance, he would have been at the local dance in the first place. They searched the town over for any guy who could be taught to dance in time for the Seneca show.

Carol had been on television once. It was when she was young and square dancing for 4H. Her club had won a blue ribbon and they had been invited to dance on a local variety show in Seneca. This was different though, and she was dying to be part of the television teen dance. The Hi Fi Hop appearance was becoming the Milton social event of the year.

In the end, Carol decided that taking Alfred as a dance partner was better than missing such an important event. At least he was tall and fairly decent looking for a brother. No one watching television would know he was her brother anyway, unless they lived in Milton and then it didn't matter.

Then came the dreaded question from Glady,

"Carol, what are you going to wear to Hi Fi Hop?"

Carol had in mind to wear something similar to what all the other girls were planning to wear. Something like they saw girls wearing every day on the show. Flats, a cute skirt and a nice sweater. The studio had sent a letter to the group leader recommending wearing something colorful to show up well on black and white television. It further advised against very light colors and any clothing that was black or white because it did not look good on camera.

Carol knew she couldn't buy anything new to wear, but she had a brown tweed skirt that had a cute pleated area in the back that she thought would look good on television. She had a fairly new green sweater that would go good with the skirt. Glady had other ideas.

"Now, I am not gonna let you go over there to Seneca if you're gonna to wear some old everyday school clothes!" Glady flatly stated. "Show some respect and dress nice. You're gonna be on television."

Carol cringed and said,

"Mom, all the other girls are just going to wear nice school clothes!"

"If you go out that door, you'll be dressed nice."

When Carol left the house for Seneca to be on Hi Fi Hop, she had on a pale beige heavy brocade sheath dress her mother had borrowed with a long sleeved, black velvet bolero jacket over it. Tied around her neck was a pure white, fluffy, rabbit fur collar with two large white pom pom fur balls hanging on each end of the bow.

Alfred looked nice in a sport jacket and tie; he was dressed like the other boys. Carol felt like she should be going to the opera in this garb that Glady had determined was right for a television appearance. She knew better than to cross Glady at this point though. She couldn't risk a big temper blow-up and be forbidden to even go.

On the way to Seneca, some of the girls commented on how dressed up Carol was. Carol knew they weren't being complimentary when they pointed out the studio's recommendation of not wearing black or white on camera.

They arrived at the studio and got out of their cars and went into the building. Since it was a live telecast, the teens were given a brief training session. They were told that they were not only the show but also the advertising for the show. They were advised that they must never stand around and they had to dance every dance, smile, and show everyone watching what a good time they were having in the studio.

Then suddenly, the program started. The teens were awed at the way the emcee chattered brightly while he appeared to be looking directly at no one. He was looking into the camera, but from in the studio it looked strange for him to babbling away and with no one in front of him.

Carol kept her mind on showing everyone she was having fun while she was dancing every dance, fast and slow, with her brother. The floodlights were bright and hot, and after the first few minutes the rabbit fur collar began sticking to her neck. About halfway through the show the song was very fast and the velvet jacket started to stick in her armpits.

Carol didn't even think of taking the jacket or collar off though, the dress was low necked and sleeveless. She knew Glady would kill her if she exposed her bare arms to the whole television audience.

The half hour program rushed by quickly and was soon over, and they were clearing the studio. Carol, while grateful to get outdoors and cool off, was sad that the big event was over so quickly. There was a letdown feeling among the whole group on the long drive home to Milton. When Carol arrived back home Glady exclaimed,

"Oh Carol, you looked so nice on television. You were dressed so much nicer than all those other girls. They say a person looks heavier on television, but that outfit I picked looked so nice your arms and legs didn't look any heavier than usual."

***

"It says 'no diers' license!" Glady firmly stated in her legal-authoritarian tone of voice. "So what kind of a charge is that? Diers? The ticket doesn't say anything about driving!" Carol felt like dying of embarrassment as she listened to her mother argue with the judge. She had finally been caught driving without a license.

Glady had taught Carol to drive on country roads when she was fourteen and now at seventeen, she had been driving regularly for years. Usually she drove Glady around, and rarely took the car alone except when her mother sent her into Milton on a quick trip to the grocery store. Apparently, one of the town's older boys had heard that Carol was driving without a license and gossiped to the deputy sheriff. The deputy had stopped Carol one evening as she was coming home from the store alone with bread and milk.

Carol had been hoping for a long time now that her mother would consent and let her take the driving test. Glady always made excuses about their family car, saying that the brakes were bad, the muffler was loose or the tires were bald. It was always something even though she drove the car herself every day. Glady convinced Carol that they would give her a ticket over at the testing center if the car wasn't in perfect condition. Carol took her mother at her word and time had gone by with Glady making excuses. Here Carol was in trouble now, standing before the small town judge, mother at her side, and wishing that Glady would shut her mouth about the poor penmanship of the deputy and pay the fine.

The judge ignored Glady and read over the ticket and asked Carol if she had a driver's license.

"Ten dollar fine!" he barked and loudly rapped the gavel when he heard the negative reply.

Glady got up and tersely wrote a check for the ten dollars, muttering about how she had ten kids at home to feed and how the judge was robbing them all of food. Carol finally got Glady out of there and out to the car.

"That plumb wore me out Carol, drive me home."

Carol just stared at her mother.

Glady knew she would be stuck running all the little pissy errands if Carol didn't get her license. She asked a friend if she could borrow her car to take Carol over to Rockwell the next week. She took Albert at the same time so she wouldn't have to go through the same thing with him. Carol and Alfred both passed the driving test with flying colors and Carol drove home legally. She finally experienced the freedom of driving without worrying and constantly watching the rear view mirror for cops.

***

"Where in the hell have you been? I've been worried sick about you." Glady yelled at Carol as she walked in the door just before midnight.

"I was out riding around with Joe and Lewis," Carol said trying to push past her mother who was blocking her entry into the house.

"I've called everyone I knew that was over at the gym. No one knew where you were. They didn't say anything about you leaving with Joe or Lewis," Glady's voice raised several octaves in pitch.

"You called people?" Carol paused and asked in a horrified tone and then Glady grabbed her by the hair.

"You goddamned slut, how dare you question me! You knew good and well, I'd be worried sick. Where in the hell have you been?" Glady was holding Carol by the hair while pushing her against the refrigerator as she slapped her face. "You filthy whore, what have you been doing?"

"I told you what I was doing," Carol insisted in a subdued but angry voice, trying not to cry. "I left the gym a little after ten thirty when everyone else did. I just felt like riding around, that's all."

Carol was going through a separation anxiety though she could have never expressed this to her mother. For six years, she had been close to her classmates and the boys were more like brothers to her. She had never dated any of them and she was feeling an unidentified anxiousness that she may never see them again after high school graduation. She dreaded they would all leave town and she would be left behind in Milton with no identity except in her family.

"We rode around town the Joe dropped Lewis off clear out where he lives and we drove back to town. When we got back I told him to take me home. We only left the gym a little over an hour ago; I figured you'd be asleep."

"Don't you ever pull that on me again," Glady screamed and raised her arm and slapped Carol again. "Now get upstairs, out of my sight. Maybe now I can get some rest, you worthless bitch. I'll be so goddamned tired tomorrow, I won't be able to see straight"

Carol escaped up the stairway wondering what important things Glady had to do tomorrow that she would need to see straight anyway.

A few months later, Carol got her last hair pulling and slapping around from Glady. It was in the summer after she had graduated high school and she was a month past her eighteenth birthday. Carol stood for it, somehow knowing that she would never get out from under if she couldn't tolerate a little bit more. Pay now for freedom later. Not that Carol had it all worked out that way at the time. After all those years of living with Glady, she just knew when to shut up, stand still and take it. It finally paid off.

Glady had been anxious and occupied all spring and summer because of Hank's health. All those early years on the farm were taking their toll now that he was well over forty. The migraines had gone away when he went to work at Lin-Aero, but the stomachaches still plagued him off and on. Finally, the old ulcer scars had welded his stomach together and he couldn't eat much of anything anymore.

Carol had graduated and after coming back home from her senior trip, she began to think more about what would happen to her in the fall. Her dad had been tested and diagnosed and was scheduled for surgery. She was concerned about her dad's health problems, but now that school was out and the excitement of her senior year was over, the nagging in the back of her head wouldn't leave her alone.

After her little sisters went to sleep at night, Carol would read for awhile but then her mind would stray from the book and she would wonder what would become of her. She didn't even consider college, Glady always told her kids that it was a good thing none of them were very good in school since only rich parents could afford college any way.

Both of Carol's older girl cousins had gone to the hospital nursing school in Rockwell, and that path had been discussed off and on as a good one for a girl to take. As far as Glady was concerned, it had never been a consideration for Carol and no action was ever taken.

Toward the end of her senior year, various classmates had asked Carol what her plans were after high school graduation. Just for an answer, Carol had alluded that she was probably going to nursing school, as if the plans were being made.

When the seniors were passing around their yearbooks for everyone to sign, one of Carol's classmates jokingly had written on the back of the inside cover: 'don't chase too many doctors under the bed up there in Halsey'. That entry had prompted several more classmates to inquire and comment positively about her plans for nursing school.

Carol didn't tell anyone that there were no real plans, and let her classmates and under-classmen go on commenting. Carol didn't have any idea how to go about getting into nursing school. Glady had always made the decisions, even telling Carol what to wear to school from day to day all through high school.

There had been no discussion at all about Carol's future. Glady certainly was not aware that Carol had any thoughts about such things. Carol knew better than to bring it up, she just waited for Glady to say something. She began to see her future in dark gray tones, but the underlying unrest kept her thinking about how she might get away from home somehow.

Hank's stomachaches had been close to intolerable after the first of the year when Carol was a senior. He never had much fat on him, and he ate much less once he went to work at Lin-Aero but he smoked more and drank more coffee. When his stomach began to hurt more, he ate even less and Glady would yell at him to eat more. Finally, in the spring Glady insisted that Hank see a doctor. She sure as hell wasn't going put up with a bunch of fighting brats and that skinny old son-of-a-bitch with his aching gut all summer long.

Hank flatly refused to see the doctors in Rockwell, so Glady yelled for him to go see one over in Halsey. Hank's pain was so bad by May that he finally made an appointment with a specialist there. After many days of testing, Hank was diagnosed with stomach ulcers and scarring from years of having ulcers. He was told the only thing that would take care of the pain would be an operation to remove the scarring which also included removing a portion of his stomach. He was put on a medication and scheduled for the operation the second week in June.

The surgery was a major procedure and Hank took weeks to recover and return to work. Glady played the dutiful wife and drove Hank over to the hospital the morning of surgery and waited outside the operating room. After he came out of the recovery room, she stayed by his side until late in the evening and then visited him every day while he was in the hospital.

Every day alone in the car, all the way over and all the way back, she cussed at the old son-of-a-bitch for going so far away to have surgery. Rockwell was just not good enough for him, the old bastard. Making her drive all the way over to Halsey to see him every day. Of course, Hank told Glady every day she came that she didn't need to come over the next day, but she would come every day any way, cussing all the way over and back.

Glady thought he looked awful with that tube up his nose draining all that blood from his stomach. What if he died? What in the hell would she do with all those goddamned brats to raise? She couldn't work with all those little kids, and she sure as hell would never accept charity. Not on your life, she thought, she would rather see all those kids dead than on welfare.

Hank came out of the hospital three weeks after the stomach surgery and now he had finally been released to go back to work. He would soon be leaving soon for his first day back at work, still on second shift. It had been ten weeks since his surgery and Glady had gotten mean as a snake having him around the house all the time.

Glady hadn't been able to sneak away at all since Hank had come home from the hospital. She would go to town and get the mail, pick up a few groceries and come right back home. Glady knew damned good-and-well that the sick old son-of-a-bitch would glare at her if she tried going out at night leaving him there with the kids. She couldn't even use Carol as cover because school was out and nothing was going on in Milton. Glady had been able to catch Bud up at Granny's house for an occasional quick chat, but there had been no intimate meetings.

The day Hank was going back to work, Carol finally ran across her yearbook again. Spring and summer had been so hectic, the book had gotten buried on the dining room table under a pile of clutter that hadn't been moved in awhile. Glady noticed it in Carol's hand and asked,

"Is that your annual? I never did get to see all the pictures and what the other kids wrote to you in it." Glady took the yearbook from Carol and sat down on the couch and began to leaf through the pages, looking at the pictures and messages from classmates. When she got to the inside cover on the back, she used her gruff-put-out tone of voice to say,

"What the hell did old Nora write that for? Where did she get that notion? Did you say something about nursing school?"

"Uh, w-well, yeah," Carol responded.

"What in the hell did you mean, tellin' 'em somethin' like that? You don't want to be a nurse! Just because your cousins are! Why, I've never heard you say you really wanted to be a nurse. And why Halsey? Just because your damned dad went over there?"

"Well, no, it's—it's just—" Carol stammered.

"Goddamnit! What in the hell were you thinkin'?"

Carol was embarrassed that her mother had discovered what she had told her classmates, but a kind of antagonism suddenly seized her. She leaped up from the couch and stormed out of the room saying,

"You don't care what happens to me!" She went up the stairs to her room and closed the door, wondering what had gotten into her.

Suddenly, Carol panicked as she heard heavy lumbering footsteps coming up the stairs, then panic turned to terror. The terror had a name and that name was Glady. Glady shoved the door open and came screeching into the room, grabbing Carol by the hair and slapping her face. When Carol tried to cover her face, Glady pounded her shoulders and back with her fist over and over.

"I'll show you who doesn't care, you goddamned slut! You bitch; don't ever tell me I don't care. I'm your mother. And don't you ever talk to me that way; I don't care how old you are. I'll show you who cares, you worthless slut."

Carol bent to the repetitive blows, crying yet knowing that the storm would blow out if she would just hang on and take whatever Glady was throwing at her.

"You goddamned yellow-headed hussy! You whore; don't ever tell me that I don't care. Now just stay in your room outta of my sight. I'm sick to death of you, you goddamned slut."

The whole incident took less than ten minutes but would be the deciding factor in Carol actually getting out of this hellhole with Glady.

Hank had been dressing for his first day back at work. He pulled on his white T-shirt and jeans while the hair pulling, slapping, punching, cussing and screaming were going on upstairs. Hank wanted to help, but he feared that he might make it worse for Carol if he interceded. He quietly walked up the steps when he thought Glady had come down and gone into another part of the house. Opening the door Hank saw a red-faced Carol sitting on the bed with her head bent down weeping. He spoke quietly to Carol.

"Get dressed and I'll take you over to your grandma's house on my way to work. You can stay there for awhile."

This offer was unexpected and Carol didn't respond right away. She felt a strange ambivalence and just sat there. Then from downstairs Glady screamed up the stairwell,

"Stay out of this, you old son-of-a-bitch! Get your goddamned ass out of here and go to your precious job, where it's all clean and nice. This is none of your goddamned business!"

Carol regretted she could not respond to her dad's offer of help but she knew from years of experience that Glady had blown herself out.

"I'll be alright dad, I don't want to go to Grandma's," Carol said. She knew that her dad didn't really have time to take her anywhere, and she didn't know what a few days with Opal would buy her anyway. Hank spun on his heel and left for work, saying nothing more to anyone.

Next thing you know, Carol's door opened again and Glady stood there as if nothing had happened. She immediately began to tear Hank down.

"That old son-of-a-bitch! Take you to grandma's, what the hell does he think? Go to grandmas, what was that supposed to do? What would you do over there all day anyway? Grandma doesn't have any room for you to stay there. She doesn't want you there. What did he think anyway? That you wouldn't be safe here with me? I'm your mother, the old bastard.

"Tell you what, lets go over to Halsey tomorrow and see about getting you into nursing school. If that's what you want, that's what we will do. Now what should we wear over there to Halsey?"

Carol was relieved. She felt so sorry for her dad and she knew he was trying to help in the only way he knew how. But in the end, Hank had helped in a way that taking her to grandma's would never have done. Carol had suffered the blows, and the last slapping had been her ticket out, but only because Hank had interceded. Her mother would have done anything to show up her dad as a son-of-a-bitch. Taking Carol to Halsey instead of a dead-end trip to grandma's was a way to win a battle with Hank. Glady smugly drove Carol over to Halsey to meet with the nursing director, mentally declaring a victory over Hank.

Carol wished she could fall through the floor as Glady raised her right hand and said,

"I swear to God, Sister, her hair is not bleached."

Carol and Glady were sitting before the Irish nun who was agreeing to take Carol into nursing school the following week. Sister Moira had been telling Glady and Carol that the fee to enter the hospital nursing school must be paid in full, but that Glady could make payments for the three years Carol was in school. Further, she said that Carol would be responsible to pay any balance due within one year after graduation.

Carol would live in the hospital nursing school dormitory for the full three years, observe all the rules, which included signing in and out, and meeting curfews. She would be free to come home on weekends and holiday breaks. Carol sat there, listening to Glady answer all the questions and agree that Carol would follow the rules. Given the chance, Carol would have agreed to anything and would have gladly signed in her own blood. She practically had her fingers crossed, hoping nothing would go wrong that would interfere with this chance.

Sister Moira had a heavy Irish brogue and she announced,

"Well, I'm sure she's a fine girl. Helpin' her mother to raise such a big family and wantin' to be a nurse. But I don't like that bleached hair."

Glady had immediately forgotten about the beating she had inflicted on Carol the day before and had taken on the challenge of grooming her to be accepted into nursing school. Glady reckoned that Carol should wear a suit and picked the lavender one that she had worn during her senior trip in May.

Then she had looked a Carol's hair and decided it was a too long for nursing school and insisted that a new shorter curly hairdo would make the best impression. She went to the drugstore and bought a strong, home permanent then came home and whacked off Carol's hair to a suitable length. These days she assumed she was an expert now that Arlene had shown her some tricks to working with hair.

Glady thought a good tight curl would be best, so she left the solution on the maximum time. Carol had natural ash blonde hair that was baby fine, so of course, the permanent had dried and lightened her hair significantly. It now had a fuzzy-yellowed look to it as she sat there during the interview.

Now here was Glady, swearing before the nun with her right hand raised, that her daughter did not bleach her hair. Carol was mortified, but in another way she was thankful, she thought that it was a good thing there wasn't a Bible within easy reach. Her mother would have grabbed it up and would be swearing on it.

CHAPTER TWENTY-SEVEN

Glady was reading the Seneca Eagle one day. She bought the paper once in awhile and she liked to read the personal columns. She would imagine the people who might have written them and dream up stories about their lives and wonder how close she was to the truth.

Today, as she read the column, she came upon a personal ad that read: 'a recent illness forces me to think about the past. Would like to hear from anyone who remembers Earl Pepaw.' A Seneca address and a phone number was printed afterward.

Glady remembered she had gone to grade school with an Earl Pepaw over in Rockwell. She wondered if it could possibly be the same one. Rockwell was miles away from Seneca and it didn't say where this Earl Pepaw had gone to grade school.

"Well what the hell," she muttered. "It can't hurt to call."

Glady picked up the phone and dialed the number and a woman answered. Glady told her that she was calling about the newspaper ad she had just read.

The woman said her name was Janie Pepaw and that Earl had placed the ad. She said she would put him on the phone. Glady waited on the line and in a minute a raspy voice answered.

Glady told the man who she was and how she had gone to school with a man in Rockwell that had his same name. Sure enough, it was the same man, and he and Glady ended up talking for close to an hour. He sounded sick, but he was talking her leg off. Glady enjoyed gabbing with him about old times.

Glady finally told Earl that she would like to see him, if it was all right with him. They made plans for her to come over to Seneca for a visit. Glady liked to have a good reason to go to Seneca.

When the kids were younger Glady remembered she would have been scared to death to drive over to Seneca. Even though Hank drove over there every day to work it was a considered a long ways to go to casually. Driving even less traveled highways used to scare her too. It was early 1966 and

Glady would be forty-four years old in May. Over the years she had gotten more comfortable driving and didn't mind it at all.

These days she waited for a good excuse to go somewhere further from home, especially to a big place like Seneca. That snotty Carol was married and living over there, but Glady would never drop in on her, and she didn't waste her time trying to get invited to Carol's home. Carol was always too busy with work and all the other things she and Harold had to do. Glady could take a hint. To hell with Carol, there were people in Seneca that wanted to see her.

The next week, Glady took off alone to visit the Pepaws using the easy directions Earl had given her over the phone. When she arrived at the Pepaw address, she marched up to the door with a composed friendly, good old gal look on her face. She was appalled at how old Earl looked when he came to the door. His lungs were real bad and he had slobbers down his shirt. His wife, Janie, was clean, but she seemed like a simpleton to Glady.

The Pepaws lived in an old house that was tidy, but it was all run down and had a strange musty smell. Every room needed paint and the furniture was worn out and broken down.

The Pepaws had four sons ranging in age from seventeen down to seven. Glady suspected that the two younger boys must be retarded as she watched them play. Earl confided to Glady that the oldest boy had gotten in with a wrong crowd but he had convinced him to join the Navy before he got into any more trouble and ruined his life permanently.

Glady observed the oldest boy and thought it likely that he was simple, like his mother. The second oldest boy seemed normal and decent to her. His name was John.

"John was sort of a pitiful kid." Glady mused to herself on the drive home as she reviewed her visit. "Too bad he's stuck in such a damned mess of a family!"

Glady happily drove over to Seneca to visit the Pepaws again the next week. A sick man and a simple wife were a great excuse to get away from that old son-of-a-bitch and all those screaming brats in that filthy house. Earl Pepaw really was sick too, he was disabled and the family was on county assistance.

Janie and Earl Pepaw had a lot to manage. Glady didn't tell them, but she was concerned about John. To her he seemed to be smarter than the rest of the family. But there he was, living in a place with retarded and sick people. What chance did the poor kid have but to get into trouble like his older brother? Glady would hate to see that happen.

Glady hit upon an idea and on the way home. She called Earl after she got back home and campaigned for him to let John come out and live in Milton with the Wilkey's for a while. She said that it would give the Pepaws one less mouth to feed, and they might avoid any trouble like they had with the older boy. Glady bragged that one more boy wouldn't make any difference to her since she had six sons of her own. It didn't take much to convince Earl, so John came out to live with the Wilkeys'.

It had never occurred to Glady to ask Hank what he thought of taking on another mouth to feed. The old son-of-a-bitch wasn't entitled to an opinion any more any way. He hardly ever said a word, just brought home his paycheck and threw it on the buffet. She figured that meant she could spend it any way she wanted too. Good thing the old fool didn't know that half their bills had been turned over to collection and she was skimping on the payment she agreed to pay them. To hell with him, let them put the old bastard in jail!

The Wilkeys' had moved into a bigger farmhouse a year or so ago. It had more bedrooms that they'd ever had before and some of the kids were already gone from home. Glady put John up with Henry since they'd be in the same year in high school. It was already half way through the school year, and she thought being with Henry might make John feel more at home.

Glady took John out shopping for new clothes. She was explicit that he pay attention to colors and she guided him as to what colors and patterns went with what. John liked the attention and the new clothes. He had grown taller over the past year and his old pants and shirts were getting way too short.

Glady warned John about Hank's behavior. She said that he had been an old bear for years and just to stay out his way and pay no attention to him. John worried at first, but then he noticed that Hank treated him much like he did his own sons. Hank completely ignored them all.

Adding John to the family seemed pretty easy to Glady. George had served three years in the Army and then found some quiet dark-haired girl and married her in a small ceremony. When Carol had announced that she was getting married, Glady was determined to do a big, beautiful wedding for her. Carol was the oldest girl and Glady wanted to do it up right and impress everyone.

Glady had almost killed herself and nearly went blind with all the sewing. Now, that damned Carol would hardly ever call her, let alone come out and visit except for holidays. Then Alfred and Dale both had to get married to tramps that had got knocked up, so they were gone too.

Alfred was married to some little slut who had really tricked him good. Glady suspected that the girl was pregnant when Alfred first brought her home. She'd raised holy hell with Alfred when she realized they were engaged to be married.

"How long have you been goin' with her, anyway? And what in the hell would you want to marry her for any way? She's been screwin' around all over town since she was twelve years old. I knew both of her folks over there in Rockwell when I was growin' up. They are nothing but trash, and now you are marryin' into that outfit? Why the little slut must be six months pregnant from the looks of her belly."

Alfred glared at Glady.

"I've been with her over three months. She says the baby is mine, so it's mine!"

"Oh yeah, well just be stupid! I'm just tryin' to warn you for your own good. Well, I tried to tell ya. Just lie in the goddamned bed ya make."

***

It was summer again.

"Goddamned hot weather" Glady announced. She had not seen Bud for a long time now. When his mother had died, he had become depressed and stayed home most of the time with his damned old wife. Glady sometimes suspected the truth was that Bud had another woman, probably someone younger than her. If she had only known it at the time, she'd have really told the old bastard off that last time she had been with him. What the hell, he hadn't been that much fun anymore anyway. But it had been so

179

long now, Glady thought she should have a climax soon or she would go completely nuts.

Glady thought about John and was proud that he had really bloomed here in the Wilkey household. He had finished his junior year and was raring to get back to school and get on with his senior year. Glady took him to visit his folks in Seneca on a regular basis. That Pepaw family gave her something to be interested in and someplace to go that Hank couldn't question.

On the way home from visiting his family, John would always tell Glady how much he appreciated what she was doing for him. She would feel good about her charity work and think about how she had saved him from all that mess with his family. Glady often wished her own kids were as grateful toward her as John seemed to be. He would beam with pleasure when she noticed him.

"Damn, those new clothes really make you a handsome dude!" Glady complimented one day as John came in the house from running an errand into Milton. "Did ja drive all them country gals wild down there at the store?"

John smiled and blushed at her words.

Later, that same day Glady was doing a load of wash and she was teaching her five-year-old daughter, Gail how to fold clothes. John came into the room and Glady teased him.

"Well do you have a country girlfriend picked out yet, Dude?"

"No!" John retorted, sounding to Glady's ears amazingly like one of her own boys.

"Well, then, do you even know the facts of life yet?" Glady probed further. John looked at her in a puzzled way, so Glady pushed on.

"Well I believe in tellin' my boys certain facts, and since you're gettin' to be my boy, I was just checkin'. Go on Gail, I want to talk to John alone."

Glady entered into a grilling mode, questioning John about sexual matters. She asked him if he knew where babies come from and if he knew how they got there, like he was a first grader.

John was shy and replied using only 'yes' or 'no' monosyllables, leading Glady to surmise that he was probably sexually inexperienced. She finished their conversation by telling

John that if he ever had any questions, she believed that she should be the one to answer them for him. It was her duty as his adopted mother.

As time passed Glady stopped treating John like company. She began to talk to him like one of her own boys and called him some of the same names she called her sons when he did anything she didn't like. Other times she made time to talk with him alone and he was soon developing into her new confidante. She had begun to ask him more specific questions.

One morning Glady went upstairs to seek out some items of dirty laundry to round out a load of whites. John and some of the other boys were lazing late in bed. Glady looked at the sleeping boys and noticed through the sheet that John had an erection as he slept. She stared at the sheet, and found herself aroused just looking at it. Glady hurriedly picked up some dirty underwear off the closet floor and went back downstairs to the washer.

"I see by your outfit that you are a cowboy!" Glady sang leeringly at her son when he came in from outdoors that afternoon. Henry had heard his mother and Arlene singing that line since he was a baby. He just ignored her, figuring she probably still missed Arlene. Most of the boys had learned long ago that ignoring Glady was the best approach. She may make rude comments about them ignoring her, but at least she would move on and pick on someone else.

"Oh you old bear, you're so much like that goddamned dad of yours! You can't even take a joke, you prude."

John entered the room shortly after that and since she had gotten no response from Henry, Glady repeated the phrase.

"I see by your outfit that you are a cowboy!" John looked directly at Glady and blushed instead of ignoring her.

Suddenly Glady knew that John had seen her upstairs that morning looking at him! As sure as she was sitting here. It was Glady's turn to be embarrassed, but she covered it quickly by saying,

"Oh, you'll just have to get used to teasing! We do a lot of that around here."

The kids were engrossed in television and Glady told them that she was going to bed with Gail that evening. Little Gail had been irritable all day and Glady had given her a baby aspirin. She told the kids she was tired anyway and was going to read some magazines and not to bother her the rest of the night. Glady was hoping that Gail would fall asleep early so she could read in peace and quiet. She had a new kind of cookie hidden in her room and she wanted to enjoy them without sharing with brats.

About nine o'clock some of the younger kids were going on up to bed at their appointed hour. There was a movie coming on that looked interesting so the older kids were stretching out into the places the younger ones had vacated. Glady looked at the clock when heard a soft knock on her door. Who in the hell could be bothering her she wondered, as she slid her cookies under her pillow. Glady spoke lowly so she wouldn't disturb the sleeping Gail.

"Who is it?"

When it was John who answered her, Glady went on.

"Come on in, I'm decent."

Glady had on the same garb she had worn every hot summer. She had worn it only in her bedroom since John had come to live there but she looked down at herself in the old slip and shrugged.

"I'm as decent as I get in hot weather in my own home anyway. It's about time you got used to it."

CHAPTER TWENTY-EIGHT

Years went by and Hank had been in the hospital off and on for most of the year. He had almost fainted one day at work and they'd sent him into the emergency room there in Seneca. After some tests, he was referred to a cardiologist who then referred him to the cardiovascular surgeon. They discovered such an extensive blockage of his coronary arteries that they told Hank that it was a miracle that he hadn't already had a heart attack. They said it would be a second miracle if he made it to the operating table without one. The doctor told Hank to not consider smoking another cigarette. Hank took the freshly opened pack of Camels out of his tee shirt pocket and handed them to the surgeon.

Hank's by-pass surgery had gone pretty well. They also did what they told Glady was a 'pop-fem bypass' at the same time. She explained that it had to do with some blood vessels in his legs and up behind his knees and in his groin. Everything had gone pretty well for a few days after the surgery, but then Hank's groin area started bleeding and they had to take him back to surgery to fix it.

Then damned if it didn't open up again after he'd come home. He had gone back in the hospital for quite a while before they sent him home after that happened and they'd had to fix it the second time. He was still having a lot of pain when they did finally release him.

Hank never complained but he was obviously hurting. Glady convinced him to let her drive him over to a chiropractor she had heard was pretty good. She told him she was sick of him sitting around hurting all the time but refusing to take the pain pills anymore.

Hank screamed out loud when the chiropractor tried to extend his leg fully out. The chiropractor looked worried and advised Glady to get Hank back over to Seneca to his surgeon as soon as possible. After they left Hank told Glady that the chiropractor's opinion was worthless and he refused to go back to the surgeon.

Two days later Hank almost bled to death in the bathroom at home. The same place on his groin had opened up again and he hemorrhaged, and blood spurted all over the place.

Luckily some of the girls were home and they helped get him up and called the ambulance. This last time the surgeons took off Hank's leg below the knee, but it looked like everything was finally going to heal.

Hank had spent most of his time worrying about when he could go home the first two times he was in the hospital. But the last time had scared him and he was glad to be here and know that he was finally healing. He hated to think about crutches and a wooden leg, but the physical therapist was nice and told him that he would get used to it in time.

After a while Hank grew accustomed to being in the hospital. Everything was always clean and smelled nice and fresh. The food wasn't bad and they let him pick from a pretty good-sized menu every day. The nurses were always pleasant and seemed glad to see him from day to day, asking him how he was, and chatting about the weather.

Maybe he shouldn't have pushed so hard to be released after the bypass. If he had stayed in the hospital then he might not be in this fix with only one leg. He realized he had pushed to leave these comfortable surroundings only to go back to the filthy, cluttered house, dirty linens, and bologna sandwiches with Glady riding his ass all the time. He began to dread being released at all.

With all of his surgeries they had finally told him over at Lin-Aero that he might as well take the early retirement. Not that there was much to retire from anymore. Lin-Aero had cut back and laid off so much over the last few years. He'd even been laid-off a few years back, but they had recalled him. It had been good to get back to work, but it was never quite the same again. There at the end his regular job was picking up trash.

Hank had been home from the hospital and retired for some time before he really noticed the relationship between Glady and John. It took him awhile to see it, but it took him much longer to believe it, and even longer to admit to himself that he cared.

Just when he thought his suspicions were fact, he could talk himself out of it. He'd figure out that Glady had been about forty-four when John had come to live there as a junior in high school. That made Glady twenty-seven years older than John.

Hank would see Glady yelling and cussing at John, just like she did her own boys.

Hank recalled two instances that he thought were telling, but he was able to dismiss them with logical reasoning. One was that Glady had insisted that John move back to the Wilkey home after he got out of the Army. He reasoned that Glady must feel sorry for John because of his family situation. The other glaring thing that made him wonder was that she finally went out and got false teeth just before John came home. She seemed especially proud of them when John saw them the first time. Hank reasoned that she must be thrilled that they turned out better than she always thought they would and was showing off because he'd been gone so long.

Other times Hank considered that he might be jealous of John because Glady paid him so much attention. He'd truly loved Glady when they were young. He knew he was not much of a conversationalist, nor a lover, after they were married. But he did the best he could by working hard to take care of her and the kids.

Hank had worked so hard at farming and had countless worries about providing for his young, ever-growing family. All those kids came along so fast, and he worried night and day about earning enough to provide for their basic needs. He tried to ignore any thoughts about sex but Glady would always talk him into it.

Glady had gained an enormous amount of weight over the years, but Hank knew having babies had caused most of it. Her teeth were in bad shape, and she continually refused to get false ones for thirty years. She only rarely bathed or washed her hair. Hank had lived with Glady so long that he didn't really notice how much her looks had changed over the years until he really thought about it.

How could a man as young as John have gotten involved with an older woman who had the personal habits she did? Hank would tell himself he was crazy that there could be anything going on between Glady and John. He would forget his suspicions until something gripped his attention again.

Hank recalled one Christmas, Carol had come home for the holidays. She bought them all fairly lavish gifts that year. Carol showed Hank a diamond ring she had brought for Glady.

"Since mom never had a real wedding ring, I picked this out for her. I thought it looked similar to the one she always described that you guys bought when you got married."

Hank looked pleased and smiled at Carol as he gazed upon the shiny line of twelve real diamonds on the ring that Carol had bought for her mother. Carol showed the ring to some of the other kids and to John before she wrapped it and put it under the tree.

Carol anxiously awaited Christmas morning as the gifts were being opened. She especially wanted to see her mother's expression when she opened her new diamond ring.

"My God! I can't wear this!" Glady wailed loudly, as she opened the ring box on Christmas morning. The expectant look faded from Carol's face as Glady continued.

"What will people think? I'll go into the post office and they'll ask me if I just got married. You're goddamned dad never bought me a ring, so why in the hell would you buy me a wedding ring now?"

"We-well it's not necessarily a wedding ring," Carol told her mother. "You can wear it on your right hand, more like a nostalgia or remembrance ring."

"Oh it looks *just* like a wedding ring. I'm not gonna wear it! Havin' people askin' about it?" Glady said in her disgusted-society-matron tone of voice.

It was then that Carol seemed to notice what Hank had noticed long before and tried to never think about. The carved silver band on Glady's third finger, left hand. Carol didn't inquire, but Hank knew that it had been a gift from John. He had brought it back from Europe when he was stationed there in the service years ago. Glady had worn it faithfully.

Glady had made excuses when she first put on the ring John bought her, saying that it was too small for her right hand but fit her left hand perfectly. She left it there and proclaimed she would get it sized for her right hand some day. She never did though, and few years later she complained that she couldn't get the ring off anymore. More than once she had announced for all to hear,

"Thank God! It's not shutting off the circulation to my finger, so I'll just leave it alone 'til it does. I might hafta get it cut off someday."

Hank watched, as Glady got up off the couch after her other Christmas gifts were opened. She casually opened the buffet drawer and tossed the ring and box into the drawer. She had never even tried it on.

CHAPTER TWENTY-NINE

"That bitch Carol!" Glady muttered as she watched her redheaded eighteen-year-old granddaughter moving off the plane and toward her. "Sendin' those kids back here again for a whole month! She did that to me three years ago and now she's done it again. I thought I had told her in such a way then, that it was hard on me to have them here so long. Always havin' to keep the house picked up, and think of things to eat, and keep them entertained.

"The boy is timid and not much trouble. But that girl is so snotty, pretendin' that California's so much better'n the state she was born in. Always actin' bored, hardly ever talkin' and askin' to stay with everyone else the whole time she's here. Then, when her cousins come around she perks up and talks her silly red head off.

"God knows we couldn't let it get back to Carol that her kids hadn't had a good time here. And what would I do if they got hurt here? It scared me to death watching them land in that lightening storm."

Glady worried all the time the plane was circling and landing in the storm. When it safely touched the runway, she breathed a large sigh of relief. She figured the kids would be scared to death when they got off the plane. Poor kids, sent so far away for a month, by their own mother.

You would never catch Glady flying in a plane. Not on your life.

"Goddamned things! Never, never, never! Like that old sayin' 'if God had wanted people to fly He'd have given them wings!"

It really pissed Glady off when one of the boys would counter with,

"You're always gadding around in the car, did God build those wheels into your butt?" Always the smart remark. Just like their dad would say, if he ever talked!

"Well!" Glady said, using her pleasant-shrill-knowing tone of voice. "What did you think of all that lightnin' n thunder?" She just hoped the teen-agers were scared so she could comfort them in grandmotherly fashion. Then that hag of a granddaughter piped up to say,

"Oh we have lightening in California too, Grandma!"

Those little fools of Carol's didn't seem to be afraid at all. They were oblivious to the dangers of the world that their mother had sent them out into on their own. Carol probably hadn't even warned them about such dangers as lightening, always too busy working. She obviously just let them fend for themselves.

Carol had left those children for their dad to raise. Poor kids, raised by that fool, chicken-shit Harold. Glady had nearly killed herself with that big wedding for Carol when she married Harold. Then, a few years later she up and left him when the kids were little. Carol told her she'd just moved up the street and saw the kids and fixed their meals every day, but who knew? It had taken Carol over a year to admit to Glady that she had split up with Harold.

Glady called Carol's house quite a few times over that year too. It seemed like that fool Harold, would always make up some excuse that Carol would have to call back later. He sounded kind of funny and Glady wondered what the hell was going on. Carol would call back later and act like nothing was wrong. During one call, Glady asked Carol in her most pleading-martyred tone of voice,

"When are you movin' back home? You went clear out to California so Harold could finish his schooling, and you said you were going to come back home after that. It's been over six years now and Harold never did finish any school. I just miss you so much all the time, when are you comin' home?"

Then that bitch had the nerve to reply, in that tiresomely patient tone of hers that Glady hated.

"Mom, I am home! And to tell you the truth Harold and I are not even married any more. We split up over a year ago."

"What about the kids? You're not leavin' them at night when you work, are you Carol?" Glady asked shrilly.

"They live with their dad," Carol said. "I pay child support."

Glady couldn't believe her ears.

"What in the hell kind of state are you livin' in anyway? Paying child support! And what the hell kind of mother are you anyway?"

Glady was just happy that Carol lived so far away. No one around here would know about this ridiculous situation and ask Glady pointed questions. It was bad enough that Carol worked full time, now something like this. Children needed their mother at home. You wouldn't have caught Glady out working and leaving her kids at home.

And now this offspring of Carol's, stepping off the plane and having the nerve to say, 'We have lightening and thunder in California too'. There she was dressed up, looking all California and fit to kill. Glady knew without a doubt that Carol had picked out the outfit her granddaughter wore. It was a short, white knit dress with white lacy panty hose and big, pink-dangling earrings. The girl was obviously thinking she was too good to be in this hick state, even though she had been born here.

Glady chose her moment several days later. She led her granddaughter into a nice conversation at the kitchen table. Glady was using her soft-inquiring-interested grandma tone of voice, asking all about California and what high school graduation had been like.

Glady showed her granddaughter the current fashions in the Spiegel catalogue and asked her what she thought about them. Then Glady looked over at her granddaughter and said,

"Your hair is just so pretty! You know that your grandpa has sisters who have red hair that shade. Course, you've never seen them since you live so far away. Your mom and dad took you clear out to California when you were just a baby.

"Your hair was dark like mine when you were first born. Then, when you were about two months old, your hair started to turn red. You know that your mother never did like red hair.

"Carol was so disappointed when your hair turned out to be red. I think that is why she left you. She just never got over the fact that you had red hair."

CHAPTER THIRTY

Glady was staring into space. She listened as Trudie sang her childhood songs for the fifth time in a row and then she had fallen asleep. She thought it was funny how time had changed things for her and Trudie. Trudie was Hanks' aunt, his father's sister. She was the old maid schoolteacher who had taken Hank and his sister's in as children when their mother had died suddenly of a ruptured appendix.

The old house that Glady had languished in as a much younger woman had been owned by Trudie and her husband, Bill. Thanks to them, four years of her life had been spent in lonesome isolation. If they hadn't offered Hank the house when he got the job at Lin-Aero, she would have never gone through all that misery.

Trudie did get married, but everyone knew that Bill had his eye on Trudie's ranchland more than the bride when he asked her. They had adopted a daughter and been together for years when Bill died at the age of 71. Trudie was much older than Bill, and she had continued living on the ranch years after he died. When she became unable to care for herself and didn't seem to know where she was any longer, her daughter had placed her in a nursing home.

The doctors said that Trudie's mind had regressed back to when she was a little girl. She was never any trouble to the nursing home staff as she sat and rocked and played with her dolls from long ago. She ate her meals, accepted her bath and stayed in her room except when they took her to the dining room. Though limited by arthritis in her knees, Trudie could walk. She got around the room, but as far as leaving, she seemed to prefer staying within sight of her own belongings.

Glady watched as Trudie napped with her mouth moving. She seemed to be silently repeating the song she had been singing earlier. Glady thought back to the time when they had first moved to Trudie and Bill's rental place and she was alone evenings with the kids. That damned old house was a nightmare. It did have electricity, but little else. Back then Glady had dreamed of owning a refrigerator.

Hank knew that Glady wanted a refrigerator and had told her if things stayed the way they were with his job at Lin-Aero they could afford a refrigerator before too long. Glady was impatient however, she knew summer was coming before any bills would be paid off and she wanted ice and anything else that would make the hot humid days more bearable.

Glady remembered the day she was reading the Rockville paper. She was very interested in an article about a contest that was being held by a local appliance store. The first prize would be a new Shelvador refrigerator! They would be giving the prize in a month, well before the heat of summer. Glady thought she could win her own refrigerator, let Hank take his promise and shove it!

Glady sat down with some notebook paper and pencil that very day. She thought about the reasons she wanted a new refrigerator. Chilled foods, cold drinks and ice in tall glasses, the vision came streaming into her head like a cool breeze. However Glady figured that the winning poem would need something more to get the judges' attention. She followed those thoughts to what the judges might be most impressed by. What had life given her but a bunch of kids?

Glady put pencil to paper, she had a clear idea in her head now. A poor woman was she, with lots of little children, sweltering in the heat. Good children with a good mother, poor little fellas needed coolin' down, bless their hearts, if only they had a refrigerator. She rhymed several lines and strung them together. It sounded good! Glady ended the poem with the line 'there is not one thing that I want much more, than a brand new gleaming white Shelvador!' Totally satisfied she folded the paper and put it into an envelope. She took it out to the mailbox with the postage pennies pinched on the envelope with a clothespin and put the red flag up. Glady just knew that Shelvador was hers; she just had to wait a month for it.

Glady diligently waited a couple of weeks the she started going out to the mailbox as soon as the mail was delivered. Each day, she tentatively opened the mailbox and peered in. No mail from the appliance store came. The local paper came, but the store just had the regular advertisements in a small space at the bottom of page 2, nothing about the contest for three weekly papers.

Sure enough though when the month was over and Glady tore open the paper to page 2, the ad had changed back to a quarter page. In bold letters: Contest Winner Announced. Glady held her breath as she read the line below the headline: Winning poem below: Glady's heart lurched and then pounded in her chest as her eyes moved down to the page. 'I'm an old gray haired woman and…'

Wait! That was not the poem she wrote. Where was her first line about the good children and the good mother? Her eyes raced down the lines, this couldn't be happening. When she got to the line about the author of the winning poem, her eyes froze. Trudie had won! Goddamn her to hell. She didn't need a refrigerator. She already had one! And if she didn't she could afford to buy one.

Glady was fit to be tied. She was so angry she sat all the older kids down and read both her and Trudie's poems to them.

"Now tell me which one sounds the best?" Glady harped. "Which one sounds like it should win a new refrigerator?"

Glady read both poems again to be sure the kids picked up on each word. She heard the murmured reply to her query.

"The first one, Momma."

"That's right, my poem is best! And they picked Trudie's. She was a schoolteacher, and I suppose they know that. But goddamned it, they should give the first prize to the best poem."

Glady looked at Trudie's lips moving in her nap. God, she looked old, every minute of her 93 years. And even if she was a schoolteacher she should have never won that contest. I needed that refrigerator, and she didn't, it just wasn't fair.

Glady's eyes moved around the room. Trudie had a lot of old things in here. It was nice that they let old people bring in their own things in to the rooms to make it more personal. There were the dolls and some of their furnishings, there were some knickknacks and old books on the shelf above the bed. Glady thought Trudie would probably never read again since the old hag didn't even know she was old enough to read anymore.

Glady wondered about the books. She wondered if there were any she knew from her school days. She couldn't see anything that was written on the ends of the books that were showing because they were so faded. Glady got out of her chair and quietly crept up to the head of the bed. Trudie remained asleep.

Glady cautiously reached up, pulled out a book and read its title. Nothing I have ever heard of she thought and pulled out a couple more. The second book was nothing either, and the third one was falling apart in her hand. Glady pushed back the second book as she held together the pieces of the third one. She carefully brought the loose page down to her and held them to her chest when Trudie moved her head. Glady quickly moved back to her own chair and sat still until Trudie quieted.

Glady laid the pages out on her lap. She began to read. Why, it was poetry written in Trudie's own handwriting. Glady read some lines in a couple of the poems and wondered if Trudie had written them herself or had copied the works of others that caught her eye over the years. It appeared that Trudie had been keeping this book for years and some of the dates went way back to when she was teaching school.

Trudie slept as Glady read on. She began to believe that these were Trudie's own original poems as she read further. They detailed the life and thoughts of a God-fearing woman and her life on the prairie.

Trudie stirred and it appeared she might be through with her nap. Before her eyes opened however, Glady had squared the pages and slipped them under her sweater.

CHAPTER THIRTY-ONE

Glady had cancer. She was pissed off because Dr. Tott had always told her she would never get breast cancer. He delivered one baby after another and always said,

"Well Glady, one good thing about having all these babies is, that you'll never get breast cancer!"

Glady would laugh and wonder how bad her bowels would be after this one. Now old Dr. Tott was dead and she couldn't even challenge him about that statement he always made as a fact. Even though she'd had cancer twenty years before, she couldn't believe it had happened again.

That time she'd had her left kidney removed when she peed blood one morning and they'd found a cancerous tumor in it. She had always heard that being pregnant was hard on kidneys so she just chalked it up to having all those kids. She had suffered through the surgery and radiation and beat the kidney cancer. Now, here she was with breast cancer, something she was never supposed to worry about.

Glady had broken her hip the year before, and she hadn't been able to get around very good after that, even with the wheelchair. In fact, her wheelchair was a big problem when she was home in the trailer house. Glady got in the habit of sitting in her easy chair all day long and watching her favorite television programs.

Several times over the previous winter, Glady had noticed the puckering in her skin, drawing in above her left nipple. Since it was always so goddamned cold, she didn't want to undress and wash up very often. She would see that damned spot puckering her breast and avoid going near it with the washcloth. Then she would dress and forget about it until days later when she washed up again.

Glady's broken hip had long-since healed, her blood pressure and diabetes were under control, and she didn't feel like bothering with any new problems right now. She decided she would see a doctor in the spring when it was warmer out. For now, television could take her mind off anything that was bothering her.

Glady loved the talk shows best. She especially loved watching Oprah Winfrey's show and looked forward to it every day. The people on the show had so many problems. Glady marveled how they talked openly on television, right there in front of everyone, about such terrible problems.

"Too bad I worried so much about so many things for so many years," Glady thought as she watched charming Oprah with her beautiful smile.

When the talk show topics dealt with child abuse, Glady would listen with morbid fascination. Pitiful tales from children who had been burned with cigarettes or scalding water, or left in rat infested apartments alone in the city, while their mother went out on the town.

"Those mothers are sick!" Glady would mutter when she heard those unspeakable horrors, then she would comfort herself by saying, "At least, there never was anything like that goin' on in my house!"

Glady sat in her wheelchair. It was Monday and she was facing the whole week home alone in the trailer house. Days on end with no one around to talk to, waiting for evening when John came home. Then the weekends went so fast because John would load her in the Blazer and push her around the grocery store and Wal-Mart while she shopped. Weekday television programs got awful boring except in the afternoons when real people came on the talk shows. Glady pulled the gray notebook out from beside her in the wheelchair. Maybe she would write today since it was early and her favored programs wouldn't be on for hours.

Kids, grandkids, brothers, sister, nieces and nephews, friends, scores of people and not one visitor had darkened her doorstep for close to a year now. Those damned kids of hers, what was the use of having so many if none of them ever came over to visit? They all thought they were so damned important, she would show them by God! She intentionally let it be known that she was writing a book of poems.

Glady knew damned good and well that her kids would be happy to see her in her grave. She would show them, she would leave a book of poetry that would surprise them all. The poetry would balance whatever they might say against her after she was gone.

Carol especially, let her put her nose in the air and never come visit, she would see right away that the poetry was good and be surprised that her mother could think that deep. Glady thought that Carol would probably get the book published. Carol would give all the kids a copy and they would pass it on to their children, a published book of poems, now that would really show them.

Only Glady knew where she got the poems she was rewriting. When she had taken the pages from Trudie's room in the nursing home, she carried them home under her sweater and then had hidden them. She faithfully copied them down word for word and was able to get them back into Trudie's room before anyone missed them. When Trudie died in the nursing home, Glady did her best to find out what had happened to her things that had been with her in her room.

Glady asked Trudie's daughter specifically about the dolls but she was trying to find out about the original poetry. She was pretty sure the daughter was saying Trudie's things had been buried with her, when she replied that,

"Mother wanted those things with her forever."

Glady knew she couldn't get a clearer answer without coming right out and asking about the books so she chose to believe that Trudie's original poems were in her coffin with her.

Glady pulled out the new handwritten copy she had made of Trudie's poetry. She read through several poems before finding one that sounded like she felt today.

"I could have written this poem." Glady muttered to herself. "I have felt like this many a day. I could even do better with this line! Why, that doesn't even make sense, let along rhyme."

Glady put the pencil to paper. She copied the poem again in her gray notebook on the small special-sized paper. This time however, she changed two of the lines.

"Now that's better," she said aloud. "Now it makes sense." Just wait until those sonsabitches see this. They will find out that their mother could write with the best of them!"

***

197

Glady was losing the battle. Those damned anti-cancer pills that she had been taking for a year now had quit working. In spite of the fact that she played the good old tough gal who had licked cancer before, the tumor had grown. The latest mammogram showed that the growth was bigger for the first time since her diagnosis a year ago so now she would have to take heavy intravenous chemotherapy treatments.

Glady set her mind that she would once again beat the 'Big C'. In fact, it would be easier than the kidney cancer treatment had been. She didn't even have to go in the hospital this time and the doctors said they wouldn't be doing any surgery. She would go to an outpatient clinic for the IV medicines.

When Glady sat in the comfortable clinic chair getting her IV chemotherapy treatment, she liked to review the good times in her life. This time she closed her eyes and thought back to last July when she had held a reception for Carol. It had been real nice, but Glady had been disappointed because some of the people who had promised her they would come had not shown up or even called to cancel.

Glady was getting a simple cancer treatment pill back then. She recalled she had kept phoning Carol to tell her about her cancer treatment and trying everything she could think of to make Carol want to come back for a visit. She told Carol how the younger girls kept saying that her cancer was terminal and that's why they weren't doing much to treat it. Glady would tell Carol that she'd never heard the doctor say anything like that.

Glady said she always listened close to what the doctors said each time so she knew she would have heard that kind of news. She appealed to the professional in Carol and hinted that since she was a nurse she should come back and talk to the doctors, get the medical facts and straighten everyone out.

Glady could tell that Carol was listening carefully to her over the phone. But then she would say some big medical words that Glady only half understood. Carol told her the name of the pills she was taking was 'Tami' something or another that Glady couldn't even remember and didn't know why she should have to. All she wanted was Carol to come home and she would never say she would definitely come back to see her.

In the past Carol had mentioned that she might come back sometime to see where her dad was buried. But, he had been dead for over a year and she had never set a date yet. Glady half suspected Carol planned to come home when it was time for her funeral.

Glady was having none of that and she finally hit on an idea. The more she thought about her idea the better she liked it.

For some reason Carol had always loved having birthdays. It never even seemed to faze her when she was getting older; she always looked forward to her next birthday. The fact that Carol was turning fifty in July helped Glady with her scheme. The half-century mark was such a significant milestone that Glady figured that Carol would probably be delighted about turning fifty.

Glady had called up several girls and teachers that Carol used to know from school. Then she contacted some distant family members of Hank's that she thought might impress Carol. She reasoned that the more names she could drop on Carol, the better her chances of getting Carol to come see her.

Glady told each person she called that Carol was planning to come back for a visit in the summer around the Fourth of July. Further, Glady told them that she was planning a big a surprise reception to honor Carol's fiftieth birthday. Some of the people seemed lukewarm to Glady's call but they told her to let them know when she had a firm date and they try to come.

Gladys spirits were undaunted as she set about planning the reception. The more people Glady told about the reception, the more sure she was that the scheme would work.

Glady had dialed Carol's number one evening hoping she would be home. She was determined she wasn't going to leave a message on any damned answering machine but Carol picked up on the third ring. Using her soft-but-firm-controlling tone of voice, Glady said,

"Well you said you were coming home in July, so a whole bunch of people are getting together for your fiftieth birthday. There is a reception planned and a lot of people want to honor you. Everyone's looking forward to seeing you again. I have spoken for the Community House, and we need to give them a firm date soon. When will you be here?"

Carol was floored. She didn't remember being so definite about going back to visit that Glady should have told anyone, let alone arrange a big gathering like this. Carol sighed but quickly thought matters through: it had been close to three years since she had been back, she hadn't seen where her dad was buried and her mother had cancer, she decided she'd better get it over with.

"Well, alright. I'll call you when I get the arrangements worked out." Carol conceded.

When Glady hung up the phone she felt exhilarated that her plan had worked like a charm. She had won again!

Glady had sent Carol's picture to the paper the week before the reception and they had printed the article just like Glady had written it. Now that she thought about it though, the write-up had made Carol sound like such a hotshot. Maybe some people thought Carol was too high-falutin' now and they wouldn't want to see her after all these years. Carol had never come home for school reunions, so why would people even bother to come and see her? It sure wasn't Glady's fault, she had done her best to keep Carol informed after she moved away.

Carol had seemed happy during the reception though. She was surprised and she hugged the old teachers and schoolmates who did show up. Carol's new husband looked real nice and was friendly and talked to everyone. The decorations that the younger girls had put up looked really pretty, all decked out with balloons and crepe paper streamers.

Glady smiled thinking that overall, the reception had turned out pretty well.

"Good thing I pushed Carol into coming back for that visit," Glady thought with a satisfied air. "She really had a good time in spite of herself, and I made it all happen."

Glady opened her eyes and watched the medication drip into the tubing. Drip, drip, drip. The IV was getting closer to the end. When this pouch was empty, they would take the needle out of her arm and Glady could go home. For now she closed her eyes and continued thinking about the picnic they'd had after the reception for Carol last July.

That damned Carol hadn't shown up until right at the time the reception was supposed to start that morning at the Community House, then she'd left right after it was over barely even speaking to her mother. Later that afternoon, Carol had shown up for the family picnic and stayed only a couple of hours.

Glady remembered she had come up with a great plan about how she could be comfortable at the picnic yet be in the center of the action. Her wheelchair wasn't very good outdoors on uneven ground, and it wasn't comfortable for long periods of time either. Glady had hit upon an idea the week before the reception and picnic. She was sitting in her easy chair, so comfortable watching Oprah, when the idea came out of the blue. Why in the hell couldn't she just take her easy chair? It would fit in the back of the Blazer and they could set it out in the park for the picnic. Glady reckoned that those damned kids could just wait on her; they could bring her food and talk to her as she sat there in comfort at the center of activity.

Glady envisioned herself in the shade of a big tree. She would be able to see everything from that vantage point and everyone could see her. They would take turns coming up to her chair to visit and talk to her.

Then, that damned Carol had ruined it all. She hadn't come near her mother's chair at all. Carol had stood over by a patch of bright flowers and people were coming up to her instead of Glady. Glady told Dale and John to get Henry and one of the other boys to come over and move her chair. She would show that bitch Carol.

Four of the boys had come over and at Glady's command and each one took hold of a chair leg. They hoisted her up, carried her to the place she indicated, and deposited her near the patch of flowers where Carol was holding court. Carol hadn't even noticed her mother nearby and had just drifted off to another spot where Glady couldn't hear a word of what was being said.

After a short while she determined that Carol was standing in one place again so she called her crew of boys and made them carry her again but was immediately dissatisfied. It was in a hot spot and Glady had to boys move her again and place her under another shade tree.

Glady heard someone say that Carol had already been out to her dad's grave and she wondered just how long Carol had been in town. She sure as hell hadn't bothered to call her mother to say 'hello' or that she'd arrived safely. She just showed up at the reception in the nick of time.

When Carol announced she was leaving the picnic Glady had demanded to know what time she could expect Carol and her husband to come to her house the next day. Carol said they might be able to get over for a little while. Carol seemed to evade the issue when Glady asked how long she could stay.

Glady remembered waiting for Carol to come and visit her new home. The house wasn't really finished yet, even though John had begun working on it over two years ago. However she and John had moved out of their cramped trailer and into the unfinished house several months ago anyway.

Glady had bragged to Carol over the phone about how nice it was to get out of that small single wide trailer and back into a real house again. She told Carol that even if the rooms weren't finished, the space was nice and she could get her wheelchair around in any room she wanted. Glady had described it in great detail over the phone and in letters to Carol to show she could also have a new home built for her.

Glady had invited all of her children and grandchildren to be out at her house for Carol's visit that day. It was a workday though, so most of them couldn't come; only a few of them made it. Even though she hadn't mentioned it, Glady hoped Carol and her husband would stay for supper. She had bought extra food and planned a meal, just in case.

Glady harped at John and the visiting grandchildren.

"Now don't mess up Grandma's house. Keep everything nice 'til Carol gets here. Clean up after yourselves, and don't use anything that you don't have too." Glady admonished from her wheelchair and doled out little chores to everyone near her.

"Dammit. Get over there and straighten up that stack of magazines. What will Carol think with a mess like that on that table? Shirley, get a rag and get that smudge off the window over there."

Glady had rehearsed carefully for Carol's arrival at her home. She replayed her planned scene many times over in her mind. She would act bon vivant and say just the right thing when Carol stepped in the door.

To prepare her for Carol's visit, Glady had John stack a big, tall pile of pillows into her easy chair then carefully spread a new blanket over the high throne of pillows. When she determined that it was ready, Glady commanded John and Dale to lift her up out of her wheelchair and place her in a queenly pose, high upon the royal pile. When she heard someone say Carol was coming up the driveway Glady mentally rehearsed her greeting statement again.

Glady waited atop her throne and watched out the window as the rental car came down the driveway and parked. From her royal perch, Glady saw Carol and her husband get out of the car and come toward the front door. Glady admonished the other visitors to be quiet so she could tell when Carol was at the door.

"Come in!" Glady yelled in her good-queen mother tone of voice when she heard the knock. Carol entered and glanced around fleetingly at Glady's home that she had been told so much about.

"Welcome to my Mountain Home!" Glady trilled.

CHAPTER THIRTY-TWO

Carol stepped into her mother's home wondering where in the world Glady had ever come up with that greeting. There weren't even any hills in this godforsaken state, let alone mountains! Glady prattled on to Carol, making excuses as to why things were so unfinished and in such a mess. Then she patted the seat next to her.

"I haven't really got to talk to you at all since you been here. Come, sit by me and talk. Then I want you to tour my new home."

Carol sat down and looked up into the eyes of her mother. She had known from the time she first looked into her mother's eyes at the reception that Glady would not last until the end of the year. She wondered if she should care more that her mother was dying. No matter how many times she asked herself the question, no answer would come.

Carol couldn't really say she felt happy that Glady was dying, but she wasn't feeling sad either. No feeling, was more what she felt. Glady's hazel green eyes that once held the light that terrified Carol were subdued and faint. In fact, they held no spark at all and appeared to be more bluish-gray than hazel green. Carol wondered if Glady had somehow contrived to look that way so that she would feel sorry for her and stay longer.

As Carol looked more closely around the room, she saw that Glady had certainly embellished her stories about her new home over the past two years. The dry wall was up, but the nail heads and seams were showing and the floors were bare plywood. Glady had given ongoing reports of John's progress on the building describing in great detail the colors she had picked out for the walls and curtains. However there wasn't any paint on the walls and there were old sheets hanging over the windows.

Carol sat beside her mother for a few minutes and then got up at Glady's urging to take a tour of the house. Carol tried to make positive comments as she looked around at the half done work. When she asked to use the bathroom to relieve her bladder, Carol noted that a mildewed shower curtain was hung over the doorway instead of a real door. No wonder Glady never sent any pictures of the place. Carol was embarrassed for Glady.

After the grand tour, Carol walked back into the unfinished living room. She looked over at her mother sitting in the corner. There was Glady, sitting high up on an old, moth-eaten easy chair, with ragged, dirty pillows showing from underneath a skimpy, cheap, new blanket: A pitiful looking old hag, the self-appointed queen of nothing, sitting up there on a makeshift throne, slowly dying. Suddenly, the scenario overcame Carol and she knew she had to get out of there!

"But you just got here!" Glady wailed. "I thought you'd stay and talk to me. Have supper here with me. I bought the things you like ta eat."

"No," Carol lied. "We've already made plans for dinner with some friends of ours in Seneca. We have to get back there over there because we have reservations at a new restaurant. We have to leave now to make it on time."

"But when are you flying back?" Glady asked pitifully.

"We are leaving tomorrow evening," Carol replied, as Glady reached out for her hand.

"Will ya come back tomorrow? I've hardly seen ya at all. It's been three years since you last came back home, and I don't want to wait three more years to see you again."

Twenty-five minutes from the time she arrived, Carol was headed toward the door to an appointment she had never made. She forced a cheery smile as she looked back across the room at her mother.

"Oh sure! We will probably have time to come out. I'll call you tomorrow and let you know what time we'll be here. Really, we have to leave now though because I have to change clothes and get over there to the restaurant. I'll call you tomorrow, I promise," Carol said. She lied straight into her mother's dying eyes, knowing she had no intention of following up on her empty promises.

"And you old bitch," Carol muttered to herself as she hurried out the door, "The only people you'll be seeing in three years will be the ones there with you in hell!"

CHAPTER THIRTY-THREE

A little over five months later, Glady lay dying and in a coma. She thought it wasn't so bad, going into a coma just before Christmas. She was being attended by so many nurses and doctors and was getting attention from the huge family that she had brought into this world.

In spite of her coma, Glady would become aware in her mind off and on. She first noticed that her boys were trading off in shifts, then another time she saw that some of the boys wives and her own daughters and granddaughters were hovering as well. Two visitors at a time, family members only, that was the rule in the intensive care unit.

Glady tried to wrinkle up her nose at Billy Totten when he was standing beside her bed looking lost and forlorn. She thought that last wife of his was going to straighten him out, but they'd begin arguing a lot when her kids got to be teen-agers. She hadn't liked the way Billy T was dealing with her son's rebellious nature and moved out one day then asked for a divorce.

Billy Totten, her youngest son, the poor little bastard. He had been so constipated in infancy and then had been bothered as he grew up that Hank ignored him. Hank never paid any attention to anybody, but Billy Totten seemed to always hope. He hoped his dad would come to a game and watch him play when he got pretty good at baseball in high school.

Glady knew Hank probably knew Billy T belonged to Raymond, but he would have ignored him even if he'd been his own. Even as an adult Billy T worked real hard on a relationship with Hank. He told Hank he would like to buy a riding lawnmower and together they could earn some money doing yard work around town. They had just begun to find a common ground when Hank had to go and die in his sleep.

About a year and a half ago now Glady had called Billy T and insisted he go over and check on Hank. She hadn't heard from him and he was supposed to call her in the morning sometime. He hadn't answered all day in spite of her attempted phone calls to see if he was all right. He had died sometime in the night and laid there all waiting for poor emotionally neglected Billy Totten to find him all stiff in his bed. Billy T was still having nightmares to this day about finding the dead body. In Glady's opinion, he'd probably never get over it.

She looked at poor pitiful Alfred standing there beside Billy T. Alfred, who had looked just like his dad from birth on up. White hair, blue eyes and all, Glady knew Hank could never doubt who Alfred belonged to. The old son-of a bitch hadn't paid any more attention to him than he had to Billy Totten though.

Alfred, the hardest to break to the toilet, and the hardest to raise. He had been such terrible teenager; he'd actually had the nerve to shove Glady back away from him when she attacked in a fit of rage. She had never let him forget that either. She reminded Alfred, and everyone else in the family, on a regular basis about that time when he had shoved her.

Alfred had been married and divorced three times now. He had beaten the shit out of that first wife of his. One time, he claimed she had fallen over a rock in the yard, when she had gotten stitches on her upper lip. Glady had known it was a crock that no one believed. That damned Alfred had ended up being such a loser. She lay there wondering how in the hell a person could have so many damned worthless kids?

CHAPTER THIRTY-FOUR

Glady slipped away into grayness for what seemed like only a few moments. When her mind became aware again, she saw that a nurse was changing her IV. She could see George there now, stepping back out of the way of the nurse. Of course Glady couldn't talk since she was in the coma, but she wished she could come out of it if only for a few minutes. She wanted to talk to people; she had questions to ask and comments to make.

He was moving up close to her bedside again, George, her oldest child. Steadfast, loyal and brave, she always thought of George when she heard those words. When he was first born, he had been so ugly, like someone had bopped him over the head, and then under the chin. But in just a few days, he became such a sweet and precious baby as he lost that newborn ugliness. Unbeknown to anyone but Glady, she had named him after her lost love of so many years ago.

Glady remembered she cried the first day George had gone to school and he had cried too. As he grew up, George never really gave her any trouble even though he didn't do all that well in school. Thinking back though, he did have that weird nervous rocking motion he would go through when he got excited or anxious. That had worried Glady at times when George would firm his mouth a strange way as he stood and rocked back and fourth with one foot in front of the other, his fists tightly clenched.

Come to think of it, she did have another concern about George. He was insistently bullying to his younger brothers especially when she wasn't around. More than just teasing and taunting, he had really hurt them sometimes. George had barely scraped by with his grades and when he graduated from high school he was unable to find work for almost a year. Glady had grown tired of his bullying and finally convinced him to volunteer for the draft and he went into the Army for three years.

Suddenly a wave of sickness washed over Glady. She worried if any of these nurses around here were dealing with her bowels while she was in this coma. Glady drifted into grayness again.

When her thoughts returned Glady could see Henry standing there now. Henry who wasn't the 'junior' that everyone always thought he should be. Henry was the same age as John, her 'adopted son', and they had both been drafted into the service at the same time. Glady thought she would die when John left for basic training and she feared for his life every day during the two years he was away. She just knew if he was sent to Vietnam that he would never return. Luckily, John and Henry both were sent to Germany and spent their whole time overseas together there.

The problem with Henry and John going into the Army at the same time and being sent to the same places was that Glady would have to check her letters to them both to be sure she didn't get them mixed up. She wanted to write to John frequently so she covered herself by writing to Henry frequently as well. She usually wrote brief letters to Henry, telling him bits and pieces of news and then asked him a bunch of questions. Henry didn't write back much or often however.

On the other hand, John received long love letters from Glady once or twice a week. She would describe in great detail how she missed him and longed to have him back in her arms. Glady made damned sure that she was the only one who picked up the mail every day. She would quickly scan the letters from John while she was in the car, at the post office. If anything looked suspiciously incriminating she would tear the whole letter and envelope up into tiny pieces and burn them when she got home. She hit upon the idea that John could write a general letter that anyone could read, and then would include a separate page written just for her to read.

One time John wrote privately to Glady that he was sure Henry had seen part of one of her letters to him. Henry had come into his room and innocently picked up a page from his bedside table wondering what his mother had to say to John.

John told Glady he had snatched the letter away, telling Henry it was an old one. He wasn't sure if he had gotten it away from him in time or not. Glady worried that Henry had seen some of the things she had written to John. For a while she wrote both boys the exact same letters in case Henry came snooping around again.

Through the grayness of the coma, Glady determined she could see the evergreen swags and colorful glass globes decorating the window over the nurse's station. She thought she could make out one of her sons in the dimness. He was standing beside her bed, and it looked like he was holding a wrapped present. She couldn't really tell which one of the twins it was though. They had always looked so much alike, but they had acted so differently.

Some fool nurse had gotten mixed up the night her twins were born and had thrown out the afterbirth so Glady never knew whether they were identical twins or not. She always figured if they were identical, they should act a lot more alike than they did though. Glady guessed that nowadays, they could probably tell with blood tests, but she always forgot to ask the doctors about it. She hoped she could remember to ask about blood tests for twins when she came out of this damned coma.

Glady suddenly knew that it was Dale standing there because he was crying. She loved him more than all the other children put together. She had always heard that a mother can't help but have a favorite child, and Dale was hers.

Dale had always understood Glady best and as he got older and he was the one sitting in the car talking with Glady while she smoked. They would talk and talk and listen to the car radio like she had with the older kids. Glady would not allow Dale to smoke; she would not even let him take one drag off a cigarette, not that he'd ever asked for one.

Although she hadn't thought so at the time it happened, it turned out that Glady was thrilled that Dale was the twin who got rheumatic fever. Back then she had been worried sick when the doctor diagnosed Dale, and secretly wished that it had been Kayle who had gotten sick. For a whole year she gave Dale his penicillin and faithfully did everything else exactly like the doctor ordered. Dale got well even though he had to continue the penicillin for several years longer.

Years later, when Kayle was drafted into the Army, Dale got to stay home from the war because of that rheumatic fever he'd had when he was in junior high school. Kayle had been sent to Vietnam and spent his near the Mekong delta. Kayle got shot in the leg and Glady wept with joy that it was him, and not Dale.

She could not have stood it if Dale had been wounded or, far worse, killed. What would she have done?

Glady never could interest Kayle in chumming around with her, but Dale had always seemed to be on her wavelength. Glady and Dale had talked openly about sex when he got a little older. Glady would describe graphically how a woman feels during sex and how she really needed it every so often.

After Carol left home to go to nursing school, Glady confided in Dale about her affair with Bud. Glady repeated many of the stories to Dale that she had told Carol. She convinced Dale she needed his confidence so he could drive her out when she met Bud and drive back out later to pick her up. She told him the cover stories to use.

Glady never would forgive that first little bitch Dale had married. The slut had trapped him by getting pregnant. Glady had always told her boys,

"No sense turnin' it down if it's offered, especially if you know boys have been there before. But never force a girl, and be sure to always use protection. You don't want to get trapped by some girl who just wants to get married."

Then that little whore Dale was seeing turned up pregnant when he was only nineteen. Glady figured the girl must have lowered Dale's defenses and caught him unaware in a weak moment. That was all she could figure out since she'd brought her boys up right. Glady was sure the little slut wasn't a virgin when she met Dale.

Glady could see his face better now that the gray haze had eased and he had moved away from the bright light. He was standing there gazing down at her, looking like his favorite dog had just been hung. Glady loved him so.

Dale lived within ten miles of Glady's house and had called her or came to see her twice a week for quite awhile now. He visited her at every holiday and birthday, and was so attentive. Dale's second wife had been a real bitch and had convinced him to move almost two hundred away from his mother and she hardly ever saw him back then.

Dale met and married his third wife shortly after his second one ran off. They had had a baby within a year and now Glady thought this marriage was getting rocky. She was pretty sure Dale was screwing around again. As Glady watched Dale through her comatose eyes, she looked at the gold and green foil package tied with a huge green bow that he was holding. She wondered what her darling boy had gotten her for Christmas.

Dale's twin, Kayle, was a whole different story. He'd been sent home after he was wounded in Vietnam and then he had gone to college for a while. Even though he never graduated, he had met a real nice girl at college and married her. The most amazing thing was that Kayle and Pat were still married. Except for Vera, who had never married, Kayle was the only one of her kids who wasn't divorced at least once.

Kayle had just never warmed up to Glady though. Only once did he sit in the car with her to smoke and talk and he hadn't even talked much that time. He acted like he was too good to be there and seemed anxious to get away.

Glady had always gone out of her way to be nice to Pat and Kayle. They came out to visit on holidays and always bought nice gifts, but that was probably because Pat had a mother who had raised her right. Early in their marriage, Glady consented to let them go over to Pat's folks one Christmas morning. When they got over to Glady's she let them open their presents out of sequence just to show them that she was a good sport. They never stayed long though, and Glady recalled that Kayle always acted like they were doing her a favor when they came to visit.

Glady wished to hell she would remember to get blood tests to see if Kayle was identical to Dale. If she could just get somebody's attention, she would have them write it down so she wouldn't forget to ask when she was well.

Glady drifted in again and remembered that she had been thinking about Kayle. It hadn't been much of a surprise that Hank had named Kayle the executor of his will. Not that there was much of anything to execute since Hank didn't owe any money and he didn't have any property. He had saved up enough to pay for his own damned funeral and left enough to pay Glady's Medicare and medical bills, but she felt entitled to that much. After all, she was the old son-of-a-bitch's widow!

There had been money left over and even though Kayle didn't come right out and say it, Glady figured there was enough to bury her too. Hank had probably saved and hoped to see her in the ground first, all buried and put away.

Too bad she'd spoiled his plans but the old bastard had died peacefully in his sleep, not even disturbing his covers. She didn't begrudge him that, but just let him try and glare at her now!

CHAPTER THIRTY-FIVE

Back when Hank died his funeral had an unexpected influence on Glady. At first she had mused that for an old son-of-a-bitch he'd actually had a beautiful service. Some of the boys did a nice job picking out the casket and making all the arrangements. Glady had stayed out of it and played the grieving widow while secretly gleeful that Hank had died before her. Now she would have a nice social security check to spend any way she wanted.

Then people had come from all over the countryside to Hank's funeral services. Such nice people, saying such nice things, many of them distant relatives of Hank and others from his long ago past. Glady hadn't seen most of them for many, many years and she sat up in the widow's seat, looking sad and aggrieved. The casket had been so beautiful, a deep iridescent blue-green with a low luster shine, arranged with a huge wreath of sunflowers and wheat, and just a hint of reds and blues in the other flowers.

As she sat at his funeral Glady seemed to realize that Hank was well respected and was over all a decent man. He never drank alcohol, nor ran around on her. He'd had an ironclad sense of duty to support his family and brought his paycheck home to her every time. He had never harshly disciplined the kids and had never laid a hand on her. Well, there was that one time, but it didn't amount to any thing.

Glady had been lost in thought during Hank's funeral services. She looked up when there was movement at the front of the church and imagined that all the people here were united in the same thought.

"Look at those boys. Just the right number to carry him, six fine sons, raised to carry their daddy's coffin." Glady's chest had swelled in a widow's pride because she also reckoned they were thinking what a wonderful job she had done raising those sons.

Glady had known that she had cancer at Hank's funeral. She had finally quit ignoring the puckering on the side of her left breast and gone to see the doctor just the week before they found Hank dead in his bed. The mammogram had shown a big growth in there. They had these new pills though and the doctors wanted to try those, and they didn't even want to do any surgery.

Twenty years earlier, when Glady'd had kidney cancer she had to go through the surgery and then radiation, which was a lot worse and bound her bowels up something terrible. Glady was happy there was an easy treatment these days, but she wondered if the pills would cure the cancer fast.

Glady had read in magazines and heard on TV talk shows that the best thing to do when you have cancer is to think positive. Glady put on the happiest face she could find every time there was anyone around. When Hank died she easily took on the role of the good old brave widow gal who was facing life head on.

Glady knew that those nice people who had come to Hank's funeral didn't know he'd left her three years before he died. He had finally been unable to ignore the undeniable facts about Glady and John and had moved out suddenly one day and into a little house on his own. Even though it blindsided her, she was relieved when Hank announced he was moving out. Now she and John could finally be in their home together without the constant worry of getting caught.

Glady was careful to keep her public relationship with John just like it had always been though. All those years, Glady had always acted like John was one of her sons whenever anyone was around. She worked hard at convincing everyone that he was like her adopted son and she didn't want people putting two and two together about what had been going on in all those years. Nobody ever said anything or seemed to notice anything unusual about an older woman out with one of her boys.

Glady knew she had to be extra careful to protect her reputation and she needed to keep up appearances, just in case things got worse with the cancer. She didn't want people to turn off toward her now; she couldn't have people thinking bad things about her in this stage of the game. Glady wasn't planning to die anytime soon but she was determined to do whatever necessary to have an important funeral like Hank's had been.

CHAPTER THIRTY-SIX

Glady's comatose thoughts waxed and waned. Sometimes she knew who was at her bedside and sometimes she wasn't aware, but right now her mind was active. She thought back to last Memorial Day when it had been a just over a year since Hank's impressive funeral. She developed a pattern of visiting graves and putting out bouquets ever since baby June died back in '51.

Back then Glady learned to make crepe paper roses and she recalled that she and the kids would sit for hours at night making paper roses every year.

First, the folded roll of crepe paper was cut using a cardboard petal pattern. Glady had to do that part herself, because the scissors were so old and the paper was so thick only she could do it right. Then the petals would be peeled off and curled one by one and then stretched at the base. The older boys could do that, but you had to watch them every minute to be sure they only got one at time and curled and pulled them right. Each petal had to roll on both sides, just so, to make a nice looking rose.

Glady would become frustrated with all the close work and having to watch those damned fool boys so they wouldn't ruin her handiwork. She used her tired impatient tone of voice during flower petal curling and would to slap them when they didn't listen to her and do it right.

Carol and George were able to help with the next step and they could take the curled petals and wrap each one around a long wire that had been bent into a small loop at the top. Holding eight to ten petals firmly in place, a strip of green crepe paper was tightly wrapped twice around the base of the petals, and then in a whirling twisting motion, the strip was wrapped down the wire to the end. The end was gently crimped so the whole thing wouldn't fall apart.

After many flowers were made up, Glady would melt paraffin in a coffee can and dip each rose into the hot wax. She had to hold each flower in the middle of the can to let the paraffin drip back in, then carefully stand the flower up so the wax would cool and harden, yet not stick to any other flowers.

Making crepe paper flowers was a long tedious process. Carol watched her mother take each flower and carefully dip it into the hot wax. As she stood there, she said,

"Mama, the flowers look prettier before they're waxed, don't they?"

In her extremely irritated tone of voice, Glady yelled,

"Are you nuts or somethin'? What in the hell are you talkin' about?"

"W-well, ju-just that the colors are prettier before they're waxed," Carol stammered.

Glady reached out and slapped Carol hard on the face, losing her grip on the rose she was waxing.

"How in the hell would you keep the rain off them? They would get soggy and the colors would run and they would turn to mush. Now look, you've made me ruin one. Get the hell out of my sight."

Glady and the kids spent several weeks before Memorial Day making, white, yellow, pink and red roses in two sizes, one tiny size for baby June's grave in pastel colors, and then making a lot more of the regular size. After a year or two, Glady learned to fasten the paper roses together to make wreaths and sprays. These were more complicated and harder to work with especially when it came to the wax but she mastered it and got to where she made up extra bouquets and wreaths to sell.

Glady drove around the countryside selling bouquets to earn extra spending money that Hank didn't know about. Over the years the neighbors bought a lot of flowers, sometimes several bunches in a household. Glady liked to brag as the neighbors commented on her homemade flowers.

"Yeah, the kids and I make these up every year. In our family we like to remember the dead on Memorial Day. They are pretty flowers aren't they?"

Whether the neighbors bought the flowers because they thought they were pretty, or they felt sorry for this woman with all those kids, coming begging up the driveway, no one knows. Anyway, baby June had many handmade bouquets and little wreaths of crepe paper flowers on her grave for years.

Glady hadn't done up the crepe paper roses for a long time. They had come out with inexpensive artificial flowers over the years. These days there were so many pretty colors, all done up in silky fabrics and colorful plastic, and of course they stayed nice most of the year, rain or shine.

Last Memorial Day, Glady had already put bouquets on her parents graves and had visited baby June's gravesite in Rockwell. She was riding out in the country to the last cemetery she intended to visit that day. She was sitting in the passenger seat of the Blazer, traveling up the graveled country road toward the cemetery where Hank was buried.

As John drove her slowly up the road, Glady looked on up ahead. She saw that the fence around the cemetery had been cleaned up of brush and that some of the straggly trees had been removed and trimmed. It made it look neat and more open this way and she could see the tall old cedar trees lining the driveway.

Glady was admiring all the colorful flowers on the graves as they drove in the gate. It had rained day before yesterday and the lawn on the cemetery grounds had just been mowed. Flowers of all colors lay out on the graves with that green new mown lawn as a backdrop. As John pulled into the inside road nearest Hank's grave, Glady glanced over to where her husband was buried. She gasped and couldn't believe her eyes.

A new head stone had been placed on Hank's gravesite. It was a large, rose granite stone with a sunflower and a windmill carved in it, but what had got her attention was that it was a single stone. It only spanned his grave and had only had his name carved with the dates of his birth and death. It made her plot next to Hank look sunken and bare, out of place; somehow unbalanced and wrong. Glady's first thought was that Kayle had sneaked out and bought a stone for his dad without telling anyone. That little bastard, how dare him make a decision like that?

John once again helped Glady out of her seat but this time she quickly placed the flowers on the graves and asked to get back in the Blazer immediately.

"To hell with this! I'm tired, let's go home," she announced to John as she began to plan her investigation of this new development.

As soon as Glady was back at home she dialed Kayle's number. She intended to get some answers, but he and Pat must have been out because their answer machine picked up the call. Glady was not going to leave a message on his damned machine and hung up on it. On toward evening Glady dialed for the tenth time and Pat answered the phone.

"Hi, Pat. How are you doin'?" Glady eased into a conversation. "It sure was nice out today, did you guys get out to the cemeteries? Oh, you didn't go? Is your husband there, I wanna ask him somethin'."

"Haay-lo," Kayle said tentatively. Glady had heard Pat tell him his mother wanted to ask him something and figured he would know something was up so she used her low pleasant tone of voice, "I went out to daddy's grave today," then unable to fully control her emotion, her voice picked up in pitch, "He has a headstone!"

It turned out that Hank had ordered the head stone for himself months before he died. He had gone over to Rockwell and picked it out and paid for completely. Kayle said he figured Glady already knew about it since it had taken care of it so long ago. He said that he had the stone placed a couple of months after Hank's funeral and he had gone out to check the workmanship shortly after and really hadn't thought any more about it.

Glady figured it must have been just after last Memorial Day. She kept calm and was about to wrap up the call when Kayle's next statement sent her into orbit.

"Yeah, dad told me he'd ordered the headstone and just before he died he said if anything happed to him to go ahead and sell the plot next to his."

"What in the hell are you talkin' about? It's our plot. Your dad bought it years ago so he and I could be buried out there around his family." Glady said as the tension in her voice began to rise.

"Well, I guess he changed his mind when he found out about you and John," Kayle said pointedly.

Glady didn't want to continue the conversation with Kayle and used her most tired, worn-out tone of voice.

"Oh well, I guess it just took me by surprise 'cause no one had mentioned it to me. It's really a pretty stone, I didn't know the old fart had such good taste." Then she said she'd had a big day and was so beat that she had to go to bed right away and get some rest.

"Goddamned that old son-of-a-bitch!" Glady raged as soon as she hung up the phone. "I don't believe it! How dare him do this to me?"

Glady fumed. That old bastard had felt obligated to pay for her medical insurance and put away enough for her funeral but he obviously made a point to tell Kayle that he wanted to spend his eternal rest in peace. Without her! What in the hell would people think about him laying there without her beside him?

Glady felt like her recent plans had been dashed. She hadn't even known that stone even existed, let alone being already placed out there for everyone to see for a year now. Glady had been hatching a plan to order a double stone for Hank's grave with her name and date of birth already carved. This would ensure her eternal rest site with her reputation intact.

All those nice people who had been there at Hank's funeral would continue to think of her as his grieving widow. They must not turn against her now, she couldn't let them find out that she had been living in sin with someone she had always introduced as her 'adopted son'.

Glady never hid from being seen with John. She let on to people that she went places with him because he had a Blazer and she could get in an out much better and her wheelchair fit in the back. No one ever questioned the relationship and thought John was being kind to Glady as she took his arm for assistance. John had never married; they all figured that he had plenty of time to devote to her. Many women thought it was sweet that an adopted son would remain so attentive to the old woman.

After years of pretending he was her secret husband Glady hadn't even considered marrying John after Hank died. By God, she was entitled to those widow benefits and she wasn't going to marry and give those up. Later on she was glad she hadn't risked her reputation when the doctor told her the anti-cancer pills didn't seem to be working anymore and she would need strong IV chemotherapy.

***

Glady knew some of her kids would be skeptical if she told them she wanted to be buried beside Hank when the time came. The two youngest girls wouldn't even discuss her death, telling her she would get well like she did with the kidney cancer and live for many more years. She knew that it would take an effort to get her way in this matter.

Glady practiced her soft-kind-convincing tone of voice to make them see that a wife had the right be buried beside her husband of almost fifty-three years.

"Well actually," she muttered, "the old son-of-a-bitch left me right before our fiftieth anniversary, but he never divorced me and that's all that matters."

Glady continued to obsess, thinking that every time someone who knew her and Hank was at the cemetery, they would see Hank buried there by himself with a single headstone. All of those people who had known the Wilkeys' for years would wonder why that was so; they might start asking questions so Glady thought she'd better hurry up and get to work on the problem.

She decided to work on George first since he was probably the easiest to convince. She figured Hank had chosen Kayle to execute the will because of his lesser sense of obligation to Glady, but she thought George would have the most influence on Kayle.

Glady planned to convince George that his dad was just mad at her when he bought that stone for himself and told Kayle to sell the plot. She would say that it didn't make sense for Kayle to sell the plot only to buy another one with the little bit of money that Hank had left for him to manage.

Glady thought she would put it in such a way for George to consider what would have happened if she had died before Hank. Did he really believe that his dad would not have buried her in the plot he had bought long ago for both of them? She would also remind George that Hank was dead; so why would he care who was buried next to him anyway?

Glady replayed her angst while trying to fall asleep at night. All those nice, lovely people who had come to Hank's funeral must be there for her too; she needed them to be there. They needed to see Glady's six sons carrying their beloved mother in her coffin, and to see her daughters weeping for their mother, like they had wept for their father. The people needed to look at all those bereaved children and determine for all time, what a fine, loving mother she had been.

"I know that you might not understand everything that went on between me and your dad. But you already know some of the ups and downs a couple goes through." Glady campaigned to her girls separately on the phone. "Daddy and I went through so many, many things in that fifty-three years."

Glady could tell the girls felt sorry for her as they listened to her go on about her long marriage, obviously thinking that she was reviewing her life and perhaps trying to make amends. Glady thought she might be winning them over, and with so many in her favor they wouldn't let Kayle sell the plot beside Hank.

Then the news came during her clinic visit that the cancer tumor was growing in spite of the IV chemotherapy; Glady knew she'd better get the convincing done soon.

CHAPTER THIRTY-SEVEN

Glady's thoughts transitioned from the Memorial Day scenario and she was aware and back in the present again. Too bad being in a coma made a person feel so helpless. There were no windows in intensive care and she couldn't tell if it was day or night. Glady couldn't even make out the clock well enough to see how much time passed between her awareness and the grayness. She wanted to know what day it was and how long she had been here.

She could still see the Christmas decorations outside the window over the nurse's station and she saw a fat nurse helping herself to a big box of candy.

"Good God," thought Glady, "she's big as a cow now, she doesn't need all that damned candy!" Then some nurses came by the window, wheeling a hospital bed with a sick person into the cubicle next door. They were practically shouting 'Merry Christmas' to each other, so Glady thought it must still be Christmas Day.

Glady couldn't see anyone near her bed though, and she wondered where in the hell all of her kids had gone off to. She didn't remember being left alone anytime since had been in here. She thought she might be getting better if the kids had left her all alone.

Soon after, Glady heard a machine beeping next to her and thought,

"That usually brings the nurses running." Then she could make out someone in a chair in the corner. "My God," she thought, "its Vera! How in the hell could I have missed her? She's been as big as a whale for so damned long, I don't know how I could have missed seeing her even in the shadows. Alvera! That damned Hank had saddled that poor newborn baby girl with a name like that!

Alvera! Glady had given in to Hank over the name because she'd felt half sorry for him since he had taken baby June's death so hard. Well anyway, even if it was her legal name on the birth certificate, Glady never called her Alvera, she always called her Vera.

Hank told Glady in later years when Vera was older that she reminded him of the pictures he had of his own mother. Hank didn't often mention his mother who had died screaming in agony with a ruptured appendix when he was five years old.

Hank had confessed to Glady early in their marriage that he craved mothering and liked hugging better than sex. She turned it against him many times over the years screaming at him in front of their children.

"The goddamned old son-of-a-bitch wanted a mother, not a wife. Look at him, the poor pitiful orphan."

Vera had grown up bashful and shot up tall and gangly when she was in her teens. In high school she put on weight and, though she wasn't exactly fat, Glady ridiculed her about the weight gain. Glady would announce to the sensitive teen on a regular basis, that tall, fat girls never got any dates.

She delivered plenty of hair pullings and slappings since every thing Vera did seemed to set Glady off. She would grab her by the hair whenever she got frustrated.

"You worthless hag. You're about as worthless as tits on a boar hog!" Glady would scream. "You're as big as a cow now, when in the hell are you gonna do something? You'll never amount to anything."

Other times Glady would say to Vera in her expert-matter-of-fact tone of voice,

"It's true that Carol had those terrible saddle bags on her thighs, but you could hide those flaws under the right clothes. What are we supposed to do with a figure like yours? Ya just can't hide that."

Vera wouldn't say much, she just steadily gained more weight and by the time she graduated high school, Glady had pretty much given up on her and wanted her out of the house. Carol had one time mentioned cosmetology as a possibility so Glady picked up on that as a career for Vera. She called a distant cousin of hers and arranged to have Vera live with her so she could go to beauty school in Seneca.

When Vera got her cosmetology license Glady demanded that she come back from Seneca to live and work near home. Vera felt indebted to her mother and complied by taking a station in Rockwell. She fixed Glady and the younger girls hair on a regular basis and was never offered a dime.

Vera lacked confidence in her work and was devastated if a customer didn't like the hairdo she had just labored over. She would go into the bathroom and worry that she couldn't face the next customer. One day Glady witnessed Vera in an anxious moment and she harped,

"Well, don't take it so hard. What did she expect, anyway? You're doin' the best you can. I've known that old bitch for a long time and she would gripe if you hung her with a new rope. Why don't you try and lose some weight, that would probably help your confidence more than anything."

Glady would harp and Vera would try to lose weight. She would get started on some radical diet and be so hungry. Then one of the other beauticians would order a pizza and Vera would give up the diet and gorge herself.

Next thing you know Glady would figure out Vera wasn't losing weight and harp at her again. Once she tried prescription diet pills and she was losing enough weight that even Glady noticed. Unfortunately Vera's blood pressure shot up and the doctor wouldn't give her any more pills. Vera gained back her loss and then damned if her knees didn't give out. She ended up going in debt to have surgery on them and that gave Glady another reason to harp about her weight.

As Glady lay comatose in her intensive care bed studying Vera, she thought,

"That goddamned cow never would lose weight. I begged and pleaded with her over and over. She's ruined her whole life, here she is over forty already. She'll never find a man to marry her!"

CHAPTER THIRTY-EIGHT

Glady's thoughts were fading more often now. It seemed like she could only think about things for a few seconds before she would fade out again. She didn't remember when big ole Vera left the room, but now there was Shirley looking down at her.

Glady loved Shirley's ribald sense of humor. Beginning in about the fifth grade, Shirley would come home and tell her mother all the dirty jokes she had heard at school. She and Glady always laughed loudly together when humor was of a graphic sexual nature. Come to think of it, Shirley reminded Glady of her good, long dead friend, Arlene.

Shirley belonged to Bud, no doubt about it. She looked just like Bud's mother, old Granny, with those soft brown eyes, sweet face and dark hair. Glady wondered if Shirley remembered when they used to go out to see Bud when she was still little, or when they would run into him 'by accident' over at Granny's. Bud had been so proud of Shirley on these sneaky visitations.

Glady admitted that Shirley had turned out to be her favorite daughter. Even if Shirley wasn't as smart as the others and had to go to Special Education.

"She is not retarded and I won't have her going to Rockwell on a bus," Glady had proclaimed loudly to Mr. Bellen, the superintendent of schools, thinking if she persisted he would change his mind.

"Now Glady," Mr. Bellen had said, "I have known you and worked with your children in the school system for many years. I want you to listen to what I'm saying. No one is saying that Shirley is retarded, but she needs special attention. She can only get that attention at the special school in Rockwell. There's a strong probability that, if she goes now, she will get some remedial lessons and can come back to Milton to graduate. If she doesn't go to Rockwell, she may never graduate high school."

"But, it will make her sick to ride the bus. All those kids on that bus, they mess their pants and it stinks to high heaven. She's much smarter than most of my boys, and they didn't go to school with retarded kids," wailed Glady, trying to negotiate a better deal.

"Shirley doesn't have to ride the bus. If someone wants to drive her over to Rockwell every day, that is perfectly acceptable Glady," Mr. Bellen stated in his smooth unruffled way.

Glady shut her lips tight, mashing them together over her snaggled teeth. Her face looked like a dark cloud getting ready to hail. Mr. Bellen further explained that these were new programs designed to help students learn the subject material. He reasoned that Glady would certainly want Shirley to complete her education and be able to graduate.

Glady hadn't liked what Mr. Bellen was saying one bit. However, she knew Shirley would not be admitted into high school here in Milton, so she gave in and set her goal to get Shirley back here as soon as possible. Glady helped Shirley with her homework daily and kept encouraging her to improve and continue the program. Shirley had made Glady proud, riding that bus over there to Rockwell like a trooper every day for two years.

"That's my girl," Glady had said to Shirley when they heard the news that she was getting transferred back to Milton for her junior year. "Let's go out and get you all new clothes."

Glady had cussed at the three younger girls as they grew up. She called them names but she was worn out and rarely smacked them around. If she tried to discipline them, they just laughed at her and got out of her way. Once in a while she had been able to catch them off guard and grab their hair and give it a good yank before they escaped.

Glady faintly saw that Shirley still at her bedside. Shirley had been married four times and had lived with five other men. They would promise her the moon in the beginning, and she would be so happy for a while. The next thing Glady would know, Shirley was leaving the guy, or he was leaving her. Shirley always had another man in short order though. Glady wondered how come Shirley had such bad luck with men.

Glady could see Tammy standing beside Shirley now. Two visitors at a time in the intensive care unit, Glady knew that was the rule. Glady'd liked it much better in a regular room like she'd had a couple of years ago when she'd broken her hip. You could have all the visitors you wanted during visiting hours in that kind of a room.

In the regular room all the kids could cluster around he during visiting hours and bring in flowers, balloons and stuffed animals to put around her bed. The nurses would compliment Glady on her lovely, big family and Glady would brag about how much her kids treasured their mother. She would tell the nurses that she had another daughter out in California who was a nurse too, and they would beam at her.

The lights dimmed in Glady's unconscious state and then brightened immediately. Shirley and Tammy were still there. Tammy was kind of like a middle child if you didn't count the boys and baby June. Two girls older than her, and two younger. The night after her high school graduation Tammy ran off and married some guy from Minnesota that she had just met driving around. A few months later he dumped her and she called wanting to come home. They'd had to drive clear up to Minnesota to get her and have the marriage annulled. Tammy looked awful when she got back home, and though she was never overweight, she looked positively anorexic now. She was smoking one cigarette after another.

Glady thought Tammy looked the more like her than any of her other daughters. One day she had run across that picture of herself from the fair so long ago, when she's had on the Mexican hat and weskit. Glady was surprised to see her younger self, but mostly how much Tammy resembled her.

Tammy gained virtually no weight over the years and she seemed deathly afraid of getting fat.

"She still smokes like a goddamned chimney. I bet she's dying for a butt right now," Glady mused, "but at least she never got fat."

Tammy had gone to college for a while after they'd brought her back from Minnesota. Then she dropped out to marry another loser. The guy never did drugs or drank; he was just a real psycho who beat up her and their kids regularly. He beat them so bad one time that Tammy called the cops and had him committed. The psychiatrists tested him and told Tammy that he was pretty bad off mentally. She filed for divorce based on his violent nature. Over the years when Tammy heard they might be letting him loose, she would take the kids and hide out. They never had let him go even after all these years. Glady had to admit that Tammy was a single mother who took good care of her kids while holding a regular job.

"I wish to God Tammy'd let Vera cut that straggly hair off," Glady thought. "Some shorter style that would fluff around her face. Maybe put in some reddish coloring to cover up that mess going gray on her head now."

As Glady watched she thought,

"Now that I look closer, Tammy is startin' to look bad now that she's gettin' older. Maybe she *should* gain some weight with that long skinny face she looks kinda like an old horse. Look at her teeth; they're so stained with all those years of smoking. I hope she doesn't try to kiss me. Even if I am in a coma, it would probably make me puke. If she doesn't watch out, she'll never find another man who'll want to walk her down the aisle."

Glady faded and then roused slowly from the deepening gray haze.

"Well shit, I'm still in intensive care, I can see Gail and there's Billy Totten here again. Gail was her youngest daughter and her youngest child.

Damned if Gail hadn't begun to climb while she was still in infancy, before she could even walk. She was the only one of Glady's kids to ever climb. Glady knew she would have died of heart failure at a young age if any of her older kids had climbed like that.

Gail climbed out of her crib, up on chairs and tables, and you would find her into the highest cupboards. She climbed up on the toilet seat, onto the tank, up to the sink and got to the medicine cabinet after lipstick before she was a year old. Gail fell and banged herself up on the head and face so many times that Glady was surprised she was normal.

Gail had slept in Glady's bedroom for years. Gail was the youngest child and no one had come along to bump her out of the baby crib like all the kids before her. Glady said there was no sense crowding Gail in the girl's room and leave Glady in a big bedroom by herself. They had moved a little bed into a corner of the room when Gail outgrew the baby crib.

Secretly Glady and John had used Gail as a front so they could be in the bedroom together. Glady reasoned that no one would suspect that her and John were up to anything indecent with a kid in the room. Every few nights, when it was little Gail's bedtime, Glady would announce to the kids who were always watching TV that she was so tired she going to her room and read.

In a while, John would get up and nonchalantly announce that he had to get up for work so he needed to turn in early. He would tell the others he was going in to check to see if Glady needed anything and then he was going up to bed.

Glady and John would talk in low voices until they thought Gail was asleep. Then they would get in a quickie before any one came blundering into the room looking for her. Though Glady hated to lose her cover, she finally moved Gail out to sleep with the other girls. She had looked over for the third night and saw the child curiously watching her and John.

Glady washed out briefly and then became aware for the last time. She saw a black haze slowly filling the corners of the room and looked up at Gail again and wondered.

"What in the hell is a person supposed to do with a kid like that? She got into drugs and screwing around when she was barely thirteen."

The room was nearly full of the black haze now. Glady's final thoughts escaped her mind just before the thick blackness completely enveloped her.

"Ya do the best ya can ta raise 'em, but ya can't be there with them every minute, that's for sure. Now, what's the matter with that fool Billy Totten? Here I'm the one in the coma, and he's standin' there bawlin' his eyes out!"

CHAPTER THIRTY-NINE

Carol was out in her garden. It was late December, but here in California there was always something that would grow year around. Pansies, peas, and beans grew best in early winter. Carol looked at the green grass coming up all over the hills. She had found out, living here so many years now, that California was called the Golden State because of the wild oats all over the hills. They dried out in late spring, making all the hills turn a golden straw color. There were oak trees out here with dark green leaves that contrasted with the golden hills of summer. Then in late fall, it would usually begin to rain, the trees would lose their leaves and the hills would turn green with new wild oats.

Carol thought it was funny that long ago she thought that California was warm all year around, but it sure was cold here today. She now had lived in California a few months longer than she had lived back home in the Midwest. She claimed that made her almost a native Californian.

As Carol dug she wondered why she had planted the lilac bush so close to the hydrangea. Now that they had grown some, they were starting to crowd each other. Well of course, she did know why she had done it. Watering in the summer was such a bear of a job. You had to nurse every living thing so carefully in the hot months here. Young trees, bushes, pets and of course, people suffered through the high temperatures of summer.

A lot of plants just didn't make it through their first few years, even with a lot of careful tending. So to keep from killing yourself, you planted them close together to share the water. Right now it was Christmas time and everything was lush and green. You could forget about those hot, dry golden hills of summer at this time of the year. As Carol dug up the dormant lilac, her thoughts turned to Glady.

Lilacs and Glady. Kayle had called earlier in the day and said that Glady was in intensive care. He said that Glady had been feeling pretty good the day before yesterday and had made John take her out to do her Christmas shopping. She had shopped all that day and felt fine.

Kayle said that yesterday Glady still felt fine when she went to Seneca to the clinic for her chemo treatment. On the way home she was tired, but when she got in her bed she started to feel a lot worse. John got her up and took her back over to see the doctor and he'd put her in the hospital. The doctor explained that her blood count had dropped down too low and they needed to observe her for a while. Glady had lost consciousness some time in the night, they'd put her in the ICU and said she was in a coma.

Lilacs and Glady. Carol remembered that Glady always loved the lilacs and yellow roses that bloomed by that godforsaken house they had lived in for years when her dad first went to work at Lin-Aero. Carol especially remembered the lilac bush. It was a huge old thing that had hundreds of lilac blooms on it every spring. Carol also remembered springtime because of all those countless tornado warnings and watches. Glady had never sighted a tornado in all those years.

Glady had been very disturbed when Carol moved to California in the late 60's. Her mother was appalled that her own daughter would shun her family and leave her home state. The spring after Carol moved Glady was on the phone complaining about how far away Carol sounded. Carol retorted that at least she wouldn't have to worry about tornadoes this year.

After she hung up Glady became inflamed over Carol's remark. Carol received a long letter from her mother shortly after the phone call. Glady had gone into great detail with a nine-point argument of why tornadoes were better than earthquakes.

Lilacs and Glady. Carol remembered Glady told her children every spring about what to do during a tornado. She always said if you didn't have a cellar you would be safest in the northeast corner of your house, but if you were in the yard, head for the lilac bush. Glady drilled them every night they spent under the cushioned dining room table where they hid from the killer funnel cloud that lurked out there in the dark to whirl them away. Carol's husband had heard her relate numerous Glady stories over the years. He told Carol one time that none of the kids would have had a chance of getting the best lilac branch to hold onto, their mother would have sucker punched them to get it for herself!

Lilacs and Glady. California's great singer and prolific songwriter, John Stewart, was a particular favorite of Carol's. She enjoyed his songs and thought Glady might enjoy his style. At Christmas one year Carol bought the newest album and carefully wrapped it and sent it to Glady. The next time she called, Carol inquired if Glady had liked the songs. Glady became incensed.

"Why in the hell did you think I'd wanna hear in a song that we blew away? I don't know why you always think that California is so much better and make fun of us back here. I look at the weather map and our winters aren't that much colder than your precious California winters. You think you're too good for us, my God Carol, you were born here; it's your home!"

Lilacs and Glady. When Kayle called on Christmas Eve he asked Carol if she was coming back to see Glady since she was so sick and in the hospital. Carol replied,

"I came back for her in July and I'm still paying for that trip. I really can't take the time away from work either since it's right here at Christmas. Besides if she's in a coma, she wouldn't know I was there any way."

George called Carol on Christmas day.

"Mom's still in the coma and has not come out of it at all since she's been here. Are you going to come back if there's a funeral?"

Carol was tired of it all. Always having to answer to Glady as to why she wasn't coming back home. Every vacation, she had to cover up if she was going someplace else instead of coming back there. Every phone call, every letter, every Christmas card, the same damned question.

"When are you coming home? When are you coming back? When are you coming home to see me?" Sometimes when Carol let it slip that she was flying out of state to a professional conference, it seemed like Glady was slighted because Carol wouldn't ask the pilot to pull over and land so she could visit her mother.

Carol had gone back to visit every vacation the first several years after she had moved to California. It didn't slow Glady down, and it seemed like the more time she spent there, the more Glady asked the eternal question.

As time went by, Carol got better at excuses. Blaming work seemed to be the best one. Certainly her mother had never come to visit California even when Carol offered to pay for it. Glady always said,

"You're the one who left. Besides, there's so many people back her at home that want to see you again."

Carol hadn't gone back for her dad's funeral when he had died unexpectedly a year ago last March. She sure as hell wasn't going back for this one. She reiterated that she couldn't afford to come back and that she couldn't leave her work right now.

In the very early morning hours, of December 26, Carol's phone rang. It was George calling to tell her that Glady had passed away. He said they had all taken turns at Glady's bedside the whole time she was there, two at a time in the ICU. They all spent day and night in the waiting room including Christmas Eve and Christmas day when they just ran home to clean up or get a bite and hurry back in case Glady woke up. George said that Billy Totten and Gail had been there at the end, but that Glady never regained consciousness the whole time.

Carol listened quietly, and then blurted out the first thing that came to mind.

"Well then, I never have to go back there again."

Carol could tell immediately that she had hurt George when she'd said that. She thought that even though she meant it, her words were not directed at him; she should have never said such a wicked thing. When the brief call ended, Carol put down the phone and left for work, feeling nothing.

CHAPTER FORTY

When the personal effects of the deceased were divided among her children Glady's book of poems seemed to be the featured item. Her kids all knew that Glady had been writing poetry for several years now. She kept it in a little gray notebook near her side in her wheelchair and never allowed anyone access to it. In the years before her last illness, she was seen openly writing on the pages.

The gray notebook was passed among Glady's children the morning before the funeral when they had gathered to divide Glady's possessions from a list she had made. Each child took his and her turn reading some of the wonderful poems authored by their mother. Written out in their mother's hand, the poetry cited God and his movement in mysterious ways. Some poems asked for strength to carry life's burdens a little further, some asked for understanding and forgiveness from those near and dear. Poems in perfect rhythm, bequeathed to them from their mother, a most revered treasure, a legacy written in her own hand.

It was a nice day for late December. Three days past Christmas and it hadn't even snowed yet and the weather had stayed mild for this part of the country. There was a big turnout for the funeral services. Sure enough, almost the same people who had been at Hank's funeral had turned out to remember his widow.

Everyone was dressed in dark colors and they were appropriately somber even though the casket was a riot of colors. Huge bouquets and sprays of floral arrangements took every bit of space at the front of the church. Sunflowers were out of season, but there were plenty of them any way. Large sprays of gladiolas of every color, pinks, yellows, blush white and lavender stood in tall rows behind the casket. There were huge baskets of red and white carnations and yellow mums with sprigs of dried wheat, and ribbon bows in matching and contrasting colors.

"Poor Glady," was the central theme in all the mourners' minds and conversations. "Here she just buried her poor husband a year or so ago, and now she's gone too. It seems like it always happens that way when a couple is so close, one just can't seem go on without the other. And look at that wonderful huge family.

All of her children are here to pay their final respects. Too bad poor Glady had to go right here at Christmas time.

"Are all of her children are here? No, I don't see Carol. I guess she just couldn't make it back from so far away. Glady was always so proud of Carol, too bad she couldn't get back. There's the other four other girls though, weeping so hard. Look at her adopted son. All those years she treated him like he was one of her own. Why, he's crying as hard as the girls. It's so sad. All their poor hearts breaking over their dear mother.

"My, my just look at all those sons. Six of them! Bearing the coffin, carrying their mother down the church aisle, all of them so somber. What a beautiful large family. Glady was such a dedicated mother, raising all those children. She must have been a wonderful cook."

The hearse slowly left the church with the large dark family car following close behind. The parade of mourners followed in their own cars, displaying their headlights all the way out to the country cemetery. The sun shown down on the tall old cedar trees that lined the driveway as the hearse turned into the cemetery and pulled up and stopped next to the green awning. The casket was carefully slid out of the back of the hearse and borne over to the graveside. It was placed gently on the green carpet that covered the lift over the open grave.

Some of the family members continued to weep quietly as they sat in the single line of chairs, set up for them under the narrow green awning. The awning gently lifted up and settled back in the wind, shading the mourners from the weak December sunshine. The huge colorful bouquets of flowers that would soon be placed on the grave were laid or standing around, entirely covering the immediate area. The minister said a prayer for the deceased and the short graveside service ended.

As they lowered her deep blue-green, iridescent coffin into the freshly dug grave, placing her next to the man who would receive no peaceful rest from her even in death, Glady smiled to herself. Not only had she kept her reputation intact and won the hard fight for her eternal resting place, she had ruined the sonsabitches Christmas one last time.

The End

ABOUT THE AUTHOR

Francer Hope is an elder woman who grew up in hard times on the Great Plains. She has spent her adult years observing and reflecting on the nuances of the human spirit and weaving them into complex characters such as Glady. She holds a Master of Science degree and taught for many years in a university setting, spending much of her career reading and writing. Her fictional works provide glimpses into socio-historical times that help make her characters believable and provide multi-dimensional qualities to their imagined personalities.